# London's Sixties

**Capital Transport**

Front cover: A 1964 view at Brixton. London Transport's all conquering RT family buses in all their glory. RTW 449 from Brixton on the 109, Park Royal RTL 1382 from Camberwell on route 172, and Streatham RT 1388 at the back on route 159. The RTW ended up in Ceylon (Sri Lanka) in December 1966, and the RTL in South Africa in December 1964. (Alan Cross)

One of a small number of red bus routes that required low-bridge buses was the 230, which later became route H1 under the Reshaping Plan. RLH 68 from Harrow Weald garage is seen in Headstone Drive. (Capital Transport)

Title Page: RT 2293 with a Park Royal body, is in Harrow on the 140. The route was one of six to serve Heathrow at this time, and provided a link to Mill Hill. RT 2293 operated from Harrow Weald garage between July 1964 and October 1971, including an overhaul at Aldenham in August 1969. Withdrawn at Barking in November 1978, it is currently in preservation. (Capital Transport)

Above: Main Road, Romford on 5th April 1969. Two Park Royal RTs, 2221 and 4696, are from Barking and North Street garages respectively. In five days' time, RT 2221 will have a repaint and stay at Barking until withdrawn in July 1971. RT 4696 will go on to Upton Park before withdrawal in October 1972. At this time North Street operated the 174 daily with RMs, but the operation on Saturdays was boosted by Barking who provided RTs. (David Christie)

Opposite: RTL 1038 arrived at Willesden after overhaul in July 1958, and stayed until withdrawn in October 1962. It waits here at Edgware terminus ready for the trip to the Monday to Saturday terminus of Wembley on route 18 in about 1960. In January 1962, the route was altered to follow its Sunday routeing to London Bridge and used to replace trolleybus 662. The bus saw further service in Ceylon (Sri Lanka) in 1964.

First published 2019

ISBN 978 1 85414 432 4

Published by Capital Transport Publishing Ltd
www.capitaltransport.com

Printed in the EU

# INTRODUCTION

The 1960s was an exciting time in London. Indeed it is often said that if you can remember it, you weren't there. The swinging sixties and the drugs that many people experimented with seem a world away from the photos in these pages. For those of us who can remember that time, life went on in a much calmer way.

The transport scene was in a period of transition. The Routemaster began to make inroads into replacing some of the RT family buses, and one-man operated vehicles began to become widespread. The main event was, of course, the end of the trolleybus system, which had been the largest in the world. The conversion to buses was completed in May 1962. The sixties in the capital was indeed an eventful time, and these colour views capture the period perfectly. Photographers were beginning to use colour film more frequently, and fortunately for us, modern technology allows us to get the best from old negatives and slides. Memories flood back as I look at these pictures taken at a time when I used to sneak into the corners of bus garages with my note book and camera on many Red Rover trips.

I thank the photographers for their efforts, and also thanks are due to Peter Horner, Robin Newell, Jim Whiting and Alan Cross for their help. We all sincerely hope that you will enjoy the selection, even if you weren't there!

*Mick Webber*

Willesden's RTW 491 waits at traffic lights in Shoreditch High Street on route 6, next to Camberwell's Metro-Cammell bodied RTL 983 on the 35, nicely showing the difference in width between these two classes. The RTW would see out its service days at Riverside, before becoming a trainer, and the RTL would be delicensed in June 1966. (Alan Cross)

Willesden's RTW 232 works the 8B, a Sunday only route from Old Ford to Alperton, and this journey is turning short at the garage. Metro-Cammell RTL 725 on the summer Sunday 35A is in the background on its way to the Royal Forest Hotel in Chingford. (Alan Cross)

RTL 1456 left Aldenham works after overhaul in June 1964 and went to Stockwell, having been fitted with a 1947 Park Royal roofbox body. Freshly painted, it passes Selfridges in Oxford Street on route 88. It is going to Acton Green. The final destination has not been displayed neatly, often a feature of long destination blinds where the weight on the rollers caused slippage. RM 1770, behind, is returning to its garage at Middle Row, North Kensington. (Alan Cross)

It is July 1968, and buses are diverted in Oxford Street to avoid the road works taking place at Oxford Circus in connection with the new Victoria Line. RM 457 arrived at Middle Row garage in February of that year and stayed until October 1971. Here it turns from Oxford Street into Old Cavendish Street. (Capital Transport)

Metro-Cammell RTL 685 from Gillingham Street is at Warren Street in June 1966 on a rush hour short working, Despite its smart appearance, it was withdrawn later that month and sold for scrap. Buses were losing their traditional cream relief band at this time, for the new flake grey version, as seen on the 29 behind. Construction work is in hand for construction of the Euston Road underpass. (Capital Transport)

RM 9 from Riverside garage is outside the Hilton Hotel in Park Lane in April 1966. Route 74B was a Mon-Fri route from Camden Town to Hammersmith. The bus carries a 'BESI' electronic scanner between decks, which tracked the movement of each bus along its route in connection with receivers mounted on short concrete posts. (Capital Transport)

When FRM I was new in June 1966, it was hoped to be the forerunner of a fleet of front entrance Routemasters, but this was not to be. It is seen in Vauxhall Bridge Road at the southern end of its journey on route 76 from Tottenham garage. It is seen in its original condition without opening windows. After a fire in September the following year, it was fitted with quarter drops. The FRM also heralded the introduction of very small white fleet numbers on new vehicles, in place of the traditional gold transfers, a change that was short lived. (Barry Le Jeune)

Victoria in December 1965, and both buses in this view have terminated here. Park Royal RTL 141 from Walworth is ready to depart for Blackwall Tunnel on the 185, which had been a direct replacement for tram route 58 in October 1951. The bus moved on to Stockwell and Clapton before being withdrawn and sold for further service in Ceylon (Sri Lanka) in August 1968. RM 1352 from Stockwell waits on the 181 for its return south to Streatham. RMs were operated on the 181 on Sundays at this time. (Capital Transport)

Route 26 was introduced in August 1959 as part of the trolleybus replacement programme, covering most of trolleybus route 661. Park Royal bodied RT 4647 is seen at Aldgate in June 1965, looking nice and fresh just two months after its overhaul. (Capital Transport)

The low sun highlights Park Royal roofbox bodied RT 2243 from Holloway as it makes its way by St Pauls in November 1965. The bus was to last until March 1969 before it was withdrawn and sent for scrap. (Capital Transport)

Weymann RT 1303, based at Holloway, negotiates Piccadilly Circus in December 1965. Route 14 started at Hornsey Rise for its trip to Putney, and was extended to Kingston on Sunday. It was one of the routes to have a summer Sunday extension, and in the case of the 14 the extension was to Hampton Court. (Capital Transport)

Kingsway in May 1969. Merton's RT 1731 had a Park Royal body, and had been based there since June 1965. It still carries a blind with upper case lettering, unlike its newer cousin MB 177, which is behind on route 501. The RT lasted until September 1976, while the MB had gone for scrap six months before after just seven years of service. (Capital Transport)

Above: A livery experiment was carried out in May 1968, when RM 523 emerged from a repaint without the relief on the centre band. Many thought that the all over red appearance did not suit the Routemaster, but RMs 494 illustrated, 496, 508, 514 and 520 followed, and all were allocated to Highgate. The experiment was not a success, and all six were repainted in September. Back in the 1950s some RTs had had their traditional black mudguards painted red for a trial period, but this too proved unsuccessful.

Right: In August 1969 RM 1737 entered service at Riverside on route 11 elaborately painted to promote Silexine paint, having been at Aldenham for three weeks whilst the livery was applied by a contractor. Reaction was mixed, but the bus remained in this state until September 1970, when it was returned to traditional colours. The next bus to be used in such a way was not until April 1971, when RM 971 promoted Yellow Pages. Many more followed, and the practice is now commonplace. (Alan Snatt)

Route 171A was a Sunday only service between Abbey Wood and Tottenham, a route length of over 23 miles. RT 3756 from New Cross is entering Beresford Square in Woolwich from Plumstead Road. The old Woolwich Arsenal buildings are behind, all of which have now been demolished with the exception of the main entrance gate. (Alan Cross)

RTL 422 was based at Tottenham and is working route 171 in Waldram Park Road, Forest Hill nearing the end of its 91 minute run from Bruce Grove, Tottenham. The year is 1967, and the route would see conversion to Routemaster operation the following year. RTL 422 would be sold for scrap in May 1969 after being withdrawn from service at Tottenham in April 1968. (John Herting/Online Transport Archive)

Delacourt Road, Blackheath on 3rd July 1967. This terrace of shops, and many others, were swept away with the building of the Blackwall Tunnel relief road later that year. Route 108A should be diverted later that month to allow demolition to take place. Also later that month, RTL 1126 would be withdrawn.
(Mick Webber)

Blackheath Royal Standard with Sidcup Weymann RT 1117. It arrived from Aldenham in July 1968, and still looks in top condition in this view on route 228A. The route had just been permanently diverted here, via Strathenden Road following the closure of Delacourt Road, as part of the Blackwall Tunnel new approach road.
(Peter Horner)

Brookmill Road Deptford on 5th April 1968. Catford RT 1843 is on route 47. It will go in for a repaint in September and stay until becoming a trainer in 1970. The large building in the background is Carrington House, then a refuge for down and outs, and now luxury flats. (Mick Webber)

The most south-easterly point for central buses during this period was Farningham. The main 21 route from Moorgate, worked to Sidcup with a Sat and Sun extension here, and the 21A worked here from Woolwich on Mon-Fri. RT 4542 had only arrived at Sidcup after overhaul in February 1967, not long before this view was taken on 13th May. A sister vehicle on the 401 is following. (David Christie)

A busy scene at Catford, St Lawrence Church in about 1962. Two Park Royal RTLs from Walworth leave on the 185. RTL 1032 on the left is turning short at Camberwell Green, and 169 is working through to Victoria. RTL 169 was sold for further service in Cape Town in 1964. The 185 was a replacement for tram route 58. To the right work is in hand for the new Town Hall extension. (Capital Transport)

This is Sangley Road in Catford. Two Park Royal RTs from Catford, 4423 and 2189, are on route 124. RT 4423 on the left has had its last overhaul, being withdrawn in 1971, but RT 2189 will see one more trip to Aldenham before being sold in 1977. At this time route 124 was a long route stretching across south east London from Forest Hill to Woolwich via Eltham and Welling during rush hours. (Capital Transport)

The film 'Carry on Regardless' has just been released, and it is 1961. Catford RT 920 loads up at the stop outside the Lewisham Town Hall Concert Hall in Catford on route 75. The route has since been diverted from here to serve Lewisham instead of Woolwich. (Capital Transport)

The Erith to Woolwich 122A was extended to Crystal Palace on Sundays, supporting the 122's reduced frequency on that day.. Plumstead RT 4001 was allocated there after overhaul in September 1966. It had a repaint in February 1970, and finished its service days there in 1974. The first stage of the Victoria Line is advertised, and so this scene at Crystal Palace is after September 1968. (Robin Newell)

Saunders RT 376 received its last overhaul in 1965 and was sent to Merton on 3rd May. It looks splendid in this view on the 49 at Crystal Palace, using the additional stand sometimes provided on the south side of the Parade. At this time route 49 operated daily between Crystal Palace and Shepherds Bush with a Sunday extension to Willesden Junction where RT 376 is destined. (Capital Transport)

RM 1677 had been delivered in August 1963 and arrived at Peckham in September. On 12th October, new weekends only route 63A commenced to Hampstead Heath following route 63 to north of Kings Cross and then via Camden Town and Chalk Farm. This view was taken on Crystal Palace Parade on that first day. (R. P. Quinlan)

Route 37 crossed south London from Hounslow in the west to Peckham in the east. Metro-Cammell RTL 810 from Stockwell negotiates traffic at Brixton from Stockwell Road into Brixton Road. This was not the normal route for the 37, suggesting the bus is on a garage run from its home base. on its way east. The Astoria cinema can be seen in the background, it was closed in July 1972. The bus was withdrawn in June 1966, and saw further service with Barton Transport. (Alan Cross)

Also at Brixton is Saunders RT 1780 from Streatham on route 159. The bus would go for its last overhaul in September 1965, and this view dates from about 1964. In the background is a reminder of a nationalised industry - the Gas Board showroom. (Alan Cross)

Monday to Friday route 228A followed its parent route from Chislehurst as far as Greenwich, then travelled the half mile down Blackwall Lane to turn at the south side of the Tunnel. Sidcup RT 960 is standing at the Gordon Arms terminus at in Edward Road, Chislehurst. (John Herting/Online Transport Archive)

Route 182 was introduced as part of the final tram to bus conversion in July 1952 to replace tram service 46. The main weekday service from Cannon Street to Eltham was extended to Woolwich in the rush hours and on Saturdays. RT 1956 from New Cross is leaving Eltham Well Hall bus station. (John Herting/Online Transport Archive)

Route 138 was converted to one man operation on 10th May 1969. The picturesque stand in Princes Way, at Coney Hall sees MB 321 waiting for its 24 minute run back to return to Bromley North. The bus was new to Bromley in October 1968 for the conversion of route 126. (Michael Rouum)

Climbing St Johns Hill, Clapham Junction is Stockwell's RTL 1235 on the Saturday and Sunday 77C service which operated via Westminster Bridge to serve St Thomas's Hospital. Its Monday to Friday equivalent was the 77A which operated via Lambeth Bridge. The bus was withdrawn in May 1967. The route in this form lasted until 1981, the small number of other C suffixed routes having been withdrawn before then. (Alan Cross)

Route 255 had replaced trolleybus route 655 on 9th November 1960. By the time this photo was taken, Riverside had taken over operation of the route from Hanwell on 3rd October 1965. RM 231 also climbs the hill out of Clapham Junction on its way to Hammersmith. (Alan Cross)

Clapham Common in 1964, where RTs and RTLs are very much in the majority. RTLs 1105 and 359 from Gillingham Street and Shepherds Bush, RTs 189 and 3072 from Norwood and Merton and RTL 1286 from Camberwell share the same stretch of road here. The 88 extension to Banstead Hospital was a Sunday afternoon only working. The 35A was a long summer Sunday route running from Clapham Common to Chingford, Royal Forest Hotel, where it stood on the edge of Epping Forest. (John Parkin, Alan Cross x 2)

All-Leyland built RTW 130 was allocated to Walworth for its last service days, finishing in November 1965. It had travelled on route 45 from Hampstead Heath to Clapham Common, where it is seen turning right into Long Road on its way to Battersea and South Kensington. (Alan MacGregor)

Clapham Common Old Town terminus. Metro-Cammell RTL 875 has turned short here on the 137 and stands next to Merton's Saunders RT 237 on route 118. The RTL would be sold to Ceylon (Sri Lanka) in August 1967 and the RT for scrap to Wombwell Diesels in July 1972. (Alan Cross)

South Lambeth Road, Stockwell in the mid-sixties. RTL 1107 was allocated to Stockwell after overhaul in December 1962 and remained there until withdrawn in May 1967. It was sold to Ceylon (now Sri Lanka) in 1968. Both buses here are on route 2B and RM 1360 at the rear, also from Stockwell, was allocated there from new in December 1962 for route 37. It stayed until August 1967. (Alan Cross)

In their later years, some RTLs returned from Aldenham with roofbox bodies in an attempt to marry up older bodies with chassis to be disposed of. RTL 1438 was one of these, and it went for service to Camberwell with this 1947 Park Royal body in July 1964. It passes the site of the tram change pit at Gresham Road, Brixton. (Alan Cross)

Thornton Heath received RM 270 in May 1962 for daily operation on route 64, and it stayed until October 1963. It returned after overhaul in January 1964, but with the body from RM 201. It is seen here with its second body at Mitcham Fair Green on the Sunday only route 115A. (John Parkin Collection)

Metro-Cammell RTL 871 is working from Stockwell and is in Bishopsford Road, St Helier. It is working the all day Sunday working of the 88 to Belmont Station, which during the afternoons continued to Banstead Hospital. Like many of its class, it was another sold in 1967 to Ceylon (Sri Lanka) for further service. The Metro-Cammell bodies were 5cwt heavier than the standard RT family variants. (John Parkin Collection)

RTL 1436 was at Stockwell from February 1960 until it went for its final overhaul in February 1964. It stands at the Raynes Park Station terminus of route 77C just ahead of the spot in the view on the next page. The 77C was originally a Sunday only service when introduced in 1959. A Saturday service was added in 1965 and remained until the route was withdrawn in April 1981. The Stockwell RTLs were replaced by RTs in 1967 and by RMs in 1972. The route was shared with Merton. (John Herting/ Online Transport Archive)

Standing by the Southern Region South Western main line at Raynes Park are Merton's RT 2149 on route 157, with Streatham's RT 4472 behind. RT 2149 still has the old five line blind fitted which was mostly phased out in the 1950s, whilst RT 4472 displays the newer four line version including lower case letters. (John Parkin)

Mitcham Cricketers stand in about 1966. RM 1349 spent nearly five years at Stockwell. Keeping it company are Saunders RT 4233 from Wandsworth and Weymann RT 1084 from Merton. Being a Sunday (or bank holiday) all three buses are destined for lengthy runs across London. (Alan Cross)

Standing on the forecourt at Morden station is Saunders RT 4474 from Sutton. The bus would go for its last overhaul in April 1965. A five-line via blind is fitted, a style quite rare by the mid-1960s. The 164A provided the through passenger with a variety of views, culminating in the landscape of Epsom Downs at Tattenham Corner, well known to racegoers. (John Parkin)

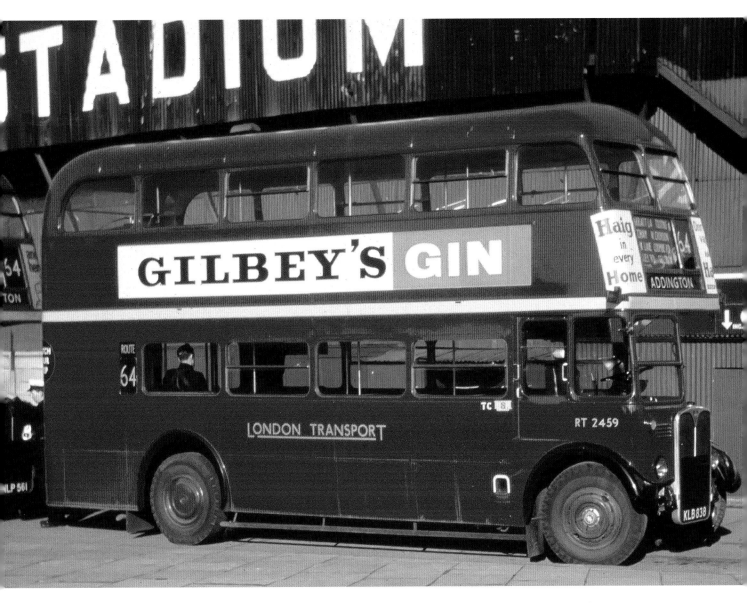

As a result of stage 7 of the trolleybus conversion programme, route 64 was extended from West Croydon over former trolleybus route 630 to Wimbledon Stadium. This occurred on 20th July 1960, although the route was cut back from the Stadium to Tooting Broadway on 10th May 1961. Elmers End supplied Routemasters, and Croydon used RTs, as shown here.

A 1947 Weymann body was fitted to RT 2636 in 1959, and in this view in 1960, it is on loan to Leatherhead for the Epsom race course special service. Many garages sent buses for this extra work, and three can be seen here at Epsom Station. The bus was sold for further service in South Africa in 1964. Route 406F provided the service between the Downs and the station, while its lesser known sister route, the 406E, provided the link from the town centre. (Alan Cross)

RM 1905 turns into London Road, Morden on route 93 in August 1969. The bus was new in 1964 and carries its original body. At this time, it was based at Chelverton Road, Putney. The brake cooling grilles either side of the radiator have now been filled in, but the between decks front ventilator has yet to be modified. Chelverton Road utilised their spare RMs on the 93 on Saturdays. (Capital Transport)

The few routes left in the 1960s being worked by TDs were at Kingston and Edgware. The former had the 215, 215A, 218 and 219, and TD 128 is seen here working the 215 in Esher, the route being converted to RFs in February 1962. This particular bus was withdrawn in September 1961. This early sixties view provides a striking contrast in bus designs operating in London during this decade with the MBS opposite. (Bruce Jenkins)

On 23rd August 1969, MBSs 550-559 entered service from Hounslow in modified form on routes 110 and 111, with split entrances for either paying the driver or using the machine. MBS 556 is pictured here at Hounslow bus station. (Alan Snatt)

Left: Kingston was the last garage to operate the RF class on central area routes. RFs 486 and 424 are working the 215 and 218 in this view in Portsmouth Road, Esher on 19th April 1969. The last RF to run was RF 507, which arrived at Kingston garage in the early hours of 31st March 1979. The advertisements on the rear panels rest uncomfortably over the beading on the bodywork. (David Christie)

Two views of a classic bus at Northwood on 4th May 1963, the last Saturday of Uxbridge garage route 225, which last ran the following Tuesday, being taken over by route 232. RT 779 has a Weymann body dating from 1951. The route had a Sunday afternoon extension to Mount Vernon Hospital. (John Cosford)

RT 3386 from Uxbridge sits in traffic in Hillingdon on route 98B. It is being overtaken by a Bedford Dormobile, a very popular vehicle in the 1960s. The 98B formed part of the complex network of routes of the 98/198 family between Ruislip/Uxbridge and Hounslow via Hayes. (Capital Transport)

Saunders RT 3062 from Twickenham is at Hayes at work on the 90B to Yeading. It passes a sister vehicle on the return trip to Kew in March 1966. This bus is now preserved. A three-wheel Reliant Regal emerges from the side road on the left)

Route 195 was introduced on 3rd October 1965 running between Perivale and Southall, with some extensions to Hayes Station and Hayes North. On 30th May 1967, it was extended from Hayes North to serve Charville Lane Estate, where RT 4462 is seen the following year. The route was withdrawn on 7th September 1968 and replaced with an amended route 105. (John Herting/Online Transport Archive)

RTL 1433 went to Stonebridge from Aldenham overhaul in August 1964, and stayed until withdrawn in October 1968. It is working the 112 and seen here at Ealing Common bound for the Broadway after travelling around the North Circular Road from Palmers Green. (John Herting/Online Transport Archive)

The Feathers Restaurant and pub is the backdrop in this view at Ealing Broadway in 1964. Turnham Green's Saunders bodied RT 1608 is turning right on route 65. It is operating one of the many short workings to Chessington Zoo, rather than the southern terminus of Leatherhead. (Alan Cross)

MBS 268 is an MCW bodied AEC Merlin delivered in November 1968 entering service at Turnham Green. A major new route revision in the Ealing area took place on 30th November 1968, and route E3 was one of the new flat fare routes to be introduced. This view is at Greenford as the bus turns from Greenford Road into Otter Road. Put into store in August 1975, after less than seven years service, the bus was sold in March 1977 to Wombwell Diesels, ending up with several operators in Australia, (Capital Transport)

Route 198 ran between Hayes Station and Uxbridge. It was a Mon-Sat route with an allocation of eight buses from Uxbridge garage on Monday-Friday but only five on Saturday. Introduced between Uxbridge Station and Hounslow West Station on 23rd January 1957, the route replaced parts of routes 98 and 220. In 1963 it reached Hounslow Bus Station before being withdrawn in June 1968. RT 4335 is seen on the original section of route not long before withdrawal. (John Herting/Online Transport Archive)

Saunders RT 1783 from Southall on route 97 has turned short at Brentford Half Acre. The bus had been at HW since its last overhaul in August 1965 and remained until December 1968. RTs had worked this route since 1954 and, apart from a Sunday allocation from Hanwell in the early 1960s, Southall was the only garage to work it until its withdrawal in November 1968. (John Herting/Online Transport Archive)

Route 268 was a replacement for trolleybus routes 626 and 628 in 1960, and was allocated Routemasters from Shepherds Bush. RTLs and, later on, RTs did however appear occasionally, and RT 2520 with a 1954 Park Royal body is an example. This is Butterwick at Hammersmith with an RMC behind on the 715. The route had quite a short life and by the end of the 1960s, its number had been reused for a new route serving Hampstead, introduced in September 1968. (Capital Transport)

Travelling through Station Road, Harrow, is Weymann RT 1881, which spent time at Edgware from June 1963 until March 1968 when it went to Aldenham for its last overhaul. It is making its way to Ruislip Lido on the 114 from Edgware Station, on what looks like a Sunday in the days when shops were all closed on the holy day. In January 1966 routes 114 and 158 had swopped their western termini to save one bus in the schedules, Ruislip Lido becoming the new terminus for the 114. (Capital Transport)

RT 693 was at Harrow Weald from September 1963 until January 1968, when it went for overhaul. It emerged from works with a different chassis and body, and returned to HD. We see it here on route 158 looking very smart with its Weymann body gleaming in the sun at Wealdstone. (Capital Transport)

In January 1966 the union representing London busmen began an overtime ban in pursuit of a pay increase. One week after this began, London Transport responded by temporarily withdrawing 44 red bus routes so that the service on the remainder could remain the same. Consent was given to other operators to cover these for as long as the overtime ban continued. Valliant Direct Coaches operated on routes 79, 97 and 230 and this 1961 Duple bodied AEC is seen on the 230 in Wealdstone in less clement weather than is shown in the previous photo. (Capital Transport)

Much has changed in London since the 1960s and this view of RM 439 on the old trolleybus stand at North Finchley in 1969 is just one small example. Now, passengers here board and leave buses in a dark and ugly covered bus station. Fifty years later, Holloway garage, from which the bus is operating in this view, was to become a major operator of all-electric buses nearly sixty years after it lost its trolleybus fleet. (Alan Snatt)

The Edgware stand in the station forecourt with Weymann RT 4075 from Enfield on the 107A, standing next to TD 114 on the 240A. The TD is a Leyland Tiger with Mann Egerton bodywork delivered in July 1949. It was withdrawn in October 1962. Route 240A was restricted to single deck operation by a low bridge at Mill Hill Broadway which was rebuilt to normal height during construction of the M1 in 1965. It was converted to double-deck operation and restricted to Sunday operation in January 1966. (Denis Battams/2RT2 Group)

RT 1932 looks resplendent after a repaint at the end of the decade. It is based at Edgware, and stands on the station forecourt there on route 240A, a Sunday only operation by this time requiring four buses. (Capital Transport)

Route 251 from Burnt Oak to Arnos Grove served some very pleasant scenery around the Totteridge and Mill Hill areas. This is Mill Hill Village, with RF 355 from Edgware garage picking up at a request stop opposite a once familiar Police box. (Capital Transport)

Route 260 replaced trolleybus route 660 in January 1962, and was extended past the old terminus at North Finchley, to Barnet. RM 907 was new in 1961, and is seen here at Barnet preparing for the return trip to Willesden Garage. The full route to Hammersmith only operated on Mon-Fri rush hours and Saturdays at this time. Although the trolleybuses have gone, a presence remains in the traction standard being used to support a street lamp. (Capital Transport)

RM 591 is still in its original condition in this 1964 view, with full depth ventilation grille between decks, brake cooling grilles, and inset number plate. It also carries a cream relief band, later to be replaced by flake grey, in this view in East End Road Finchley. Route 143 was extended from Archway to Farringdon Street on 1st February 1961 in part replacement for trolleybus routes 517/617. (Capital Transport)

Golders Green was, and still is, a major bus terminus, providing interchange with the Underground and fifteen bus routes in 1968. Weymann RT 186 from Wandsworth, leaves on route 28. The route had a Sunday afternoon extension to Putney Heath for hospital visitors. (Capital Transport)

Park Road in Muswell Hill in March 1969. RM 1964 was new in July 1964, and is working the short local route 212, taking only 15 minutes from end to end. Until September 1968 rush hour limited stop 'Express' journeys completed the journey in 11 minutes. Twelve RTs operated the route on Mon-Fri. The RM requirement on Saturdays was twelve and six on Sundays. Three months after this photo the route will be withdrawn and replaced by flat-fare route W7. (Capital Transport)

Route 188A was a Sunday only operation worked with RTs from Holloway and RTLs from Camberwell. RTL 1238 was a Park Royal bodied bus allocated to Camberwell between October 1964 and June 1966, and waits here at the Archway terminus. The route was introduced in November 1964 and formed from the southern end of route 188 and the northern end of the 172. (Capital Transport)

This is Southgate, opposite the tube station, in May 1969. Weymann RT 4093 from Muswell Hill garage has arrived from Winchmore Hill on the 244. It will move on to see its last service days at Sutton in January 1971 and will be withdrawn in the following September. (Capital Transport)

It is October 1965, and Chalk Farm's RM 1725 is on the stand at Hampstead Heath on route 24. The bus was new in October 1963, and was at CF until November 1965, when front-entrance buses in the form of XA class Atlanteans took over. Thirty buses were required on the Mon-Fri running of the route. (Capital Transport)

A month after the previous view, and the tree to the left has lost its leaves. Route 24 received the new Atlanteans on 7th November 1965 from Chalk Farm, replacing RMs on the service. The change was part of comparative trials between doored vehicles and the first production RMLs, which were introduced at the same time from Tottenham on the 76 and later swopped with Chalk Farm's XAs. This is XA 31. (Capital Transport)

Blackstock Road, Finsbury Park is the location on 6th November 1967. RT 2843 from Holloway is a Weymann bodied bus on route 4A, and following is Park Royal RTL 1446 from Poplar on the 90-minute run to Becontree on the 106. The 4A route number had a life of just under ten years, being introduced in November 1961 and losing the suffix when extended to Tufnell Park in September 1971. (David Christie)

RTL 164 carries a Park Royal body built in 1952. It is working from Hackney on route 106 at Finsbury Park on 6th November 1967. It was withdrawn in September 1968. Although operated by Routemasters at weekends for a number of years, the 106 bade farewell to RT family operation on 2nd December 1968 when they took over on Monday to Friday also. (David Christie)

The trolleybus terminus at Wood Green was tucked away in Redvers Road, buses working an anti-clockwise loop, and standing on the wrong side of the road. K1 No.1112 from Stamford Hill depot, waits on Sunday only route 649A with West Green Metro-Cammell RTL 637 behind on the 233. Route 649A was replaced at stage 11 of the conversion scheme, which took place on the 19th July 1961, the route having last worked the Sunday before. (Denis Battams/2RT2 Group)

Westbury Avenue, Turnpike Lane in July 1966. Walthamstow's Saunders RT 255 is on route 144, a route shared with Wood Green. The Mon-Fri allocation was RT, with some RM operation at weekends, the exception being Leyton who only operated the route on Sundays with RTs. The bus spent a few months as a trainer before its final withdrawal from WW in June 1970. (Capital Transport)

Bus route 253 replaced the busy trolleybus 653 on 1st February 1961. RM 837 is at Stamford Hill on its way to Warren Street, and advertising the fact that the final section of the Victoria Line is now open. That happened in March 1969. Evidence of the stable allocation of routes at Stamford Hill garage is the upper case lettering on the eight year old via blind. (Capital Transport)

Among the reds and greens of London Transport buses and coaches in the 1960s, RM 664 was a unique unpainted bus. Even before RM 1 appeared there had been a suggestion that one of the new Routemasters could be left in unpainted aluminium to see how it would fare in London traffic. This idea followed a trial with unpainted cars on the District Line of the Underground. RM 664 entered service in July 1961, an event that was mentioned on BBC television's main evening news. It worked from eleven garages until it was repainted red in July 1965. Its last route in unpainted condition was the 123 from Walthamstow garage and the bus is seen in Seven Sisters Road a few weeks before going for painting. (Capital Transport)

RT 2827 carries a 1947 Weymann body from its 1960 Aldenham overhaul in this view. The bus was delicensed and sold in November 1964. RT 2561 is travelling in the other direction in this scene on route 135 in Southbury Road by Enfield garage. The point inspector is clearly sorting out an issue with the running of the route. (Alan Cross)

Tottenham High Road and RM 715 from Edmonton passes ex-London RTW 413, which was sold to Upminster and District in April 1966. The Routemaster, which was new to Edmonton in March 1961, is on route 127 which replaced trolleybus 627 at stage 10 of the conversion scheme in April 1961. The bus spent 14 years at EM. (Alan Cross)

Angel Road Edmonton, and Tottenham's Park Royal bodied RTL 1366 has travelled from Chingford Hatch on its way to Bounces Road on the 191. Its last service days were spent at AR from July 1966 until November 1967 when it was delicensed and prepared for its sale to Ceylon in July 1968. (John Herting/Online Transport Archive)

Saunders RT 1183 was transferred from Sutton to Enfield on 22nd March 1969 and still carries its Sutton garage code. It is leaving Lower Edmonton on route 128. Only three months remain for this bus to operate on the 128 as in June 1969 it will be withdrawn and replaced by flat-fare route W8. (Capital Transport)

RML 2266 was new in July 1965 and was one its type that first entered service from Tottenham on the 76 in November 1965. A little later in its career it is seen working from West Ham garage at the stop in Chingford Road next to Walthamstow Greyhound Stadium. Route 249 was introduced in April 1960 to partly replace trolleybus routes 697 and 699 and received its RMLs in February 1966. Long after the stadium closure and demolition, the iconic sign on the right remains preserved on site. (John Herting)

The 6B was a long and fairly short lived route that ran from January 1964 to September 1968 on Saturdays only between Chingford Mount and Kensal Rise. Walthamstow garage shared the route with Willesden and the former's RM 172 carries one of the earlier RM bodies in this 1968 view, though not by this time its original one. The location is Lea Bridge Road. (John Herting/Online Transport Archive)

Enfield's RT 4557 stands at the new bus station at Chingford on route 121. To the left is RT 2050, and on the right is the new order in the shape of MB 363, a November 1968 delivery. Between August 1966 and June 1969 the Monday to Saturday 121 was unusual in being operated by one-man operated RFs on Monday to Friday and crew operated RTs on Saturday. This was necessary to balance the driver's rosters at Enfield. (Capital Transport)

Route 257 was introduced in February 1960 to replace trolleybus route 557 at stage 5 of the conversion scheme. It was extended beyond the trolleybus terminus at Chingford Mount, to Chingford Royal Forest Hotel, where this view was taken. RM 245 was new to West Ham in April 1960, and was transferred to Walthamstow in March 1964. It stands next to Weymann RT 2483 and Saunders RT 1781, both from Leyton, working the 38. (John Herting)

Old Station Road, Loughton, and RF 365 from Loughton garage has arrived from South Woodford on the 254.
It was introduced in 1950 to cater for the expanding development of the area. From South Woodford it operated
via Buckhurst Hill to Loughton Station and then around a loop via Debden and Loughton town centre to terminate
back at Loughton Station. On Sundays, it worked from Loughton to Buckhurst Hill only. (Mick Webber Collection)

Loughton Station in the early 1960s. RTL 1140 from Clapton will be the first away back to Victoria, followed by Loughton RT 4699. The running time for this route was 82 minutes. Behind is the rebuilt and resited station dating from 1940 which was completed in advance of the former LNER line being electrified and given over to the Central Line. (C. Carter)

At the terminus at the Green Man, Leytonstone is Loughton's Saunders RT 1260. The bus arrived from Aldenham in July 1965, and stayed at this garage until withdrawn in January 1969. The modern garage at Loughton was built opposite the old LGOC building, which still stands, long after the modern structure was demolished. (John Herting)

This is Balaam Street in West Ham. Weymann RTL 1362 from West Ham travels north on the 278, a route that was introduced at stage 6 of the trolleybus conversion scheme in April 1960 to part replace route 687. Principally an RM route, there were a few scheduled RTL workings in morning peak periods which were spare from route 25. Note the trolleybus overhead support poles in use for street lighting. (John Herting/Online Transport Archive)

RT 2776 is another of the unique buses featured in this album. It was one of two RTs and an RTL that toured the United States, and then Canada, in spring and summer 1952. RT 2775 was a workshop, stores and staff accommodation bus and RTL 1307 was used as an information and exhibition centre. RT 2776 was employed in giving rides to the locals in the many places visited and was always immediately recognisable by the ventilators fitted above the upper deck front windows. The bus kept its original body until its last overhaul and is seen in Wanstead in June 1965. (Capital Transport)

Route 262 commenced on 31st December 1966 between Victoria & Albert Docks and Leyton, being extended to Chingford in September 1968. RML 2384 was new to Poplar garage in February 1966 and transferred to Leyton garage in December 1966 and stayed until May 1970. It is captured here in Plaistow Road on its way from Victoria and Albert Docks to Chingford Station. (Capital Transport)

When RTL 1438 emerged from Aldenham in July 1964, it carried a 1947 Park Royal roofbox body. After two years at Camberwell, it was transferred to Poplar, and is seen here at the 108's northern end, Bow, on a garage journey to Poplar in November 1967. RTLs worked the 108 until September 1968, when they were replaced by RTs. Double-deck operation finished just a month later when, on 26th October, MBs took over. After a period in store, RTL 1438 was sold to Pickersgill & Laverick of Barnsley in May 1969. (David Christie)

Carpenters Road in Stratford in April 1969. Dalston RLH 58 heads for Maryland Station on route 178. The bus was a Dalston resident from May 1959 until April 1971 when it was withdrawn along with route 178, which was partially replaced by flat-fare route S3. The low bridge behind carries the main line to Liverpool Street. (David Christie)

Mare Street, Hackney is the setting for this view of Saunders RT 4813 from Leyton on the 38A. It is about to turn right into Graham Road on its way to Victoria. It left Leyton garage in February 1965 for overhaul. Clapton garage is just under the railway bridge and to the right. (Alan Cross)

The 253A was a short lived Monday to Saturday route. It replaced most of the 170 when it was introduced in January 1964, and was operated by Clapton with RTLs until they were superseded by RTs in September 1967; its withdrawal coming in March 1968. RTL 1427 is in good condition in this mid-1960s view, after its overhaul in June 1964. (Alan Cross)

The bus map for the period says that service 100 is "irregular". The twelve minute journey from Barking to Beckton (10 minutes for the return) was certainly that. Buses from Upton Park, ex route 15, worked it, and RML 2518 is pictured here in Barking. The bus was new to the garage in July 1966 and stayed until June 1973. Had the 100 been scheduled in isolation, inefficient crew duties would have resulted thus it was linked to the 15 as a scheduling device. (Capital Transport)

RT 519 has turned at Leyton Bakers Arms, and is taking stand time at the triangle outside Leyton bus garage. The weekday only 10A provided a service from here to the country terminus at Abridge. The year is 1967. (John Herting/Online Transport Archive)

Hornchurch used four RLH buses for the weekday route 248. RLH 52 spent its last five years at the garage before being exported to America in April 1971. It is seen here at Cranham. The low height buses were required to pass under the bridge in St Mary's Lane near Upminster. (Capital Transport)

Station Parade in South Street, Romford. RT 2091 from North Street on route 247, carries one of the oldest bodies in the fleet, a Park Royal unit from 1947. Green RT 4165, from Grays on the 370, also has a Park Royal unit in this view taken around 1964. (Alan Cross)

The Park Royal body on RT 482 looks very smart on 29th May 1967, after arriving from overhaul at North Street in April. The driver negotiates the roundabout at Parkside in Romford on route 247. For many decades until withdrawal in July 1981 the 247 operated beyond Harold Wood through open country side to Brentwood. (David Christie)

# Pearson's Canal Companion

# STOURPORT & BLACK COUNTRY RINGS
# BIRMINGHAM CANAL NAVIGATIONS

Published by Wayzgoose
Staffordshire DE13 9RS
email:enquiries@jmpearson.co.uk
www.jmpearson.co.uk

WAYZGOOSE

# Lock-wheeling

Wellbeing by Water is not a new phenomenon imaginatively concocted by the Canal & River Trust's unctuous Marketing Department. Seventy years ago a series of guide books - anonymously written, but published by CRT's predecessors, British Waterways - cogently extolled the hidden benefits of inland waterway exploration to a post-war public prepared to sink their teeth into any leisure activity which could be relied upon to put austerity firmly in its place. In those halcyon days nationalised industries tended to be entrusted to the leadership of old soldiers with a proven track record in mass destruction. In his enthusiastic Forewards to the fourteen booklets constituting the series, Major-General Sir Reginald Kerr highlighted the 'invigorating physical and mental benefits' to be derived from pleasure cruising; in the same jolly hockey sticks tone with which he had once cajoled his troops into battle.

Retrospectively oozing charm and innocence in equal measure, these old British Waterways guides can be picked up on the internet for a song and provide a rewarding exercise in nostalgia, an inherent appeal of the inland waterways often overlooked in the rush to promote their contemporary relevance to an inclusive audience.

The guides' cartographically simplistic strip-maps gave no hint of the compass's cardinal points - a characteristic Pearsons themselves are occasionally lambasted for by anal-retentives - but once one has taken to the water (towpath walking was tacitly not encouraged in those days for they were not legal 'rights of way') north tends to lose its magnetism in more senses than one.

Delightful woodcuts adorned the original RAF blue covers, and if the descriptive text accompanying the maps had a tendency to wax lyrical about country houses miles distant from the canal, well that only emphasised how much easier it was in those days to get around England by public transport. Black and white photographs illustrated the boat-empty canals and their car absent hinterlands. At Wombourne, cricket on the village green implied that one only need turn up in whites to be roped in. Even the adverts oozed charm: 'Send 3d for an illustrated brochure.' How much more rewarding than clicking a mouse; the anticipation must have been nigh on unbearable.

Tending to concentrate on one historic canal at a time, prospective readers were required to purchase two or three booklets to cruise a circular route. Moreover, they would have had to have made their way blindfolded, so to speak, along the Birmingham Canal Navigations' main lines, which were deemed far too unwholesome to be delineated for the benefit of gullible holidaymakers. That minor detail didn't deter stalwarts. In *The Trouble With Canals*, John Liley stoically relates a family holiday around the Black Country Ring in 1952; ditto Andrew Dow aboard a BW hire boat on the Stourport Ring nine years later in *Memories of a Railway Childhood*. Seventy years from now, will our guides be regarded just as quaintly? We are all hostages of the parameters time has abitrarily foisted upon us, and not even an expert negotiator can free us from its clasp. Canals have a tendency to contradict the notion that they are impervious to change, and it seems likely that those we embrace today for their restorative powers will be unrecognisable in the future. Meanwhile, the past remains the place to go, and with a Pearson's Canal Companion you can venture there safe in the knowledge you're suitably armed. Indeed, there's no imperative to return if you find it conducive. Happy time-travelling!

# Contents

# RIVER SEVERN Worcester 4mls/11k/1hr*

SWAPPING the stolid waters of a canal for the less predictable currents of a river, or vice versa, is invariably a bit of an adventure. It isn't always easy to tell whether that buoyancy you suddenly feel is current flowing under your hull or adrenalin coursing through your veins. But, make no mistake, your senses are heightened.

Waterside Worcester's infatuation with the Severn is on the wane ... and has been for the best part of a century to be brutally honest. Dripping (*almost* literally) with atmosphere, old photographs depict a quayside thronged with pleasure steamers gunwale deep with hat-wearing day-trippers. Trip boats still ply spasmodically, but not with the ambition of Roberts' Castle Line of yore, who regularly steamed down to Tewkesbury or up to Stourport with their garrulous, pipe-smoking, parasol-wielding cargoes. Risk averse insurance premiums load the dice against such innocent pleasures now; plus our

attention span is demonstrably not what it was.

Downstream the river heads for Tewkesbury and Gloucester through the paired, side-by-side, Diglis River Locks as covered in our *Severn & Avon Canal Companion.* Upstream, 'Sabrina' flows past a slightly incongruous row of redbrick terraced villas, the Diglis House Hotel, and King's School's striking, prow-shaped boathouse. But these are no more than warm-up acts for the Cathedral, the juxtaposition of the noble building and the wide river being one of the great inland waterway scenes, or at least it was until someone omitted to keep the trees trimmed. For a more favourable view of the Cathedral from the river you'll have to take yourself to Madison, Wisconsin USA, where in the

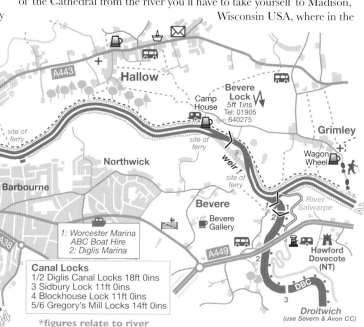

**Canal Locks**
1/2 Diglis Canal Locks 18ft 0ins
3 Sidbury Lock 11ft 0ins
4 Blockhouse Lock 11ft 0ins
5/6 Gregory's Mill Locks 14ft 0ins

1: Worcester Marina
ABC Boat Hire
2: Diglis Marina

'Passengers No More'
1: Henwick - closed 1965

note overlap and 180°
spin with Map 24

Diglis River Locks (duplicated)
7ft 11ins
Tel: 01905 354280

Bevere Lock
5ft 1ins
Tel: 01905 640275

6

**figures relate to river*

for details of facilities in Worcester turn to page 83

Chazen Museum resides one of Benjamin Williams Leader's most iconic canvases dating from 1894. On summer weekend afternoons and Bank Holidays a charming ferry operates in the vicinity of the Cathedral, rekindling scenes from days when such crossings were a common sight up and down the river. The ferrymen (and one lady!) are all volunteers and proceeds go to charity. Clinker built, the rowing boat, licensed to carry nine passengers, is called *Doris*, and the 'voyage' little less than heavenly.

The reach between the Cathedral and Worcester Bridge is designated a Swan Sanctuary in response to a period in the 1980s when swans were dying from lead poisoning; lead at that time being a component of angler's fishing weights. Fishing was subsequently banned and swans certainly now flourish on the river, as do herons, kingfishers and cormorants; even otters. Handy little bags of appropriate food for the swans and local duck population are available from riverside outlets.

Another prominent riverside landmark is the spire of St Andrew's (redundant and mostly demolished) church - nicknamed the 'Glovers' Needle' in homage to one of Worcester's old trades. Antiquated wharves and warehouses line the east bank of the river south of Worcester Bridge. Widened in the 1930s, the old parapet found its way into Edward Elgar's garden at Marl Bank, so enamoured was the composer of anything associated with his home town. Fee payable visitor moorings are provided on the city side of the river either side of the ornate, cast iron railway bridge which carries the pretty Malvern and Hereford line across the

*Cathedral Ferry*

river. A third bridge spanning the Severn is of modern origin, being a stylish pedestrian link (much used by students to reach the university) between the city centre and the west bank suburbs: the Severn Way swaps sides at this point.

Like a guest reluctant to depart, the river appears to be in no particular hurry to leave Worcester behind. One can't blame it, there is, after all, so much to see. The Pitchcroft plays host to the city's National Hunt race course which can trace its origins back to 1718. Other sports were enjoyed on these meadows. In 1824 a bare fisted boxing match went eighty-four rounds. Enviable riverside properties - some of which would not look out of place beside the Thames - look smugly down from the Henwick bank. A waterworks was opened on the Barbourne side in 1858, pumping water from the river before purifying it in filter beds. The Pump House survives and has been regenerated as an Environment Centre. Sadly, though, no formal provision has been made for boaters to moor and pay a visit; their

⚠ A pair of broad locks separate the basins from the river. Remember that they are closed overnight, re-opening at eight in the morning. Entering or leaving the river can pose problems, especially if the current is flowing quickly, and getting your crew on or off for the locks needs careful consideration. Even if you're heading upstream, the easiest access point is the pontoon immediately downstream of the lock entrance; the river's easily wide enough for you to turn once everyone's back on board. Coming downstream, turn after you've passed the entrance and you should find yourselves perfectly placed to drop your lock crew off on the pontoon. In any case, CRT often provide volunteer lock-keepers at Diglis now.

needs are seldom taken into consideration. Plans for a new footbridge at this point appear to have stalled, perhaps because the original cost of £9m stretched to £16m in 2022. Adjoining the Pump House is a pretty little park which goes by the seemingly outlandish name of Gheluvelt. Military historians will recognise this as the name of a Belgian village where the 2nd Battalion of the Worcestershire Regiment counter-attacked with such gallantry in October 1914 that Field Marshal French - not widely known for hyperbole - was heard to remark that they had 'saved the British Empire'.

Make the most of your encounter with the Severn, otherwise the three or four hours spent on the river between Worcester and Stourport are apt to flash swiftly by. Mooring can be problematical. Overnight berths on the lock pontoons are at the discretion of the lock-keepers and can't always be counted on. Similarly, though some pubs offer moorings for patrons, they're not extensive and are provided on a first come, first served basis.

Bevere Lock

The Malvern Hills slip into view in the neighbourhood of Bevere, glimpsed on the south-west horizon behind the spire of Hallow church. Queen Elizabeth I is said to have hunted for deer hereabouts; though, by all accounts, there are few places where she didn't. A loop in the river forms the three acre island of Bevere, a place of refuge for the good burghers of Worcester in medieval times when war or plague threatened. A new fish pass was opened here in 2020 to enable a rare fish called twaite shad to reach breeding grounds upstream. The revitalised Droitwich (Barge) Canal departs unostentatiously to the east, climbing through eight broadbeam locks to the former salt-making town which gives it its name, thence continuing as the narrowbeam Droitwich Junction Canal to meet the Worcester & Birmingham Canal at Hanbury Wharf - see Map 22. A full description of this enchanting Mid-Worcestershire mini-ring will be found in the sibling *Severn & Avon Canal Companion*.

Opened in 1771 and surveyed by Brindley - though actually engineered by John Priddey - the Droitwich Barge Canal flourished during the 19th century as an export route for the salt industry, an activity carried out in the vicinity since Roman times. When salt making declined this 'barge' canal fell into decay and was disused by the time of the First World War, its horse-drawn trows just a memory. In 1973 a trust was formed to restore the canal, and three decades and £12m later their laudable ambition bore fruit in 2011. And very popular it has proved too. Confirmation that canal restoration can work positively on many levels.

The village of Grimley stands nervously well back from the river, though anglers make use of the bumpy lane down to the water's edge to reach their perches in amongst the musky clumps of balsam. In the winter months cormorants occupy the high, skeletal branches of riverside trees, forming images reminiscent of Japanese prints. Yes, boating the Severn is huge fun: a treasured blur of alder and willow fringed banks broken by occasional outcrops of sandstone; caravan parks and static homes; cattle flank high in the river margin; kingfishers skimming like low flying aircraft over the water's surface; and the unruffled routine of the automated locks and their affable keepers.

*Autumn on Severn*

## Grimley
Map 1

Quiet village at the end of a No Through Road. Walkers skim it on the Severn Way, but boaters will find it hard to moor. Napoleon's brother, Lucien, lived at a house called Thorngrove for several years.

### Eating & Drinking
THE CAMP HOUSE - riverside downstream of Bevere Lock. Tel: 01905 640288. Peacocks in the garden, Bathams ambrosial beer, and authentically home cooked meals (by Lynne the landlady) render this isolated inn a veritable paradise on earth. It's been in the Wainwright family for eighty years, though sadly the rabbit and pigeon pies, once a fixture of the menu, are no longer a feature: 'Can't get anyone to shoot 'em!'. Limited moorings for customers. WR2 6LX
WAGON WHEEL - village centre. Tel: 01905 640340. 15th century thatched pub opposite the church. Closed Mondays. Lunches 12-2pm, dinners 6-9pm, Tue-Sat. Two sittings for Sunday lunch. WR2 6LU

## The Holts
Map 2

Cluster of settlements spread about both banks of the Severn. Lamprey fishing, employing putcheons, was a pastime on the river hereabouts. Holt itself lies on the Severn Way, and boasts a Norman church and the tower of a 14th century castle incorporated into a later house. Cafe and farm shop at Top Barn.

### Eating & Drinking
THE HOLT FLEET - west bank. Tel: 01905 620286. Prior to its architecturally ostentatious rebuilding in the Thirties, this riverside inn was a popular destination for steamer trips. Nowadays it's a comfortably furnished and family-owned inn/bistro. Limited moorings for patrons. WR6 6NL
THE WHARF INN - east bank. Tel: 01905 620337. Food and B&B. Moorings for patrons. WR6 6NN
LENCHFORD INN - Tel: 01905 620229. Breakfasts from 7.30am (8am weekends), meals 12-3pm and 6-9pm (5-8pm Suns). Moorings for patrons. WR6 6TB

### Shopping
Convenience store (gas, coal and logs) at Holt Fleet. The apple growers, Broomfields, have a farm shop and tea room on the (pavemented) road up to Holt Heath where there is also a post office stores and bus stop for services between Worcester and Stourport.

## Astley
Map 2

The centre of the village lies two miles west of the river. Glasshampton Monastery is nearby.

### Eating & Drinking
HAMPSTALL INN - The Burf. Tel: 01299 879884. Food daily from noon ex Sun evening. Mooring pontoon for patrons. DY13 0RY

### Things to Do
ASTLEY VINEYARD - Hampstall Lane. Tel: 01299 822907. Established in 1971, output is limited to just nine thousand bottles a year. Shop and tours. Open Fri-Sun, 10.30am-4pm. DY13 0RU

*9*

# 2 RIVER SEVERN Holt Fleet 5mls/11k/1½ hrs

CANALS and rivers, like men and women, are inherently the same, yet intrinsically different - though you wouldn't expect us to state definitively which is which in these gender fluid days. No, we would just encourage you to savour the river whilst you're on or beside it. What is it the French say? 'Vive la Difference!'

That dyed-in-the-wool canal man, L. T. C. Rolt, certainly enjoyed the river. He knew of 'no lovelier reach of the Severn below Stourport than that which extends from Lenchford Ferry to Lincombe Lock'. Moored for a couple of days opposite Shrawley Wood he recalled 'a hot walk through narrow, heavy-scented lanes by Borely was rewarded by two punnets of ripe raspberries'. These words appeared in *Worcestershire* published by Robert Hale in 1949 as part of their County Books series. Never reprinted and long out of print, it's nevertheless reasonably easy to find secondhand, and contains much of relevance to the contents

of this particular Canal Companion.

For much of this map, the river is left pretty much to its own devices, but at Holt Fleet the main road from Droitwich comes swooping down to cross the Severn on one of Thomas Telford's marvellous cast iron bridges. This one dates from 1828 and bears more than a passing resemblance to Galton Bridge (Map 14), though it would be hard to imagine a more contrasting setting. Holt Lock shares its characteristics with Bevere downstream and Lincombe up. All three were built in the 1840s as part of a scheme to improve the river's previously unreliable navigability. Interestingly, the engineer in charge of the project was Edward Leader Williams senior, father of the brothers we 'bumped into' back at Worcester. These days, given their regular diet of cabin cruisers and narrowboats, the locks appear preposterously large, but one has to remember they were constructed

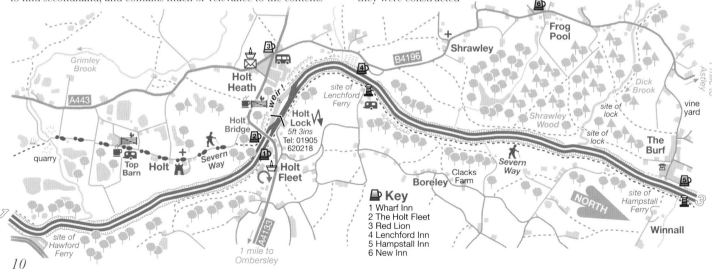

**Key**
1 Wharf Inn
2 The Holt Fleet
3 Red Lion
4 Lenchford Inn
5 Hampstall Inn
6 New Inn

with much larger vessels in mind. Indeed, just occasionally, one will come their way which does them justice. English Holiday Cruises' hotel boat *Edward Elgar* for example, which regularly cruises up and down the river. Sadly, though, the days when these gargantuan locks reverberated to the cut and thrust of tanker barges and pleasure steamers are long gone.

Dick Brook - emerging almost imperceptibly out of the shadowy trees on the west bank of the river - was once made navigable in the 17th century to serve a forge located deep in the woods. Two lock chambers were cut out of the sandstone, and cargoes of pig iron brought up from the Forest of Dean were probably transhipped into tub boats to be conveyed along the narrow stream to the doors of the forge. The brain behind this was Andrew Yarranton, a Brindley before his time.

Here and there a rash of caravan parks and shanty-like chalets mar otherwise unspoilt riverside meadows for everyone but their proud owners. Luckily this manifestation of mankind's capacity for destroying the very

tranquillity he desires is confined to those parts of the river nearest main roads. Arthritic gardening enthusiasts may recall that Clacks Farm played host to broadcasts of the BBC's *Gardeners' World* for a number of years. Stanley Baldwin - thrice Prime Minister between the wars - knew and loved these Severn reaches. He died at Astley Hall near The Burf in 1947. A small memorial to him stands beside the B4196.

Before Telford's bridge was built travellers crossed the river at Holt by ferry. Trace your finger down an old map of the Severn and you'll discover a sad litany of forgotten water crossings between Stourport and Worcester. Alas the idyllic and (to anyone ever charmed by H.G. Wells' account of 'Mr Polly's' sojourn at the "Potwell Inn") enviable lifestyle of the ferrymen came to an end once people had replaced Sunday afternoon rambles along the riverbank with a drive in a motor car. Not that there wasn't a darker side to ferrying. In 1919 the Hampstall Ferry was swamped by the waves of a passing steamer and sank, drowning nine people.

**Holt Fleet**

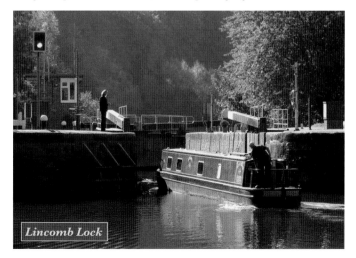

**Lincomb Lock**

# 3 R. SEVERN, STAFFS & WORCS CANAL Stourport 4mls/6lks/3hrs

STOURPORT suffers from a personality disorder: half convinced that it's a seaside town; half a rich heritage of canal wharves. But whether you have come here for a ninety-nine and a knees-up, or to pay homage to Brindley's basins, Stourport rarely disappoints. To moor in the Upper Basin, listening to time being measured by the quarter beats of the clocktower's sonorous bell, is one of the inland waterways' most magical experiences. And whatever entrance the boater makes - locking up from the Severn under the benign gaze of the Tontine Hotel, or descending into the dripping depths of York Street Lock from the canal - there will be few steerers able to resist exploration of the basins, shunting back and forth like some busy tug; turning in wide arcs or honing their reversing skills. The original and largest - known as the Upper Basin - opened in 1771, and connects through two wide-beam 'barge' locks with the river.

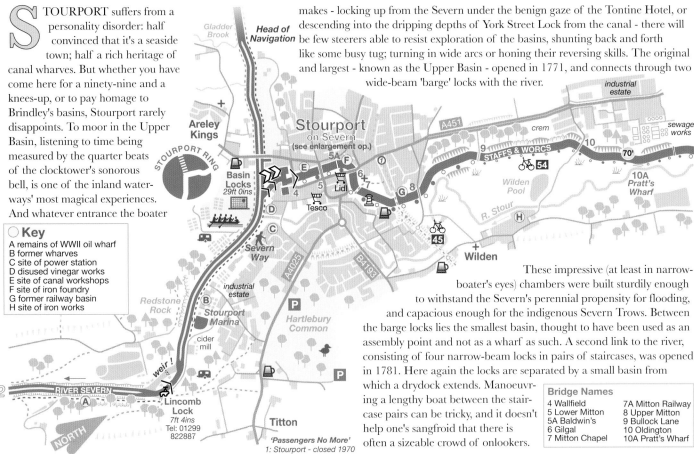

## Key
A remains of WWII oil wharf
B former wharves
C site of power station
D disused vinegar works
E site of canal workshops
F site of iron foundry
G former railway basin
H site of iron works

### Bridge Names
4 Wallfield
5 Lower Mitton
5A Baldwin's
6 Gilgal
7 Mitton Chapel
7A Mitton Railway
8 Upper Mitton
9 Bullock Lane
10 Oldington
10A Pratt's Wharf

Lincomb Lock
7ft 4ins
Tel: 01299 822887

'Passengers No More'
1: Stourport - closed 1970

These impressive (at least in narrowboater's eyes) chambers were built sturdily enough to withstand the Severn's perennial propensity for flooding, and capacious enough for the indigenous Severn Trows. Between the barge locks lies the smallest basin, thought to have been used as an assembly point and not as a wharf as such. A second link to the river, consisting of four narrow-beam locks in pairs of staircases, was opened in 1781. Here again the locks are separated by a small basin from which a drydock extends. Manoeuvring a lengthy boat between the staircase pairs can be tricky, and it doesn't help one's sangfroid that there is often a sizeable crowd of onlookers.

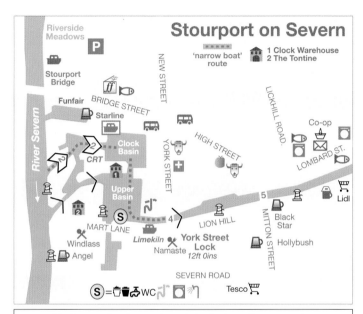

**Stourport on Severn**

`narrow boat` route

1 Clock Warehouse
2 The Tontine

Riverside Meadows

P

Stourport Bridge

Funfair

Starline

BRIDGE STREET

NEW STREET

River Severn

2

CRT

Clock Basin

YORK STREET

HIGH STREET

LICKHILL ROAD

Co-op

LOMBARD ST.

Upper Basin

2

MART LANE

Windlass

Angel

S

Limekiln

Namaste

4

York Street Lock
12ft 0ins

LION HILL

5

MITTON STREET

Black Star

Hollybush

Lidl

SEVERN ROAD

Tesco

S = 🗑♿WC

**The 'narrow boat' route through the basins at Stourport - from river to canal and vice versa - involves negotiating two staircase locks which are unusual in that there is no need to ensure that the lower chamber is empty when going down. Proceed cautiously: angles/clearances are tight!**

At the top of the narrow locks, and contemporary with their construction, lies the Clock Basin, interconnected with the Upper Basin. On a peninsula between these upper, boat-filled expanses of water stands the glorious Clock Warehouse, headquarters these days of the Stourport Yacht Club whose comparatively huge vessels migrate up-river to winter in the security of the basins.

Once there were two basins which lay to the east of Mart Lane. Known expediently as the 'Furthermost Basins', they dated from the early 19th century. The lower, reached through a wide lock, had a brief existence, closing in 1866 when the town gas works took over the site. The other basin flourished in an Indian Summer of commercial activity between 1926 and 1949 when coal boats (colloquially known as 'The Light Run') for the power station discharged in it; their dusty black cargoes of Cannock coalfield slack being unloaded by electric grab and carried in hoppers along an aerial ropeway to the power station's furnaces. Subsequently it was infilled for use as a timber yard, but it has been re-excavated as the focal point of a regeneration scheme, and is jostled by apartments now.

Another important element of the redevelopment of Stourport Basins concerns the return to life of the Tontine Hotel, similarly refurbished as apartments. It derived its unusual name from a system of speculative life insurance, the last surviving member of its original group of investors gaining full ownership of the building: fuel for skulduggery one imagines and the possibility of a plot which would inspire most detective story writers. In its heyday it boasted a hundred bedrooms, a ballroom, and gardens spilling down to the riverbank. "Pray, miss, is your dance card full?"

## The River

Downstream of Lincomb Lock there are the remains of a Second World War oil wharf. If you're walking through the woods on the Severn Way look out for the bollards to which tanker barges would moor whilst discharging their liquid cargoes.

Lincomb is the highest on the Severn. It lies in a picturesque setting dominated by one of the sheer red sandstone cliffs which characterise the river in this part of the world. There is another such dramatic outcrop between Lincomb and Stourport known as Redstone Rock, a refuge of outlaws in Cromwell's time. Opposite the rock, a well piled wharf marks the destination of the Severn's last commercial traffics above Worcester in the late 1960s. Just below Stourport Marina stands a cider mill where, towards the end of summer, you'll see thirst-inducing lorry loads of apples being upended onto conveyor belts en route to the indoor presses.

TUG
Nº 3
BRUNEL
MARKET DRAYTON

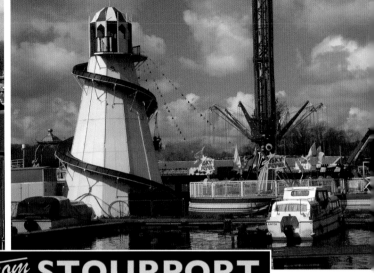

**POSTCARD** *from* **STOURPORT**

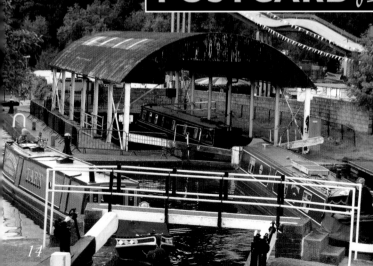

14

One of the joys of inland waterway exploration is the occasional, unforseen encounter with an historic vessel. Researching this guide we saw two for good measure at Redstone Wharf, albeit barely recognisable from their working prime. One was *Severn Traveller*, a former petroleum barge built by Hills of Bristol in 1935. The other was *VIC 99*, one of the WWII Admiralty 'puffers' built by Harkers of Knottingley, Yorkshire in 1945.

No trace now of the Shropshire, Worcestershire & Staffordshire Electric Power Company's

grandiose power station, opened with a flourish by Stanley Baldwin in 1927. During the Second World War its lofty chimneys were camouflaged in green and yellow to hide them from the Luftwaffe, a successful ruse as it turned out. Extended in 1950, it ceased generating in 1984 and has subsequently been replaced by housing. Alongside the entrance of the River Stour, from which the power station drew copious amounts of cooling water, stands a disused vinegar factory. Stourport Boat Club held their first regatta in 1876 along a mile and a half course between Redstone Rock and a point upstream of Stourport Bridge. The event still takes place every August and attracts muscular competitors from far and wide.

Stourport Bridge dates from 1870 and is the third structure to span the Severn at this point. The Severn's official head of navigation lies where the Gladder Brook enters from the west bank, though occasional convoys of shallow-draughted die-hards journey upstream to Bewdley campaigning to restore navigation to the Upper Severn. One waterway project which did not materialise was for a canal from Stourport to Leominster. A token

sod was dug opposite the basins in 1797, but the ludicrously over ambitious through route never came to fruition.

## The Canal

Above York Street Lock, the canal widens at the site of the Staffordshire & Worcestershire Canal Company's principal maintenance depot and workshops. One or two of the original buildings have been absorbed into a tasteful housing development. The crane arrived from Wombourne circa 1930. When we first explored the S&W by boat in 1980 Dartline had a hirebase here. Earlier it had been home to Holt E. Abbott, a pioneer of canal boating for leisure and an early stalwart of the Inland Waterways Association. A plaque on the towpath side commemorates his legacy, and there is another reference to this unsung hero on Map 38.

The canal abandons Stourport with the air of someone not anxious to help the police with their enquiries, and whilst sharing a wide enough valley with the Stour, tends to be masked by trees and vegetation, and as a consequence gives every indication of skulking. An old railway bridge spans the water, it carried the Severn Valley Railway between Hartlebury and Bewdley, but unfortunately wasn't part of the line to be preserved. There used to be a canal/rail interchange dock at this point. Rusty mooring rings set into a high brick retaining wall recall busier times. To the southeast, a loop line was opened in 1941 to serve the power station, and thereafter the plant received coal by both rail and water.

Another distant echo of bygone trading days is encountered at the graceful side-bridge numbered 10A. From here a branch canal led down by way of a lock into the River Stour for boats to reach Wilden Ironworks across the valley. By all accounts, steering a loaded narrowboat 'down the brook's' sharp bends and shoals was no sinecure. Coal from Highley Colliery, on the Severn Valley Railway, would be transhipped at the railway basin, carried the short distance up the canal, and thence downriver to the works. For further insight obtain a secondhand copy of J. Ian Langford's inestimable *Towpath Guide No.1* to the Staffs & Worcs Canal published in 1974, a weighty tome and model of all a good canal guide should be, though sadly the series never progressed beyond four titles.

# Stourport
Map 3

All the trappings of a seaside resort: funfairs and fish & chips, steamer trips, paddling pools and amusement arcades. Day trippers pour in from the land-locked West Midlands to let their hair down and make believe they are really in Barmouth or Weston-super-Mare. Marginally more in touch with reality, us boaters can swagger about the town pretending that we've just come up with a cargo of oil from Avonmouth.

## Eating & Drinking
ANGEL - Severnside. Tel: 01299 513172. Popular Marston's pub open from 11am daily. DY13 9EW
BIRD IN HAND - Holly Road (between bridges 7 & 8). Tel: 01299 871515. Canalside. Open from noon. Food (ex Sun eve) and Hobsons (of Cleobury Mortimer) Holdens (of Coseley) beers. DY13 9BA
BLACK STAR - Mitton Street (Bridge 5). Tel: 01299 488838. *Good Beer Guide* listed pub overlooking canal offering food and Wye Valley Ales. DY13 8YP
THE HOLLYBUSH - Mitton Street. Tel: 01299 827435. Black Country Ales and guests. DY13 9AA
NAMASTE - Lichfield Street. Tel: 01299 877448. Indian restaurant adjacent Bridge 4. DY13 9EU
RISING SUN - Lombard Street (canalside Bridge 5A). Tel: 01299 822530. Little Banks's backstreet local offering good value meals. DY13 8DU
THE WINDLASS - Stourport Basins. Tel: 01299 871742. Cafe/restaurant housed in former canal workshop and stable. Open 10am-4pm. DY13 9EW

## Shopping
Co-op (with post office), and Lidl supermarkets are most easily accessed from either side of Bridge 5A. Tesco superstore on Severn Road. On High Street look out for Gough's, a butcher/greengrocer featuring gluten-free pies. Two launderettes on Lombard Street.

## Connections
BUSES - Diamond 3 links Stourport with Kidderminster every 20 mins Mon-Sat and approx. hourly Sun. Local independent Services 294/6 run half a dozen times a day ex Sun to/from Worcester via Holt Heath. Tel: 0871 200 2233.
TAXIS - Terrys. Tel: 0771 235 1111.

TWO isolated locks, couched in the gloom of sandstone outcrops and bereft now of the lock-keepers' cottages which long ago presided over them, commence the canal's slow, steady climb towards Wolverhampton. They are separated by the lofty seven-arches of the Severn Valley Railway's Falling Sands Viaduct, which was threatening to fall down before being rescued by donations and a grant from the National Lottery Heritage Fund. Serendipitously, you may be treated to the nostalgia-evoking sight of one of the SVR's vintage trains crossing the viaduct en route for Kidderminster or Bridgnorth.

Carpet-making Kidderminster has had its canal-front regenerated. All the usual suspects: fast-food outlets, supermarkets, ring roads and retail parks. Yet one or two of the carpet factories remain intact. Treat yourself to a browse along Castle Road which crosses the canal on Bridge 15. Here, in quick succession, you'll chance upon the Art Deco facade of a former swimming pool, the impressive, 'low-relief' frontage of Brinton's

erstwhile carpet factory, and an octagonal tower, a leftover fragment from a vanished castle. Returning to the canal, note the roller-coaster sequence of side bridges, hinting at basins which used to serve various works.

Kidderminster Lock is squeezed between the town's busy ring-road and an aqueduct over the Stour. The traffic roar is deafening. Ear muffs for lock-wheelers wouldn't go amiss. Or mouth a lip-reading prayer in the direction of the splendid parish church of St Mary's (the largest in Worcestershire) with its attendant statue of Richard Baxter, the 17th century preacher, teacher and pastor who wrote the words to several well loved hymns such as *The Saints Everlasting Rest* and *Ye Holy Angels Bright*.

Regrettably, the ring-road gobbled up Mill Wharf, centre of

## ○ Key

A site of sugar beet works
B site of tram depot
C sites of carpet works
D site of gasworks
E site of Mill Wharf

| Bridge Names | | |
|---|---|---|
| 11 Falling Sands | 15 Caldwall Hall | 20 Wolverley |
| 12 Caldwall Lock | 16 Kidderminster | 21 Wolverley Forge |
| 13 Round Hill | 17 Limekiln | 22 Debdale |
| 14 Caldwall Mill | 19 Wolverley Court | |

**'Passengers No More'**
1: Foley Park Halt - closed 1970

(S) = 🗑♿WC

*Falling Sands*

lies in a seemingly remote parcel of scrubland in an area once extensively used for sand extraction. Wolverley Lock is overlooked by a quaint pub, with a canalside patio which has the potential of transforming your lock routine into street theatre. North of here, delving into glades of balsam and convolvulus, bluebells and foxgloves, the canal is at its most beguiling.

The Elan Valley water pipe-line used to cross the canal between bridges 21 and 22, now it is culverted beneath it. Completed in 1907, this 73 mile pipe brings water from reservoirs in the Rhayader Mountains of Wales to the bathtubs of Birmingham. The pipe-line's construction at the turn of the century was a huge undertaking, and one of the last great adventures of the 'navvies': "rough, violent men, whose speech had foreign inflections and whose corduroys were caked with the mud of four counties," wrote Francis Brett Young in the preface to one of his most enjoyable novels, *House Under the Water* which was inspired by the project.

canal commerce in its heyday. Archive pictures in Langford's *Towpath Guide No.1* depict the wharf chock-a-block with coal boats and backed by handsome warehouses. Coal was the predominant cargo, but carpets were carried too, notably in Shropshire Union flyboats, which would depart promptly at 6pm en route to Wolverhampton, where the consignments were put on a train the following morning. Why not simply take the carpets to Kidderminster station, you may well ask? Well, that belonged to the Great Western Railway, and the flyboats were operated by their rivals the London Midland & Scottish. Think DHL and UPS if you want a modern equivalent. But a large percentage of the town's carpets did go via the GWR, not least on 23rd June 1923 when 26 tons of them were despatched bound for Macy's department store in New York.

New housing is spreading out north of Kidderminster, but the canal quickly establishes its more obvious rural charms. Wolverley Court Lock

*Kidderminster*

18

# Kidderminster
Map 4

Newcastle for coal, Northampton for shoes, Burton for beer, and Kidderminster for carpets: once upon a long lost time towns were feted for their stock in trade. Nowadays you need to repair to the charming Museum of Carpet to be able to contextualize Kidderminster's former status as a world epicentre of floor covering, and to grasp visually how its sky was held aloft by a forest of factory chimneys. All bar one felled now, alas, but what a beauty the survivor is, soaring above Slingfield Mill, tapering to a lofty 180ft pilastered and duo-toned. The adjoining mill has gratefully found new use as a shop and hotel. Also spared redevelopment is the so called 'Piano (due to its shape when seen from above) Building', a former wool warehouse dating from 1867, once penetrated by a subterranean canal arm, but now a college. Carpet remnants apart, Kidderminster repays exploration, and it's intriguing to see at intervals how the River Stour keeps appearing, as if playing peep-bo! By the Town Hall a statue commemorates Sir Rowland Hill, born locally in 1796 and buried in Westminster Abbey eighty-three years later in recognition for his invention of the modern postal system; though not necessarily its present unreliability. A plaque on the former dance hall next door recalls appearances by such illustrious acts as T. Rex, Fleetwood Mac and Captain Beefheart ... and whilst on the subject, it shouldn't escape your attention that Kidderminster was the home town of Led Zeppelin stalwart, Robert Plant.

## Eating & Drinking
BISTRO PIERRE - Exchange Street. Tel: 01562 813530. French chain. Open from noon daily. DY10 1BY
COFFEE 1 - Riverside. Tel: 01562 745192. Nice coffee shop overlooking a stretch of the Stour. Open from

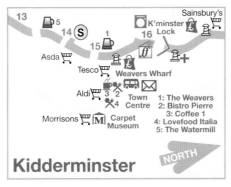

**Kidderminster**

7.30am (9am Sun) until 5.30pm (5pm Sun). DY10 1BY
KING & CASTLE - Comberton Hill. Tel: 01562 747505. SVR refreshment room featured in the *Good Beer Guide*. Food 10am-4pm. DY10 1QX
LOVEFOOD ITALIA - New Road. Tel: 01562 60610. Delightful restaurant open Tue-Sat 5.00-9pm for dinner. DY10 1AF
THE WATERMILL - Park Lane, Bridge 13. Tel: 01562 66713. Canalside, all-day Marston's pub/restaurant housed in mock watermill. Food from noon daily. Limited off-side customer moorings. DY11 6TL
THE WEAVERS - Park Lane (Bridge 15). Tel: 01562 742305. Quaint canalside pub featuring Hobsons, Wye Valley and Woodcote ales. DY11 6TG

## Shopping
The shopping centre is comprehensive, lively and largely traffic free. Markets on Thur & Sat. Post office in W. H. Smith on Vicar Street. M&S, Boots, T. K. Maxx and Debenhams at Weavers Wharf. Launderettes on Park Lane and Comberton Hill.

## Things to Do
SEVERN VALLEY RAILWAY - 01562 757900. One of

Britain's premier preserved railways, the SVR runs up the valley via Bewdley to the Shropshire market town of Bridgnorth, a delightful ride in its own right, never mind the fun of being hauled by steam. DY10 1QX
MUSEUM OF CARPET - Green Street. Tel: 01562 69028. Open Tue, Wed, Thur & Sat 10.00am-1.30pm (3pm sch hols). Enjoyable insight into the history of carpet manufacture appropriately housed in the former Stour Vale Mill. Loom demonstrations at noon! Admission charge. Entrance via Morrison's. DY10 1AZ

## Connections
BUSES - Diamond service 3 links Kidderminster with Stourport at 20 minute intervals Mon-Sat, hourly Sun. TRAINS - frequent local services to/from Birmingham Snow Hill and Worcester etc. Tel: 0345 748 4950. Taxis - Central Taxis. Tel: 01562 515131.

# Wolverley
Map 4

A fairytale village snuggled in sandstone and watered by a trickling brook, Wolverley is worth every minute of the five or six it'll take you to wend your way there. Dramatically perched on an outcrop, St John the Baptist's church is most engagingly reached via a rocky, lichened, zig-zagging path known as 'Holloway'.

## Eating & Drinking
GIL'S - Queen's Head Terrace. Tel: 01562 850499. Charming cafe open daily 10am-4pm. DY11 5XB
LOCK INN - canalside Bridge 20. Tel: 01562 850581. Pretty canalside pub which also operates Old Smithy tea room (featuring Marshfield Farm ice cream) on the far side of the lock. Take-aways. DY10 3RN
QUEEN'S HEAD - village centre. Tel: 01562 229081. Pretty 17th century village pub open from noon daily. Food served 12-3pm and 6-8pm Mon-Sat and 12-4pm Sun. Banks's/Marston's beers. DY11 5XB

## Things to Do
MINI-PRO GOLF - 18 hole course. Tel: 0783 025 9766.

**W**E'VE pondered, rhetorically, through eight editions, if there's a prettier length of canal in the country than the Staffs & Worcs in the vicinity of Kinver? And in over thirty years no-one's got in touch to contradict this notion. There are rivals of course - we've vouchsafed as much - but it's the unanticipated shock of this loveliness which takes the breath away. No quango has seen fit, as yet, to burden the Stour Valley with spurious accolades. Do we really need to be told when somewhere is an Area of Outstanding Natural Beauty? Can't we be relied upon to use the evidence of our own eyes!

Kinver church looks kindly down from its rocky outcrop, but to our mind the most alluring length of all lies between Hyde Lock and Dunsley's diminutive tunnel. Here, bordered by deciduous woodland on one side, the canal glides past meadows backed by a conifer plantation. It would be difficult to imagine a more pastoral scene, yet a huge ironworks stood in the vicinity for two centuries. In its heyday twenty puddling furnaces produced wrought iron and the premises lined the canal for some distance. But only the manager's house remains, and nowadays butter wouldn't melt in its mouth, innocent in its setting beside the towpath above Hyde Lock. Less innocent is the discovery that three and a half miles of underground chambers were hewn out of the area's soft sandstone during the Second World War to create a 'shadow' factory for Rover who were engaged in the manufacture of aircraft machine parts. Even more

**Bridge Names**

| 24 Austcliff | 27 Whittington | 30 Hyde |
| 25 Clay House | 28 Whittington Horse | 32 Stewponey |
| 26 Caunsall | 29 Kinfare | 33 Stourton |

The towpath is in pretty good condition for a rural canal, and used by walkers and cyclists alike. Short walks abound in the vicinity of Kinver where good car parking is available or you can use the bus from Stourbridge and walk back via Stourton Junction.

**S** = 🗑🚮♿WC 🐕

unnervingly, these subterranean labyrinths - known locally as the Drakelow Tunnels - were earmarked as a seat of regional government in the event of a nuclear war. Nowadays the tunnels are used more peacefully for wine storage, whilst a trust are working towards opening a museum to preserve and interpret the facility's history. Inland waterway crime writer Andy Griffee's novella *Devil's Den* is set in the vicinity.

Barely had the ironworks' pandemonium ceased, when a new interloper arrived on the Stour Valley scene, in the shape of a curious little narrow gauge railway operated with electric trams. The Kinver Light Railway opened in 1901 and lasted only twenty-nine years, but in its short existence brought thousands of delirious day-trippers from the Black Country to Kinver, vaunted by the operating company as the "Switzerland of the Midlands". The 3ft 6ins gauge track (along which through cars ran from as far away as Birmingham) crossed the canal at Stewponey, ran alongside it at Hyde, and terminated at Mill Lane, Kinver where the pumping station now stands. What an attraction it would be now had it only survived.

Stewponey was a focal point for boat traffic on the Staffs & Worcs. Facilities included a wharf, stables, toll office, workshop and employees' cottages. Even after the Second World War, in excess of fifty boat loads of Cannock Chase and Baggeridge Colliery coal was being worked through here to Stourport Power Station each week. But in 1949 the National Coal Board announced a florin surcharge on each ton of coal loaded on to boats. Predictably the traffic rapidly transferred to rail. A few years of desultory day boat trading to Swindon Steel works, 'railway' boats off the Stourbridge Canal, and occasional cargoes of baled wool to Stourport from 'up north' followed, and then, without anyone really noticing, let alone mourning, the working boats vanished.

Stewponey doesn't find its way on to Ordnance Survey maps, but is a name of local currency, thought to be derived from an old soldier,

returning with a Spanish wife from the town of Estepona, who opened an inn here, the name of which was soon corrupted by Black Country vowels. The inn was rebuilt as a roadhouse in the Thirties, one of those huge joints which were honeypots in the early days of motoring; there was even a Lido in the grounds. Imagine that the Lido remained in use and that you could still reach it in the jaunty company of one of the Kinver Light Railway's trams, then calculate just how much Progress has defaulted on the Past.

At Stourton Junction four chambers raise the Stourbridge Canal up on its way to the Black Country. Canal junctions don't come much more enchanting than this and, even if your itinerary commits you to the Staffs & Worcs, you could do worse than spend a night in Stourbridge, little more than an hour and a half away as described on Map 38.

North of Stourton Junction, the canal - known colloquially as the 'Stour Cut' - bridges the river of the same name. The setting is idyllic, the river tumbling over a shallow weir just upstream of the double-arch aqueduct, and issuing from the adjoining bend, a broad pool. Close by, a peculiar cave is cut out of the rocks at water level. Known as "Devil's Den", it is thought to have been used as a boathouse by the Foley family of Prestwood Hall.

Southwards from Stewponey, the river is the canal's constant companion, the man made waterway keeping pace with the Stour's gradual descent to the Severn by way of occasional, isolated locks of great charm. It is difficult to think of another canal bounded by so many trees, their presence broken only by occasional outcrops of Triassic rock. The most dramatic of these - a real cliffhanger! - is near Caunsall where the Bunter pebble beds of Austcliff Rock loom over a bend in the canal. Little less spectacular is the canal's burrowing beneath the old iron-making village of Cookley, its houses precariously poised over the northern portal of Cookley Tunnel.

## Cookley
Map 5

A village with an iron-making tradition going back three centuries and where steel wheels are still made in canalside premises. Access from the canal is via paths from either end of the tunnel.

### Eating & Drinking
BULLS HEAD - Bridge Street (village centre). Tel: 01562 243468. Convivial local with a prominent outdoor terrace high above the canal. DY10 3SA
EAGLE & SPUR - Castle Road. Tel: 01562 851036. Comfortable village pub. Food lunchtimes daily, plus some evenings - telephone ahead to check. DY10 3TB
FARMERS DEN - Bridge Road. Coffee shop.
*A fish & chip shop (Tel: 01562 850554) and Tandoori take-away (Tel: 01562 850900) offer further options.*

### Shopping
Tesco Express (with ATM) 6am-11pm daily.

### Connections
BUSES - Diamond service 9A runs bi-hourly (Mon-Sat) to/from Kidderminster. Tel: 0871 200 2233.

## Caunsall
Map 5

ANCHOR INN - Caunsall Road (access via footpath from Bridge 24). Tel: 01562 850254. Quaint pub open from 11am. Cobs and up to five real ales. DY11 5YL
ISLAND POOL - Wolverhampton Road (access via Bridge 26 and pavemented A449). Tel: 01562 850311. Country pub open from 8.30am daily. DY10 3RX

## Kinver
Map 5

Kinver is well aware of its charms and flaunts them outrageously. Visitors pour in during the summer months, filling car-parks at the rear of the pubs, restaurants and cafes which provide most of the fabric of High Street. But somehow Kinver preserves its modesty and repays the ten minute stroll from the canal. In any case, the village's main asset is its superb setting beneath Kinver Edge, a dramatic wooded ridge rising to five hundred feet and the southern end of the 'Staffordshire Way' long distance footpath. For those with time and energy at their disposal, the climb to the top of The Edge can be recommended. The lofty church of St Peter is notable for its monuments and brasses of Sir Edward Grey.

### Eating & Drinking
BACI - High Street. Beautifully appointed Italian restaurant. Tel: 01384 878789. Closed Mon. DY7 6HF
BAY TREE - High Street. Tel: 01384 878888. Well thought of restaurant. Open Tue-Sat 12-2pm and 5.30-11pm; Sun 12-7pm. DY7 6HL
CROSS INN - Church Hill. Tel: 01384 878481. Black Country Ales pub which repays the climb. DY7 6HZ
HARLEYS - Dunsley Road. Tel: 01384 878899. Smokehouse grill and bar. Open Wed-Fri from noon; weekends from 9am. DY7 6LU
MANOR HOUSE - Whittington (access from Bridge 28). Tel: 01384 872110. Smartly refurbished Marston's inn/restaurant in 700 year old half-timbered property with links to Dick Whittington. DY7 6NY
OLDE HOUSE TEA ROOMS - High Street. Tel: 01384 878523. Nice tea room with outside seating to rear. Open daily (ex Wed) from 10am. DY7 6HE
PLOUGH & HARROW - High Street. Tel: 01384 872900. Unprepossessing 'local' worth patronising for the medal-winning Batham ales. DY7 6HD
VINE - canalside Bridge 29. Tel: 01384 936919. Food from noon daily. DY7 6LJ
*Plus cafes and fast-food outlets in the village centre.*

### Shopping
All the shops (and there's a good choice for such an apparently small village) congregate along the High Street. Galleries and gift shops rub shoulders with a Co-op convenience store. The Butchery offers a great range of sausages, hand-raised pork pies and cheese.

### Things to Do
HOLY AUSTIN ROCK HOUSES - Compton Road. Tel: 01384 872553. Rock houses care for by the National Trust, and open to the public Thursday to Sunday afternoons between March and November plus weekends out of season. Tearooms. DY7 6DL

### Connections
BUSES - Select Bus Services 242 operates hourly (ex Sun) to/from Stourbridge. Tel: 0871 200 2233.

## Swindon
Map 6

Not easily confused with its Wiltshire namesake - once you've seen it anyway - this Swindon barely amounts to more than a spattering of houses at a meeting of by-roads and a small housing estate occupying the site of a former steel works. To the west lies Highgate Common, threaded by the "Staffordshire Way", and, not far beyond - should you have the benefit of bicycles - Halfpenny Green and its vineyard (Tel: 01384 221122 - DY7 5EP).

### Eating & Drinking
NAVIGATION INN - adjacent Greensforge Lock. Tel: 01384 273721. One of the most comfortable of inns on the southern half of the S&W Canal. Enville, Three Tuns and guests. Food 12-3pm/5.30-9pm weekdays and 12-9pm weekends. DY6 0AH
GREEN MAN - High Street (*west* of Bridge 40). Tel: 01384 400532. Cosy & quaint Marston's pub. Food served 12-2pm/6-8pm (ex Sun eve) DY3 4NR
*Another pub, and fish & chips in the village centre.*

### Shopping
Small convenience store.

### Things to Do
ASHWOOD NURSERIES - Tel: 01384 401996. Traditional working nurseries with garden and gift shops and tea room. Ten minutes walk from Greensforge Lock. Award-winning hellebores! DY6 0AE.

*Awbridge*  *Stourton Junction*

# SCENES *from the* STAFFS & WORCS

*Hyde Lock*  *The Bratch*

23

THE countryside empties. Wales is only the width of an Ordnance Survey map away. These are the landscapes of Francis Brett Young, and no-one has ever written more vividly about the area between the Black Country and the Welsh Marches. Try and get hold of a copy of *Far Forest* or *Dr Bradley Remembers*; either would make admirable reading before 'lights out' on your cruise.

Smestow Brook, a tributary of the Stour, is now the canal's chief confidant and friend. In the woods below Gothersley Lock stood a canal company roundhouse, a twin to that at Gailey (Map 36) now restored and used as a canalside shop. Both roundhouses date from the year of Admiral Nelson's demise. The Gothersley one marks the site of an

important canal wharf provided to serve a sizeable ironworks which existed here until the 1880s. The roundhouse itself, a gaunt ruin for many years, was storm damaged in 1991 and its base is now the focal point of a picnic site and visitor moorings. The ironworks has vanished as well, its forges, furnaces, tramways and wharves superseded by ivy, ash, balsam and butterbur.

Greensforge is a delightful mooring place. Its name recalls the existence of another vanished forge, one which became a mill, the big, four square building which remains intact and glimpsed through the alders and willows lining the Smestow. Stroll down the lane and you'll discover its macey, long dry mill pond, an obvious declivity in the reed beds. Nearby an arm extends

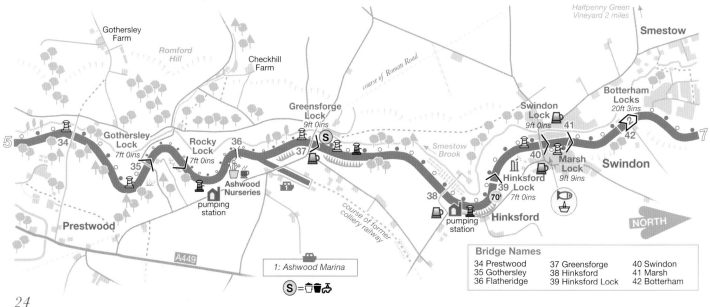

| Bridge Names | | |
|---|---|---|
| 34 Prestwood | 37 Greensforge | 40 Swindon |
| 35 Gothersley | 38 Hinksford | 41 Marsh |
| 36 Flatheridge | 39 Hinksford Lock | 42 Botterham |

*Hinksford Pumping Station*

recently as 1976 and specialised in rolling silicon steel sheets for the electrical engineering industry. Not that you would credit it now, the site being covered by the neat lawns, barbecues and conservatory extensions of modern housing. The works was owned at one time by the Baldwin family, of which Stanley became Prime Minister. Note how the towpath briefly changes sides so that it did not run through the works' precincts. Railway boats traded here with steel blooms from Stourbridge Basin. A controversial scheme for a new 200-berth marina in the vicinity of Hinksford Lock, passed by the local authority in 2010, appears to have stalled. Botterham Locks are a staircase pair, so remember to ensure that the top chamber is full and the bottom empty to start with. At the foot of the locks stood the Boat Inn.

*Botterham Staircase*

into Ashwood Basin, now a marina but once an important interchange basin with the Kingswinford Railway, a colliery line dating from 1829 whose first locomotive, *Agenoria*, is now in the National Railway Museum's collection in York. The lovely garden which borders the canal south of Bridge 36 belongs to John Massey, owner of the adjoining Ashwood Nurseries, recipients of a gold medal at the Chelsea Flower Show of 2016 for their hepaticas. The garden is private, though open to the public on Saturdays. The nurseries are best accessed from Greensforge Lock.

Between Greensforge and Hinksford locks the canal is bordered by the contrasting images of woodland and a huge static caravan park. Hinksford Pumping Station is one of several waterworks in this part of the valley. Yet another ironworks lined the canal at Swindon. This one survived until as

**D**ON'T be fooled! They may look intimidatingly staircase-like, but Bratch Locks are, in fact, three quite separate chambers 'telescoped' together, rendering it impossible to pass oncoming boats once they have begun to move up or down the flight. Notices regarding their colour-coded operation are prominently displayed. Furthermore the unfailingly friendly lock-keepers are usually in residence and dispense worldy wisdom from their octagonally shaped office on Bridge 48. At busy times do as they ask and be prepared to be patient.

If you're kicking your heels, go and have a peep through the iron railings at the positively Ruritanian pumping station erected on behalf of the Bilston (Map 11) Waterworks Company in 1895. Coal came in by narrowboat to fuel a pair of triple-expansion vertical steam engines

provided by Thornewill & Warham of Burton-on-Trent. The engines - affectionately referred to as *Victoria* and *Alexandra* - fell out of use in 1960, but *Victoria* was lovingly restored by a team led by Len Crane in the 1990s. Subsequently the old lady was occasionally 'fired-up' on selected open days, but the last of those was in 2010, and no-one seems to know if the works will ever open its doors to an admiring public again.

Below Bratch the canal skirts Wombourne, skirmishing with increasing amounts of housing and diminishing amounts of industry. The red scars

**Bridge Names**

| | |
|---|---|
| 43 Wombourne | 48 Upper Bratch |
| 44 Giggetty | 49 Awbridge |
| 45 Houndel | 53 Dimmingsdale |
| 46 Bumble Hole | 54 Mops Farm |
| 47 Bratch | 55 Castle Croft |

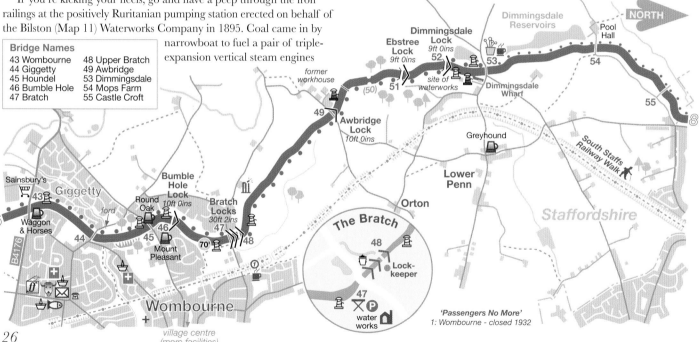

*'Passengers No More'*
*1: Wombourne - closed 1932*

26

of former sand quarries abound. Narrowboats carried sand from local wharves to Black Country forges for mould making in the casting process. There's a picturesque ford just west of Bridge 44. Bumble Hole Lock sounds vaguely Dickensian, doesn't it!

North of Bratch the countryside is open and attractively rolling and there are glimpses westwards of the Clee Hills. Indeed, given its proximity to Wolverhampton, the emphasis is deliciously rural: explore the lanes radiating from the canal and you could be lost in Somerset.

Reputedly haunted, Awbridge Lock, together with its balustraded bridge, display many of the charming characteristics of the Staffordshire & Worcestershire's engineering. A curious carving on one of the parapet coping stones (south-west side) allegedly depicts a naval sailing vessel, and is said to date from the use of French prisoners to work on the canal following the Battle of Trafalgar. A few hundred yards along the road to the south-west stand the eerily derelict remains of Seisdon Union Workhouse in use between 1860 and 1930.

The South Staffordshire Railway Walk occupies the trackbed of an old Great Western Railway line opened as late as 1925. Its shortlived passenger services lasted barely seven years, but it remained a useful means for goods trains to by-pass the Black Country until 1965. Another line, intended to reach Bridgnorth, never materialised. The dock by Bridge 53 is employed by our esteemed cover artist for the sign-writing of boats.

## Wombourne　　　　　Map 7

A 'village' of twelve thousand souls, 'One-bun' appears intimidatingly urban from the perspective of the canal, but its historic core - tantalisingly just beyond the bottom of the map - is significantly prettier and grouped about a substantial green, quintessentially bestrode by cricketers in whites all summer long.

### Eating & Drinking

WAGGON & HORSES - Bridgnorth Road (Bridge 43). Tel: 01902 892828. Marston's Rotisserie open from noon daily, food served throughout. WV5 0AQ
ROUND OAK - Ounsdale Road (Bridge 45). Tel: 01902 892083. Bank's (Marston's) family orientated pub with a big canalside garden. Food served lunch and evening (from 5pm) Mon-Thur, from noon throughout Fri & Sat, and 12-6pm Sun. WV5 8BU
RAILWAY CAFE (closed Mon & Tue) is housed in the old Wombourne station 5 mins East of Bridge 47.

### Shopping

Large Sainsbury's adjoining Bridge 43. Suburban range of shops less than ten minutes walk east of Bridge 44. Even more shops in the centre of Wombourne about quarter of an hour's walk east of Bridge 45.

## Lower Penn　　　　　Map 7

GREYHOUND - Greyhound Road (half a mile east of Br.53). Tel: 01902 620666. Comfortable country pub. Lunches & dinners Mon-Sat and Sun lunch. WV4 4UN
*Small garden centre with cafe also adjoins Bridge 53.*

## Wightwick　　　　　Map 8

Wolverhampton's most westerly suburb, pronounced 'Whit-ick'. Sneeze and you're in Staffordshire!

### Eating & Drinking

CANALSIDE BAR & GRILL - Castlecroft Lane. Tel: 01902 761360. Indian restaurant open from 5pm Mon-Thur, 4pm Fri and 12pm weekends. WV3 8JU
THE MERMAID - adjacent Bridge 56. Tel: 01902 764896. Picturesque road side pub dating from 18th century and now part of the Vintage Inns group. Open daily from noon. Food throughout. WV6 8BN

### Things to Do

WIGHTWICK MANOR - Wightwick Bank. Tel: 01902 761400. Sublime late Victorian house furnished by William Morris, Rossetti, Kempe, Burne-Jones et al. Extensive gardens, tea room (using kitchen garden produce) and National Trust gift shop. WV6 8EE

## Compton　　　　　Map 8

Another of Wolverhampton's suburban outposts and location of the Wanderers training ground.

### Eating & Drinking

FIUME - Bridgnorth Road (canalside Bridge 59). Tel: 01902 755550. Italian restaurant. WV6 8AB
*Chinese, two pubs and fish & chips also within easy reach of the canal.*

### Shopping

Spar (inc. post office and cash machine), pharmacy, launderette, off-licence, and Sainsbury's Local.

## Tettenhall　　　　　Map 8

Two green 'Tet'null' straddles its triassic sandstone ridge exuding Home Counties affluence. This was where the fortune-makers of Wolverhampton chose to erect their piles, confident that the prevailing westerlies would blow their factory smoke the other way. The shortlived railway station and goods depot (adjacent Bridge 61) host a vintage tea room (Tel: 01902 219280); transport exhibition (Sat & Sun) and gift shop. Adjoining the Upper Green is a wide choice of nice shops and eating & drinking establishments.

# 8 STAFFS & WORCS CANAL Compton & Tettenhall 3mls/3lks/2hrs

THE Staffordshire & Worcestershire Canal completes its ascent from the River Severn - having climbed the best part of three hundred feet in the process - at Compton Lock, which was completed in 1770, and is generally considered to have been James Brindley's very first essay in narrow lock construction. The chamber boasts one of the distinctive circular weirs peculiar to this canal. In Victorian and Edwardian days rowing boats could be hired for pleasure here. The summit stretches for about ten miles to Gailey - Map 36.

Visitor Moorings either side of Wightwick Bridge (No.56) offer every inducement to visit the National Trust's Wightwick Manor, a late 19th century house built for the Wolverhampton paint magnate, Theodore Mander, in beguiling Arts & Crafts style. An impressive girder bridge carries the trackbed of the Wombourne branch railway (now a well-surfaced public right of way) over the canal on the outskirts of Tettenhall, one of Wolverhampton's better-heeled suburbs.

When Pearsons draw attention to the prowess of Thomas Telford, it is usually in connection with his contribution to inland waterway engineering, but at Tettenhall New Bridge it is the road above the canal that he was responsible for. In the early years of the 19th century, communications between London and Dublin were appalling. Over twenty quite autonomous turnpike trusts were responsible for the road from London via Shrewsbury to Holyhead, the port for Ireland. Yet despite vociferous protests from travellers and the frequent failure of the Mail Coach to penetrate the wilds of Wales at all, matters were not brought to a head until the Act of Union between Britain and Ireland required the regular presence of Irish Members of Parliament at Westminster. Telford was invited to survey the route and plan improvements, which he did with characteristic

| Bridge Names | |
|---|---|
| 56 Wightwick | 61 Tettenhall Old |
| 57 Wightwick | 62 Tettenhall New |
| 58 Wightwick Mill | 62A Hordern Road |
| 59 Compton Road | 63 Tunstall Water |
| 60 Compton Lock | 64 Aldersley |

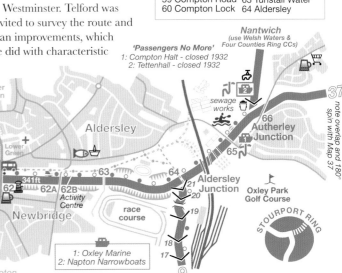

'Passengers No More'
1: Compton Halt - closed 1932
2: Tettenhall - closed 1932

*Nantwich*
(use Welsh Waters & Four Counties Ring CCs)

sewage works

66 Autherley Junction

65

37

note overlap and 180° spin with Map 37

Wightwick Manor (NT)
M

sw

7

old windmill

56 57

Wight-wick Lock 70'
8ft 8ins

58

Wightwick Mill Lock
9ft 0ins

A454

Castlecroft

59

Compton Lock
9ft 4ins

60

Compton

Tettenhall

Upper Green

A41 to Chester

Lower Green

The Rock

B4161

sw

341ft

61

2

62

62A 62B

Activity Centre

Newbridge

Aldersley

race course

63

64

21
20
19

Aldersley Junction

18

17

9

Oxley Park Golf Course

STOURPORT RING

1: Oxley Marine
2: Napton Narrowboats

NORTH

A454 to Wolverhampton

A41 to Wolverhampton

28

thoroughness; recommending widening, resurfacing and numerous gradient modifications, as demonstrated nearby in the cutting through Tettenhall Rock; though historians of late have suggested that 'The Rock' may not have exactly been the great engineer's personal choice. Nevertheless, the new road opened throughout with the completion of his famous bridge over the Menai Strait in 1826. Seventy-five years later, Wolverhampton's electric trams began using New Bridge, notable, initially, in that they collected power from studs in the road as opposed to overhead wires. Between 1927 and 1963 it was the turn of trolleybuses to silently carry Tettenhall's prosperous bourgeois to and from the commercial centre of Wolverhampton.

Another pair of bridges with stories to tell are encountered before the canal reaches Aldersley Junction. A side-bridge inconspicuously spans a former coal wharf latterly used as a base for the erstwhile Double Pennant hire fleet. Bridge 62B carried a private railway line into Courtaulds' long demolished rayon factory. The bridge-builder's plate records

that it was erected by Braithwaite & Co of West Bromwich in 1927. Two diminutive saddle-tanks, endearingly known as *Rosabel* and *Annabel*, shunted the sidings. The works was also served by Cowburn & Cowpar chemical boats, a long haul from Courtauld's chemical works at Trafford Park near Manchester. Nicknamed 'bottle boats', the fleet's eight motors, all built by Yarwood & Sons of Northwich in the 1930s, were named after birds beginning with the letter 'S', and, remarkably, all are preserved in one form or another.

Bridge 63 is an enigma. From a distance it looks like a typical hump-backed occupation bridge. In fact it carries Smestow Brook across the canal. Even more curiously the bridge plaque, an 18th century original, reads Tunstall Water Bridge, and yet the neighbourhood is known as Dunstall. An unwitting error by the pattern maker? A tradition still honoured by CRT?

The canal approaches Aldersley Junction in wooded cuttings, all but screening from view two sporting centres. To the west is Aldersley Leisure Village, home to Wolverhampton & Bilston Athletics Club and Wolverhampton Wheelers Cycle Club. To the east is Wolverhampton Race Course which has been the scene of horse racing since 1886. Apparently in more recent times it was the first to be floodlit in the United Kingdom, and now hosts regular evening meetings on its all-weather track.

At Aldersley Junction the S&W encounters the fabled BCN. The first boat emerged from the latter on 21st September 1772, six days before James Brindley's untimely death at the age of 56. The bosky junction is such an isolated, uninhabited location now that it's hard to believe that there were once a number of canal employee dwellings here, and substantial ones at that. Both companies had toll houses, and when trade was at its zenith the sense of purpose must have been something to behold. Tap 'Aldersley Junction' into your search engine and you'll be rewarded with some fascinating archive images. Better still, obtain a copy of Eric De Mare's 1950 classic *The Canals of England* and wallow in the lost magnificence of plates 56, 57 & 61.

# 9 BIRMINGHAM CANAL NAVIGATIONS 'The Twenty-one' 2mls/16lks/2hrs

**M**ORE than most, the canal traveller comes to appreciate that Birmingham and the Black Country lie atop a lofty plateau. Moreover, if that traveller happens to be boating, the appreciation will be of a markedly physical nature by the time the summit has been scaled.

Negotiating 'The Twenty-one', as it is colloquially known, is a transitional experience, whichever way you're going. Nothing could appear more rural than the sylvan purlieus of Aldersley Junction - nothing more urban than Broad Street Bridge above the top lock (Map 10). And in between, there is so much to take in, that the locks seem dreamlike, even with the frustration of supposedly vandal-proof security equipment to cope with.

The flight was completed in 1772. James Brindley was the chief engineer, assisted by Robert Whitworth and Samuel Simcock. One can picture the three gentlemen huddled over drawings. Initially there were twenty chambers, but the bottom one was so deep that it created water shortages. So in 1784 it was reduced in depth and a short cutting excavated to carry the canal to a new lock built in the intervening pound. This extra lock, No.20, gives its identity away by having only one tail gate.

In working boat days the locks were the haunt of 'hobblers', men or boys who would help single-handed captains through the locks for a small consideration, and occasionally, latter-day hobblers and/or CRT volunteers are on hand even now to provide the same service. Boat children were apparently in the habit of riding horses bareback, at breakneck speed down to Aldersley to collect upcoming boats. Galloping equines are still encountered on the flight in the slightly different form of thoroughbreds on the neighbouring race course. How many canals lie alongside race courses? One can only think of Aintree and Ripon in comparison. Newbury's surely a furlong too far from the K&A to count.

Three fast-food outlets offer the opportunity for lock-wheelers to take some sustenance on board at Gorsebrook Bridge. A Science Park borders the canal between locks 12 to 15 where Clayton tar boats used to ply to and from the gas works. The selfsame gas works, incidentally, whence, on 5th September 1862, the balloonists James Glaisher and Henry Coxwell, together with their balloon called *Mammoth* filled with gas from the works, ascended to a literally giddy height of seven miles above the earth. Much discomforted, they landed near Ludlow. A feature film titled *The Aeronauts*

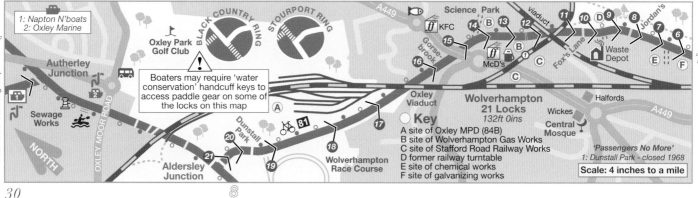

relates the adventure, albeit with typical Hollywood disregard for accuracy, Henry Coxwell has become Amelia Wren in an attempt to stimulate female interest.

Wolverhampton has always been a fascinating railway centre, and the once rival lines of the Great Western and London Midland & Scottish railways span the canal at several points, notably on a pair of fine viaducts. Lock 11 must have been a trainspotter's idea of heaven when the best of Swindon and Crewe puffed imperiously overhead. Between locks 9 and 10 the pit of an old turntable can still be discovered in the undergrowth on the towpath side. Here stood the coaling stage of Stafford Road engine shed, home to a number of the Great Western Railway's legendary King and Castle classes of express locomotives. Drifting smoke from a tall refuse incinerator chimney provides scant consolation for the loss of such scenes.

*Lock 12*

*Lock 16*

*Aldersley Junction*

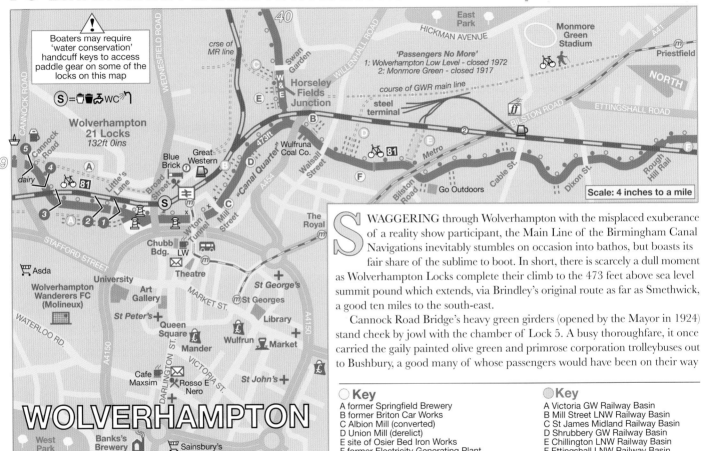

**Boaters may require 'water conservation' handcuff keys to access paddle gear on some of the locks on this map**

(S) = 🍴🗑♿WC⚓

Wolverhampton 21 Locks 132ft 0ins

crse of MR line

Swan Garden

Horsley Fields Junction

East Park

HICKMAN AVENUE

Monmore Green Stadium

Priestfield

NORTH

'Passengers No More'
1: Wolverhampton Low Level - closed 1972
2: Monmore Green - closed 1917

course of GWR main line

steel terminal

ETTINGSHALL ROAD

Blue Brick

Great Western

Wulfruna Coal Co.

Walsall Street

Metro

Cable St.

Dixon St.

Rough Hill Rail

dairy

Cannock Road

Little's Lane

Broad Street

W'ton Tunnel

Mill Street

"Canal Quarter"

473ft

Bilston Road

Go Outdoors

Scale: 4 inches to a mile

Chubb Bdg.

LW

Theatre

The Royal

University

Asda

Wolverhampton Wanderers FC (Molineux)

Art Gallery

St George's

St Georges

St Peter's

Library

Queen Square

Mander

Wulfrun

Market

WATERLOO RD.

MARKET ST.

Cafe Maxsim

Rosso E Nero

St John's

VICTORIA ST.

DARLINGTON ST.

STAFFORD STREET

CANNOCK ROAD

WEDNESFIELD ROAD

WILLENHALL ROAD

BILSTON ROAD

# WOLVERHAMPTON

West Park

Banks's Brewery

Sainsbury's

SWAGGERING through Wolverhampton with the misplaced exuberance of a reality show participant, the Main Line of the Birmingham Canal Navigations inevitably stumbles on occasion into bathos, but boasts its fair share of the sublime to boot. In short, there is scarcely a dull moment as Wolverhampton Locks complete their climb to the 473 feet above sea level summit pound which extends, via Brindley's original route as far as Smethwick, a good ten miles to the south-east.

Cannock Road Bridge's heavy green girders (opened by the Mayor in 1924) stand cheek by jowl with the chamber of Lock 5. A busy thoroughfare, it once carried the gaily painted olive green and primrose corporation trolleybuses out to Bushbury, a good many of whose passengers would have been on their way

## ○ Key
A former Springfield Brewery
B former Briton Car Works
C Albion Mill (converted)
D Union Mill (derelict)
E site of Osier Bed Iron Works
F former Electricity Generating Plant

## ● Key
A Victoria GW Railway Basin
B Mill Street LNW Railway Basin
C St James Midland Railway Basin
D Shrubbery GW Railway Basin
E Chillington LNW Railway Basin
F Ettingshall LNW Railway Basin

to work at the celebrated Fallings Park factory of Guy Motors. Butler's Springfield Brewery - 'Home of Butlers Ales - Pride of the Midlands' - opened in 1873 and brewing was continuous for a hundred and eighteen years. Following a period of decay, it was seriously damaged by fire in 2004, but happily - for it is a most handsome building in its own right - it has been repurposed as part of the University of Wolverhampton campus, a fitting role for the 21st century.

Above the top lock - with its weeping willows, rabbit burrows and picturesque pair of BCN cottages (109 & 110) - the canal widens into a landscaped area where fairly salubrious visitor moorings are provided for overnight stops. The present Broad Street bridge replaces an earlier structure that boasted cast-iron balustrades and ornate gas lamps and which now spans Lord Ward's Canal at the Black Country Living Museum. Broad Street was formerly called Canal Street, and lead to a notoriously poor slum area known as 'Caribee Island', occupied chiefly by a diaspora of Irish immigrants displaced by the potato famines of the 19th century.

Like a sizeable wedge of chocolate cake, Chubb's former lock and safe-making works dominates the horizon. These days it's home to a number of arts based studios and a film theatre. The prominent warehouse was owned by the famous canal carriers, Fellows, Morton & Clayton. Following a period of use as the unlikely venue for a nightclub, it has become a kitchen showroom. Peep through the roadside archway and you'll see that the old company name remains signwritten on the upper storey wall. Water, Elsan and refuse disposal facilities are obtainable by entering a short arm spanned by a cast iron bridge: the manoeuvring involved is fun in its own right. The arm was the original course of the canal before it was diverted through Wolverhampton Tunnel when the High Level railway station was built. Alternative visitor moorings are provided on the opposite side to the towpath at this point: hard-by the busy ring-road, they offer an enhanced sense of security at the expense of access to or from the outside world.

Beyond Mill Street Bridge, a former canal warehouse at Albion Wharf has been converted into apartments. Further redevelopment is taking place here as part of Wolverhampton's 'Canalside Quarter' initiative. Centre-piece of the development will be a former flour and animal feedstuffs mill. An atmospheric photograph of this building, together with the British Waterways motor *Mountbatten*, appears on page 144 of Mike Webb's book *The Twilight Years of Narrow Boat Carrying*.

At Horseley Fields Junction the Wyrley & Essington Canal commences its tortuous circumnavigation of the north-eastern tip of the Black Country - turn to Map 40 to learn how it gets on. Numerous industries once clustered along the canal hereabouts, amongst them Jones & Bayliss, specialists in the manufacture of ornamental fences and gates. The best the canal can come up with now is an oxygen depot, though in many respects the canal provides its own heady supply of that commodity. On the opposite bank a lofty oblong brick building was once part of Wolverhampton power station: all it generates now is melancholy. Follow Bilston Road in a north-westerly direction and you'll come upon Dixons paint and wallcovering suppliers occupying a works erected in 1885 for the carriage and Hansom cab builders Forder & Co. To the rear of that stands the former Royal Hospital, a monumental mid-19th century building. Two decades of decay have set in since the last bedpan was emptied, but now, somewhat belatedly, it is to be redeveloped as apartments.

The emerging railways of the mid-19th century quickly grasped that development of short haul traffic, to and from the numerous works firmly established beside the densely knit canals, was in their best interest. One, of what amounted to over forty, railway owned basins, remains more or less intact at Chillington Wharf and has been given Grade II listed status, though each time we pass it looks a bit sorrier for itself. Saving significant buildings for posterity requires rather more effort than the mere application of a rubber stamp. Bilston Road Bridge carries the Metro tramway across the canal. From Cable Street, a short walk eastwards will take you to Monmore Green Stadium, a venue for greyhound and speedway racing. East Park, gifted to Wolverhampton by the iron magnate Sir Alfred Hickman, originally boasted a boating lake, but the water in it kept leaking away into old mine workings. At Rough Hills Stop the canal narrows at the site of a former toll house and there are BCN cottages (23 & 24).

# Wolverhampton

Map 10

There comes a moment, perambulating Wolverhampton's inherently handsome thoroughfares, when you can't help wondering if its millennial elevation to city status didn't heap unnecessary pressure on the place: like someone promoted on merit from a job they were very good at to a position they subsequently find untenable. Who benefits from such aggrandizements? Palpably not the denizens: people in towns go about their business phlegmatically; people in cities assume airs! Wolverhampton reminds us of Wakefield, another proud and ancient borough, linked to the inland waterways, but apt to languish in the shadows of a domineering neighbour. Both so-called cities have had to come to terms with the erosion of heavy industry and to find sustainable uses for hefty legacies of flamboyant Victorian and Edwardian buildings. Should you wish to encounter Wolverhampton's faded elegance at its most plangent, make your way along one or other of the cobbled approach roads to St John-in-the-Square. Among several fine churches in the town (sorry, 'city') of varying denominations, St John's, with its slender lofty spire, dates from the 18th century and may well have been designed by Roger Eykyn who is also credited with St Paul's in Birmingham's Jewellery Quarter (Map 16). Trust us, one way or another, Wolverhampton rarely fails to steal your heart.

## Eating & Drinking

BLUE BRICK - Sun Street (best accessed from canal from Broad Street Bridge, go under railway and turn right). Tel: 01902 875301. Bistro and bar incorporated within fabric of old Low Level railway station and operated as part of Whitbread's 'Table Table' chain. Handy for breakfasts (before all those locks, perhaps!) from 6.30am Mon-Fri and 7am weekends. Main menu served from 11.30am onwards daily. WV10 0DJ

CAFE MAXSIM - Darlington Street (opposite post office). Tel: 01902 428999. Mediterranean tapas bar and cafe. Tue-Sat 10am-3pm, plus Fri & Sat evenings from 6pm. Al fresco in 'secret garden'. WV1 4EX

GREAT WESTERN - Sun Street. (best accessed from canal from Broad Street Bridge, go under railway and turn right). Tel: 01902 351090. Splendid establishment featuring railway and football memorabilia, Holdens, Bathams, guest beers, Black Country cooking at lunchtimes: grey paes & bacon, hot pork cobs, faggots & chips, fish pies etc. WV10 0DJ

MEDICINE BAKERY - Chubb Buildings. Artisan bakery/deli/cafe housed in handsome former lock works. They are also at The Mailbox in Birmingham - see page 68. Open 8am-4pm daily. WV1 1HT

MOON UNDER WATER - Lichfield Street. Wetherspoon. Tel: 01902 422447. WV1 1EQ

ROSSO E NERO - Darlington St. Tel: 01902 425031. Italian. Mon-Sat from noon, Sun 12-4pm. WV1 4HW

## Shopping

Retail market on Tue, Wed, Fri & Sat. There are no city centre supermarkets within easy carrier bag walking distance of the canal. RIP Beatties flagship department store, in the process of being converted into appartments. Coal, logs and bottled gas from the long established Wulfruna Coal Co. at Minerva Wharf, Horseley Fields - Tel: 01902 453517.

## Things to Do

ART GALLERY - Lichfield Street. Tel: 01902 552055. Dignified Italianate building dating from the 1880s; note how the first floor is windowless, because, of course, the wall space was required for hanging paintings which are top lit from the roof. Look out for the work of Edwin Butler Bayliss (1874-1950) who captured the industrial Black Country to a T. Local tourist information and excellent cafe. WV1 1DU

ST PETER'S CHURCH - Lichfield Street. Tel: 01902 422642. Imposing collegiate church in red sandstone. Visitor Centre featuring local history. Shop. WV1 1TY

## Connections

BUSES - West Midlands hub. Tel: 0871 200 2233.

TRAINS - busy railhead; local West Midlands services shadow the BCN main line through Coseley, Tipton, Dudley Port etc to Birmingham. Tel: 0345 748 4950.

TRAMS - treat yourself to a ride on the Metro, a fascinating journey by modern tram across what's left of the industrial Black Country and the opportunity to eavesdrop on oral history in the making as you go along; much of it, seemingly, in Polish or Romanian!

TAXIS - Associated. Tel: 01902 420420.

# Bilston

Map 11

What pride went into the building of these Black Country towns. What pathos now, as handsome buildings crumble from wanton neglect. Witness the terracotta Technical School, standing ruinously across the road from the Craft Gallery. What species is incapable of doing something worthwhile with a characterful building such as this? At least the offices of the once neighbouring tram depot have survived, still proudly displaying the initials of the Wolverhampton District Electric Tramways Ltd. Why not remove both to the safety of the BCLM? Thorold shared our enthusiasm for the place: 'unquestionably one of the best Black Country towns'; forty years ago it probably hadn't begun to crumble quite so much. More positively, don't miss St Leonard's - it's difficult to anyway - gleaming whitely above the town's low rooftops with a confident 19th century sense of self-worth. It was designed by Francis Goodwin. A memorial commemorates one Mary Pearce, descended from *three* children of Edward I!

*continued on page 39:*

**WELCOME to WOLVERHAMPTON**

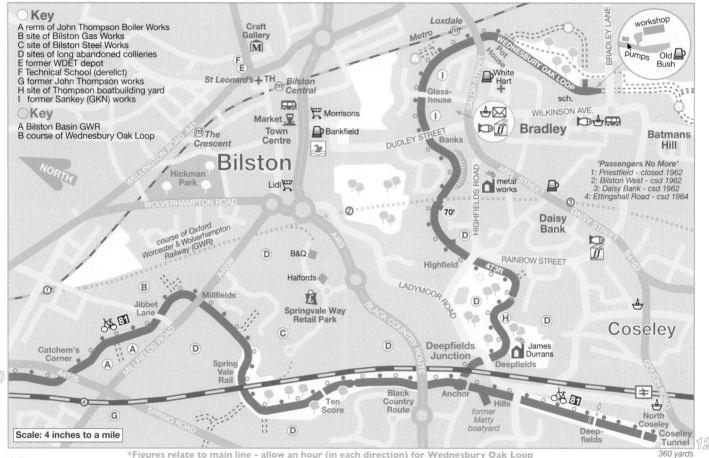

◯ **Key**
A rems of John Thompson Boiler Works
B site of Bilston Gas Works
C site of Bilston Steel Works
D sites of long abandoned collieries
E former WDET depot
F Technical School (derelict)
G former John Thompson works
H site of Thompson boatbuilding yard
I former Sankey (GKN) works

◯ **Key**
A Bilston Basin GWR
B course of Wednesbury Oak Loop

Craft
Gallery
Ⓜ

Loxdale
Metro Ⓜ

St Leonard's ✚ TH

Ⓜ Bilston
Central

WEDNESBURY OAK LOOP

workshop

pumps  Old Bush

BRADLEY LANE

sch.

White Hart ✚

Glass-house

WILKINSON AVE.

Bradley

Batmans Hill

Ⅿ The Crescent

Market Town Centre

🚌 Morrisons

Bankfield

Bilston

Lidl 🛒

SALOP STREET

DUDLEY STREET  Banks

HIGHFIELDS ROAD

ASH STREET

metal works

**'Passengers No More'**
1: Priestfield - closed 1962
2: Bilston West - csd 1962
3: Daisy Bank - csd 1962
4: Ettingshall Road - csd 1964

Daisy Bank

DAISY STREET

B4163

Hickman Park

WELLINGTON ROAD A41

NORTH

WOLVERHAMPTON ROAD

course of Oxford Worcester & Wolverhampton Railway (GWR)

A4039

A4123

B&Q

Halfords

🛍 Springvale Way Retail Park

C

70'

②

473ft

Highfield

RAINBOW STREET

LADYMOOR ROAD

BLACK COUNTRY ROUTE

D

D

H

D

Coseley

B

Jibbet Lane

Millfields

①

🚲 81

Catchem's Corner

A4126

A

A

MILLFIELDS ROAD

D

Spring Vale Rail

D

Deepfields Junction

James Durrans

Deepfields

GOUCH ROAD

10

④

G

SPRING ROAD

Ten Score

Black Country Route

Anchor

Hills
former Matty boatyard

🚲 81

Deep-fields

North Coseley

Coseley Tunnel

12

**Scale: 4 inches to a mile**

*Figures relate to main line - allow an hour (in each direction) for Wednesbury Oak Loop

360 yards

LIGHT-HEARTEDLY lockless, the canal wends its way across a landscape no longer remotely 'black'; though it would be inappropriate in a book as wholesomely chaste as this to begin calculating exactly how many shades of grey it has become. Old boatmen would be disorientated by this reed-fringed ribbon, bereft of all but the merest hint that manufacturing once went on along its banks. Should you like to see how it once looked, make a point of visiting Wolverhampton Art Gallery, where, from time to time (though not nearly often enough) they deign to hang on display examples of their substantial collection of the works of Edwin Butler Bayliss, once heralded as the Poet Painter of the Black Country. Butler Bayliss belonged to the family who made fences and gates at their Victoria works on Cable Street (Map 10), but eschewed a life in business to concentrate on his art. He deserves to be more widely known. Glibly speaking his work is a cross between the French Impressionists and L. S. Lowry, but that barely does justice to the atmosphere his canvases engender. Several of his works are recognisably located along this section of canal, and feature the once vast steel works at Spring Vale (C).

Steel production ceased at Spring Vale in 1979. It is well nigh impossible to comprehend from a contemporary perspective just how gargantuan the plant - originally owned by Sir Alfred Hickman, later Stewarts & Lloyds and eventually British Steel - was, and how completely it dominated the neighbourhood. Mull on such matters as the passage of your boat swishes the bullrushes by Ten Score Bridge, and idly wonder what'll replace the retail parks, designer outlet villages and fast food drive-thrus of the present day in times to come. One notable works which does survive, albeit disused, is the John Thompson factory at Ettingshall (G). Dating from 1948 it remains a modernistic design of ferro-concrete construction featuring copious fenestration and curved roof lines. Thompsons can trace their history back to a boatbuilding yard (H) near Highfields Road on the Wednesbury Oak Loop.

From Deepfields Junction the Wednesbury Oak Loop, the original course of Brindley's main line, departs on its foreshortened way to the Canal & River Trust's workshops at Bradley (pronounced with a long 'A' like Cradley). An arcane adventure, even by BCN standards, its

Bradley

exploration will appeal to the kind of boater who doesn't feel fulfilled until they have pointed their prow up the most obscure and unpromising of backwaters. It had been growing shallower with each passing year, but was thankfully dredged over the winter of 2018/19; not so much for the benefit of inquisitive diehards, but because of its importance as a supply channel, water being pumped from a subterranean honeycomb of flooded coal workings at Bradley to maintain the Wolverhampton Level. Initially pea soup in colour, by the time you reach the terminus the canal becomes so transparent that you can marvel at a Hans & Lotte Hass world of subaqueous tendrils beneath your hull.

James Durrans - 'one of the world's leading producers of carbonaceous materials' - works at Deepfields establishes what turns out to be a misleadingly industrial tone. But increasingly the emphasis is on housing; newbuilds drawn, no doubt, by the perception of a waterside setting, as though their occupants could somehow contrive to convince themselves they had purchased property overlooking one or other of the Italian Lakes. Joseph Sankey's (GKN) metal works once spanned the canal just east of Glasshouse Bridge. A fine aerial view of it in its heyday exists on Historic England's *Britain From Above* website.

Bradley Workshops were opened in 1961 as a replacement for the depot which had previously existed at Ocker Hill (Map 46). They are occasionally open to the public and, to contradict Dr Johnson, not only worth seeing but worth going to see. It is one of only two CRT work-shops where lockgates are still made,

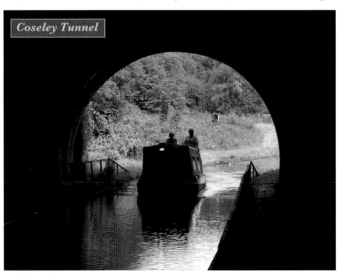

Coseley Tunnel

the other being at Stanley Ferry on the Aire & Calder Navigation in Yorkshire. The delightful scent of wood resin permeates the building. On the wall of the adjoining pumping house a plaque recalls the bizarre deaths of Maud and Frederick Fellows here on 31st January 1916. They were the unwitting victims of 'enemy action', killed when a passing Zeppelin randomly dropped a bomb on them. Scarcely any trace remains of the remainder of the Wednesbury Oak Loop on its way to rejoin the main line at Tipton (Map 12). But by following public footpaths, it's feasible to follow the Bradley Branch down to Moorcroft Junction on the Walsall Canal as depicted on Map 46.

The Wednesbury Oak Loop became of secondary status with the opening of Coseley Tunnel in 1837. Plans for a shortening of the route between Deepfields and Bloomfield (Map 12) had been lodged over forty years earlier, and arms were dug from both directions, but considerable difficulty was encountered with the tunnelling process and the project was mothballed until Thomas Telford revived it as part of his main line improvement scheme in the 1820s. It's plain to see there were towpaths on both sides of the tunnel, but the one on the western bank of the canal has been allowed to fall out of use in recent years. Houses perch picturesquely above the northern portal, reminding one of Cookley (Map 5). The neigh-bouring Deepfields Footbridge presented presumably less of a challenge to Dorman Long & Co of Middlesborough than one of their other projects - the Sydney Harbour Bridge.

# Tipton
Map 12

"Talk to the Tipton" is the local building society's encouraging slogan, and who could resist passing time with this endearing little town, surrounded by canals past and present. Back when the Tipton Green & Toll End Communication Canal was 'in water', Tipton was literally islanded by canals and had been comically compared with Venice long before the analogy was poached by Birmingham. Henry Thorold, in his 1978 *Shell Guide to Staffordshire*, considered 'there is no place more redolent of the Black Country than Tipton', and, as regular followers of the Canal Companions well know, we rarely quibble with Henry!

With its early car production line, soap, lubricants, blue bricks and sausage manufactories, Tipton had always punched economically above its weight, so it is appropriate that the little town's most famous son was William Perry aka 'The Tipton Slasher', England's champion prizefighter for seven undefeated years from 1850. His pugilistic years followed a period as a canal boatman; ideal preparation one imagines. Another sporting claim to fame is that of Tipton Harriers, the athletics club which celebrated its centenary in 2010. Their most notable exponent was Jack Holden who won Commonwealth and European gold medals for the marathon in 1950, thus covering the club - whose motto is 'Swift & Eager' - in a reflected glory never quite shaken off. Tipton Library (ex Thur & Sun) features an excellent little Heritage Centre.

Grade II listed St Paul & St Martin's redbrick church on Owen Street has found a new lease of life under the auspices of the Christ Apostolic Church. The premises next door, despite having the appearance of a nonconformist chapel, originally belonged to a bank, but now they are a betting shop; fruit for a parable there, perhaps.

## Eating & Drinking
FOUNTAIN - Owen Street. Tel: 0121 522 3606. *Good Beer Guide* listed canalside pub. Lunches Mon-Fri, snacks at other times. Banks's & guests. DY4 8HE
MAD O'ROURKE'S PIE FACTORY - Hurst Lane. Tel: 0121 557 1402. Quirkily eccentric street corner pub renowned for its gargantuan Desperate Dan Cow Pies (certificates for finishers!) and Lumphammer Ale. From noon daily, food served throughout. DY4 9AB

## Shopping
Handy convenience stores easily reached from either of the main lines. Two ATMs on Owen Street. Post office on Union Street. Small market on Tuesdays.

## Things to Do
BLACK COUNTRY LIVING MUSEUM - Tipton Road, Dudley. Tel: 0121 557 9643. Admission charge. Thrilling 'open air' celebration of a throwback world peopled by costumed characters. It will take you at least two or three hours to walk around the exhibits which include a village, colliery, school, pumping engine, boat dock and fairground. Rolfe Street Baths (which used to overlook the canal as it passed so dramatically through Smethwick) have been re-erected here as an excellent exhibition hall devoted to Black Country social history and industrial archaeology. Trams, trolleybuses and buses offer nostalgic rides from the main entrance to the village. Secure moorings (with comprehensive facilities) are available for visiting boaters, access via Tipton Junction. Refreshments include a Workers' Institute Cafe, Hobbs Fish & Chip Shop (where the fish & chips are cooked as per local tradition in beef-dripping) and the Bottle & Glass Inn. A £23 million development is underway to bring history up to date by featuring the 1940-60s period. Frankly, it would be ludicrous to boat/walk along the BCN Main Line and not call in here. DY1 4SQ

DUDLEY CANAL & TUNNEL TRUST - Birmingham New Road. Tel: 0121 557 6265. 45 minute boat trips from the imposing Portal Visitor Centre into Dudley Tunnel and its fabulous limestone caverns. Longer trips through the entire length of the tunnel, and also Netherton Tunnel on selected dates. Refreshments available at the Gongoozler Restaurant. DY1 4SB

## Connections
BUSES - services 11/11A provide a 10 minute frequency from stops adjoining Factory Bridge to Dudley (a town well worth visiting) passing the Black Country Living Museum in the process. Diamond 229 affords a similar 20 minute frequency from stops on Owen Street. Tel: 0871 200 2233.
TRAINS - local West Midlands services half-hourly between Wolverhampton and Birmingham. Tel: 0345 748 4950.

# Bilston
Map 11
*continued from page 34:*
## Eating & Drinking
MAJOR FISH RESTAURANT - Church Street. Tel: 01902 497072. Something of an 'institution' in this neck of the Black Country. WV14 0AX
TRUMPET - High Street. Tel: 01902 493723. *Good Beer Guide* listed town centre local featuring Holden's lovely beer and live jazz most nights. WV14 0EP
BANKFIELD INN - Bankfield Road. Tel: 01902 504795. Marston's new build previously known as the White Rabbit in reference to a local coal mining superstition. Open from 11am daily, food throughout. WV14 0EE

## Shopping
Thriving indoor retail market Mon/Thur-Sat 9am-5pm. Morrison's supermarket. Pedestrianised High Street.

## Things to Do
BILSTON CRAFT GALLERY - Mount Pleasant. Tel: 01902 552507. Open Thur-Sat 12-4pm. WV14 7LU

*39*

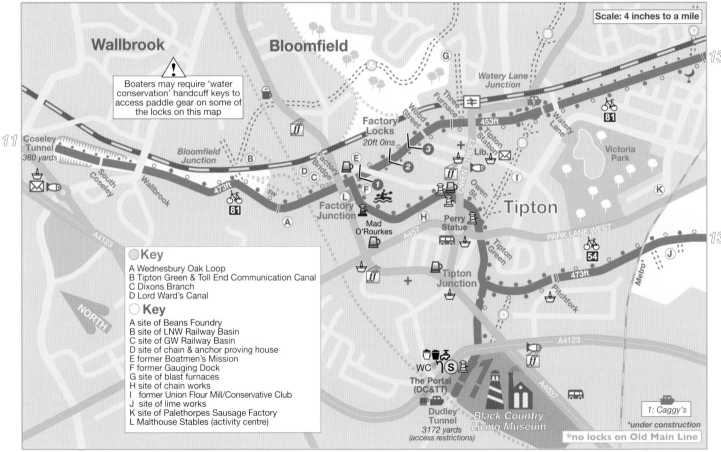

Scale: 4 inches to a mile

Wallbrook

Bloomfield

Boaters may require 'water conservation' handcuff keys to access paddle gear on some of the locks on this map

11

Coseley Tunnel
360 yards

Bloomfield Junction

South Coseley

Wallbrook

473ft

81

sw

A

Factory Bridge

Factory Junction

B

C

D

L

E

F

1

Mad O'Rourkes

Factory Locks
20ft 0ins

3

2

G

Three Furnace

Wood Street

453ft

Watery Lane Junction

Watery Lane

Tipton Station

Lib.

B

81

13

Victoria Park

Tipton

H

Perry Statue

A457

PARK LANE WEST

Tipton Green

Tipton Junction

473ft

Pitchfork

Metro*

54

K

13

J

A4123

NORTH

A4123

A4037

WC

S

The Portal
(DC&TT)

Dudley Tunnel
3172 yards
(access restrictions)

Black Country Living Museum

1: Caggy's

*under construction

**Key**
A Wednesbury Oak Loop
B Tipton Green & Toll End Communication Canal
C Dixons Branch
D Lord Ward's Canal

**Key**
A site of Beans Foundry
B site of LNW Railway Basin
C site of GW Railway Basin
D site of chain & anchor proving house
E former Boatmen's Mission
F former Gauging Dock
G site of blast furnaces
H site of chain works
I former Union Flour Mill/Conservative Club
J site of lime works
K site of Palethorpes Sausage Factory
L Malthouse Stables (activity centre)

*no locks on Old Main Line

'REISTY and wild as the midden in August' according to Liz Berry's poem *Tipton-on-Cut*. Other metaphors are available. Once upon a time Owen Street, Tipton's main thoroughfare, was surrounded on four sides by canals; nowadays it's effectively just three; though a public footpath - complete with the obvious remains of a lock chamber - faithfully shadows the course of the euphoniously named Tipton Green & Toll End Communication Canal, which sounds like something Tolkein might have invented. You can add further veracity by imagining it is 1942, and you're accompanying Daphne March aboard the *Heather Bell*, making your way towards the Cannock coalfield after discharging three hundred and fifty two sacks of flour at Tipton Green, a sequence photographed by the Ministry of Information for use as wartime propaganda, illustrating women's adaptability in the absence of men. Ah, the past, the past; it keeps bubbling to the surface of the BCN's viscous waters, as if refusing to be consigned to itself.

Emerging from Coseley Tunnel, the canal negotiates a swarthy cutting before opening out beyond Wallbrook Bridge. The exact point at which the Wednesbury Oak Loop rejoined the main line at Bloomfield Junction is difficult to decipher. Similarly, solely rubble remains on the site of Beans Foundry, a smoky, cacophonous icon in the early days of our growing familiarity with the BCN in the 'eighties and 'nineties, but subsequently demolished; and, as yet, unreplaced. In the early days of mass motoring, Beans rivalled Ford in the realms of affordable cars. Fortunately, not all their vehicles could match the speed of *Thunderbolt*, specially constructed to attempt the land speed record. It duly obliged, achieving 357 mph at Bonneville, USA, in 1938.

Nearing Tipton, a pair of sizeable railway basins provided a means of transhipping cargoes between the BCN and London & North Western and Great Western railways respectively. Railway owned boats would operate between these interchange points and 'boatage' depots which were wharves

Factory Locks 'Down'

Factory Locks 'Up'

operated by the railways but without direct rail links.

Utilitarian nomenclature abounds on the BCN, and at Factory Junction, Brindley's "Wolverhampton Level" and Telford's "Birmingham Level" are seen to meet or divide, depending on your direction of travel. Heading for Birmingham, therefore, you have the choice (always assuming both routes are free of stoppages if you're boating) between the directness of Telford's wide, embanked, twin-towpathed 'Island Line', twenty feet below through the three Factory Locks, and Brindley's original route which parallels it, hugging the 473ft contour in the shadow of the Rowley Hills. The former, accompanied by the busy railway, encounters Caggy's boatyard, named after Caggy Stevens, the BCN's last working boatman. From this point the aforementioned Tipton Green & Toll End Communication led to the Walsall Canal (Map 46) until its abandonment in 1967.

There are two notable survivals at Factory Junction. Between the pub and the top lock a former Boatmen's Mission now finds use as a workshop making ornamental ironwork. This was one of five such establishments on the BCN dispensing hot drinks, tobacco, washing facilities and a little transitory warmth and companionship. On the Sabbath the emphasis became more overtly religious, and Sunday School lessons were held for boat children. On the opposite bank of the top lock stands a former BCN gauging station where the carrying capacity of boats was calculated for toll taking purposes. Craft gained access through two arches at the west end of the building. Recently, this listed and hugely significant structure has been placed in jeopardy by a proposal that the site be cleared for a housing development. Nothing has happened, yet, but perhaps it would be sensible to move it, brick by brick, to the sanctuary of the Black Country Living Museum.

From Factory Junction the Old Main Line winds beguilingly around the edge of Tipton. Former stables have been given a new lease of life as a canoe centre - boaters should proceed with due care. Good visitor moorings are provided, courtesy of the Friends of Tipton Cut, on the offside north of Owen Street Bridge. An anchor on a plinth pays lip service to one of Tipton's old industries. Snaking round the corner, past The Fountain public house and under Owen Street Bridge, Brindley's route passes a small park featuring a pigeon-splattered statue of William Perry, aka 'the Tipton Slasher'. The other end of the TG&TECC lies scarcely discernibly opposite. BCN cottage 100 overlooks Tipton Green Bridge.

Brindley's route affords access to the Black Country Living Museum where an unusual vertical lift bridge (rescued from the Great Western Railway's Tipton interchange basin - 'C'), gives access to a section of Lord Ward's Canal which led directly from the Old Main Line to a bank of lime kilns which still forms an attractive feature of the museum. Several historic boats are usually on display - though some, like Thomas Clayton's *Stour* when we last saw it, in distressingly poor states of repair - and there is a working boat dock where visitors can witness the trades and techniques of traditional Black Country boat construction.

Beyond the museum moorings is the northern portal of Dudley Tunnel, first dug in 1775 to gain access to subterranean limestone workings. Ten years later it was extended through to join up with the Dudley Canal at Park Head (Map 39). The tunnel re-opened to general boating traffic in 1992, with the proviso that vessels be shafted and 'legged' through so as to avoid the creation of engine fumes, and that they meet the fairly restrictive gauge limitations. Since then, life has been made easier by the introduction of a tug.

Tipton

DCTT & BCLM

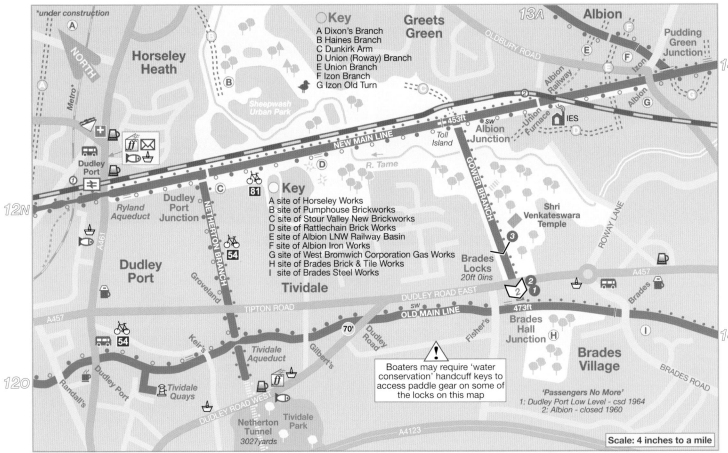

# 13 BIRMINGHAM CANAL NAVIGATIONS  Dudley Port  2mls/0lks*/1hr

*under construction

NORTH

13A

**Albion**

OLDBURY ROAD

Pudding Green Junction

**Horseley Heath**

**Greets Green**

○ **Key**
A Dixon's Branch
B Haines Branch
C Dunkirk Arm
D Union (Roway) Branch
E Union Branch
F Izon Branch
G Izon Old Turn

Albion Railway

Metro

Sheepwash Urban Park

Albion

Albion

NEW MAIN LINE

453ft

sw

Union Furnace

IES

Toll Island

Albion Junction

Dudley Port

R. Tame

D

GOWER BRANCH

**Shri Venkateswara Temple**

ROWAY LANE

12N

Ryland Aqueduct

Dudley Port Junction

81

○ **Key**
A site of Horseley Works
B site of Pumphouse Brickworks
C site of Stour Valley New Brickworks
D site of Rattlechain Brick Works
E site of Albion LNW Railway Basin
F site of Albion Iron Works
G site of West Bromwich Corporation Gas Works
H site of Brades Brick & Tile Works
I site of Brades Steel Works

NETHERTON BRANCH

54

A461

**Dudley Port**

Groveland

**Tividale**

3

**Brades Locks**
20ft 0ins

2 2
2 1

Brades

A457

**Dudley Port**

DUDLEY ROAD EAST

sw

473ft

**Brades Hall Junction** H

I

**Brades Village**

BRADES ROAD

54

Keir's

TIPTON ROAD

70'

Dudley Road

OLD MAIN LINE

Fisher's

120

Randall's

Dudley Port

Tividale Aqueduct

Gilbert's

ff

*Tividale Quays*

DUDLEY ROAD WEST

Netherton Tunnel
3027yards

Tividale Park

A4123

⚠ Boaters may require 'water conservation' handcuff keys to access paddle gear on some of the locks on this map

**'Passengers No More'**
1: Dudley Port Low Level - csd 1964
2: Albion - closed 1960

Scale: 4 inches to a mile

39

*three locks on Gower Branch

T HE old and new main lines of the BCN pursue their intrinsically different ways across the heart of the Black Country, and connecting canals come marching in from left and right, determined to jump on the bandwagon. There is so much to take in that you need to keep your wits about you to do it full justice.

## Old Main Line

Brindley's route tends to be less boated than Telford's. A narrow channel fights its way through lily beds like something out of a Rupert the Bear illustration. Moorhens and coots are confident enough in being undisturbed to build precarious nests midstream. Tividale Quays is a housing development built on the site of former galvanising works: the Birmingham Canal Navigations Society recommend this (with the usual disclaimers) as a safe mooring site for visitors, though we've never witnessed anyone other than convoys using it as such. A tad voyeuristic, perhaps.

Tividale Aqueduct carries the old main line over the Netherton Tunnel Branch. There is no waterway connection here, but a path links the two levels. Netherton's northern portal looks intriguing and sepulchural when seen from the vantage point of the aqueduct, as though it might somehow lead you into the past, if only you had the gumption to go there.

Southwards there are occasional glimpses towards the Rowley Hills and Dudley Castle. Tramways once ran down to the canal from quarries along the escarpment. At Brades Hall Junction the Gower Branch descends through the BCN's solitary 'staircase' lock to join Telford's main line, quarter of a mile to the north, encountering a magnificent Hindu temple in the

Albion

*Tividale Aqueduct*

process. A substantial bay-fronted toll house stood alongside the top chamber. In latter years it was home to Thomas William King, a prolific photographer of canals before they became popular with the public.

## New Main Line

Whilst Brindley's canal wanders about the foot of the Rowley Hills with 18th century sloth, Telford's gets to grips with the task of reaching Birmingham with 19th century urgency. This 'new' main line crosses great open expanses of wasteground where large craters recall past quarrying and brickmaking. These areas have been redeveloped as urban woodland. Inexorably the Black Country is becoming green again, going full circle back to a pre-industrial arcady.

Junction after junction - some vanished, some intact - keep the adrenalin flowing. The short Dixon's Branch served the premises of the Horseley Bridge & Engineering Company, manufacturers of the elegant iron bridges that are such a distinctive feature of the area's canals. Three aqueducts carry the canal across two roads and a railway. The most notable, Ryland Aqueduct, is a concrete rebuilding of 1968. A short loop railway once crossed the canal here, used by the 'Dudley Dodger' push & pull train which ran from the town station at Dudley to connect with main line trains at

Dudley Port. The South Staffordshire Railway burrows beneath the canal and is in the process of being refurbished as a West Midlands Metro tram route: a far cry from the days when Palethorpe's nearby 'sausage siding' was shunted on a daily basis.

At Dudley Port Junction the Netherton Branch makes a bee-line for its famous tunnel. Opened in 1858 to relieve pressure on the Dudley Tunnel route, it was the last canal tunnel to be built in Britain, going into the record books - at 3027 yards - as the eighth longest. Subsequent closures have rendered it fourth (in navigable terms) to Standedge on the Huddersfield Narrow Canal, Dudley itself, and Blisworth on the Grand Union. In the shadow of Tividale Aqueduct stand BCN cottages 174 & 175.

Perched on a lengthy embankment which crosses the infant Tame, the canal parallels the busy railway. Extol the virtues of canal boating by waving at passing trains. In 1899 over enthusiastic extraction of clay for brick-making at the Rattlechain Works caused the banks to burst and six miles of water to drain away. It's safe to say the canal was repaired rather more rapidly than the average breach today. The base of Dunkirk Toll Island all but fills the width of the new main line; an 'eye of the needle' job for nervous steerers. A Horseley cast iron bridge dated 1855 spans Albion Junction, whence the Gower Branch links up with the old main line and 'Wolverhampton Level'. Sweet peas thrive on the canal bank. The branch was used by Alfred Matty's to convey poisonous phosphorus waste from Oldbury for disposal in a lagoon at the site of Rattlechain Brick Works.

At Albion a fair degree of 'metal-bashing' is still undertaken, but old maps depict far greater complexities of industry. From Albion railway station a branch led across Oldbury Road to the London & North Western Railway's Albion interchange basin, reached via an arm off the Wednesbury 'Old' Canal. An atmospheric night-time painting of its busy interior by Brian Collings appeared in the first edition of Tom Foxon's evocative memoir of a 1950s working boatman *Number One*. Pudding Green ought to be the name of some picturesque village snuggled deep in the Sussex Weald. Instead, it's an incongruous gateway to and from the under-boated northern waters of the BCN, of which more on Map 13A.

## Great Bridge
Map 13A

The Spine Road has brought 21st century mundanity to Great Bridge, and sucked much of the life out of it in the process. Yet there are still overtones of durable Black Country character, and Great Bridge remains a more than useful frontier post for stocking up on life's little luxuries before heading off into the barbarous northern wastes of the BCN.

### Eating & Drinking
THE RIDGACRE - New Gas Street (overlooking Swan Bridge Junction). Tel: 0121 553 4910. Table Table bar/restaurant. Breakfasts from 6.30am (7am weekends) main meals 11.30am onwards. B70 0NP *Fish & chips from Frydays or The Black Country Chippy. McDonald's and KFC drive-thrus.*

### Shopping
Access between locks 7 and 8 to main thoroughfare of shops, Asda supermarket and Boots pharmacy. Small retail market Weds & Sats.

### Connections
BUSES - service 74 operates at frequent intervals to/from Dudley, West Bromwich and Birmingham, connecting with the nearest railhead at Dudley Port. Tel: 0871 200 2233.
METRO - handy pedestrian access from Black Lake station to isolated section of Ridgacre Branch.
TAXIS - West Brom Cars. Tel: 0121 553 5050.

## Oldbury
Map 14

"Of Oldbury, with its mean, blackened streets, I can find no redeeming words to say." That was L. T. C. Rolt's considered opinion in 1949 - he could be cutting when the mood took him. No longer in Worcestershire, redevelopment has radically botoxed the town's face, and since 1974 it has been the seat of power in the Metropolitan Borough of Sandwell whose pagoda-like headquarters dominate the town. The new library is housed in a building named after Jack Judge, music hall entertainer and composer of *It's A Long Way to Tipperary*, who (born here in 1872) is equally feted in Stalybridge.

### Eating & Drinking
COURT OF REQUESTS - Church Street. Tel: 0121 543 6970. Wetherspoons housed in a handsome building of 1816 which was originally a court room, but more recently the town's library before it moved - see above. Open 8am, food throughout. B69 3AF

### Shopping
The best canalside choice in shops between Wolverhampton and Birmingham, though there are no signed visitor moorings as such. The centre is most conveniently reached from the Old Main Line, but is also little more than half a mile from Telford's route at Bromford.

### Connections
BUSES - frequent links with Dudley, Birmingham etc. Tel: 0871 200 2233.
TRAINS - Sandwell & Dudley railhead by Bromford Bridge on New Main Line. Tel: 0345 748 4950.
TAXIS - Midland & Apollo. Tel: 0121 555 5151.

## Langley
Map 14A

The Black Country's pulse still beats faintly in little communities like Langley. It feels just like a village; albeit a village surrounded by heavy industry. To get the measure of the place, make a bee-line for Elaine's discount store, stockists of everything you ever wanted, and much you didn't know you ever wanted. More prosaically, there's a Londis convenience store with post office counter, a pharmacy, cash machine, a couple of Indian restaurants and several pubs and fast food outlets of varying ethnicity.

Entertainment - in addition to exploration of the Titford Canal - is provided by the Oldbury Repertory Players at their Barlow Theatre. Telephone the Box Office for performance details on 0121 552 2761.

### Connections
BUSES - service 12 operates quarter-hourly (hourly Sun) to/ from Birmingham and Dudley (via Oldbury. Tel: 0871 200 2233.
TRAINS - half-hourly services to/from Birmingham Snow Hill and southwards towards Stourbridge, Kidderminster and Worcester. Tel: 0345 748 4950.
TAXIS - Premier Cars. Tel: 0121 552 7070.

## Smethwick
Map 15

Unfathomably, Thorold overlooked Smethwick in his masterly *Shell Guide Staffordshire*. Perhaps he was nervous of parking his Bentley there, or simply misled by the fact that it had already been transferred into Worcestershire in 1966. A curse on the meddling classes! Ditto planners, who had the affrontery to demolish one side of High Street to make room for the expressway. What remains is more Asian than Anglo-Saxon, and characteristically book-ended by gurdwaras. Luke Perry's bronze statue of a Sikh soldier commemorates the contribution of combatants of all faiths from the Indian subcontinent who fought for Britain in both world wars. If you enjoy Asian cooking then this is the place to stop for authentic ingredients; the sweet shop displays are mouth-watering.

### Things to Do
GALTON VALLEY PUMPING STATION - Brasshouse Lane. Tel: 0121 556 0683. Enjoyably interpreted canal history in authentic pumphouse setting. Open selected Saturdays Apr-Oct 10am-3pm. B66 1BA

### Connections
TRAINS - frequent West Midlands services between Rolfe Street station and Birmingham New Street and between Galton Bridge and New Street and Snow Hill. Tel: 0345 748 4950

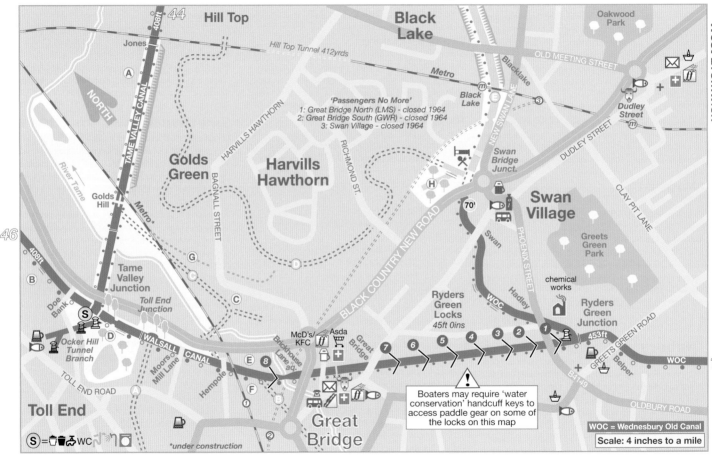

# 13A BCN WALSALL CANAL Etc. Great Bridge 2mls/8lks/3hrs

**Hill Top**

**Black Lake**

Oakwood Park

44

409ft

Jones

Hill Top Tunnel 412yrds

A

NORTH

OLD MEETING STREET

Metro

Blacklake

Black Lake

m

West Bromwich

Dudley Street

**Golds Green**

**Harvills Hawthorn**

HARVILLS HAWTHORN

'Passengers No More'
1: Great Bridge North (LMS) - closed 1964
2: Great Bridge South (GWR) - closed 1964
3: Swan Village - closed 1964

NEW SWAN LANE

Swan Bridge Junct.

DUDLEY STREET

m

CLAY PIT LANE

TAME VALLEY CANAL

Golds Hill

BAGNALL STREET

RICHMOND ST.

H

70'

**Swan Village**

Greets Green Park

46

River Tame

Metro

G

BLACK COUNTRY NEW ROAD

Swan

PHOENIX STREET

chemical works

408ft

**Tame Valley Junction**

Toll End Junction

D

C

Ryders Green Locks
45ft 0ins

Hadley

WOC

Ryders Green Junction

B

Doe Bank

S

Ocker Hill Tunnel Branch

WALSALL CANAL

Moors Mill Lane

Brickhouse Lane aq.

McD's/ KFC

Asda

Great Bridge

7

6

5

4

3

2

1

453ft

GREETS GREEN ROAD

Belper

WOC

1

TOLL END ROAD

Hempole

E

F

8

⚠ Boaters may require 'water conservation' handcuff keys to access paddle gear on some of the locks on this map

B4149

OLDBURY ROAD

**Toll End**

**Great Bridge**

*under construction

WOC = Wednesbury Old Canal

Scale: 4 inches to a mile

S = 🗑🚮♿WC

ATMOSPHERE seeps from every cavity (and there are plenty of them) on the canals depicted by Map 13A, and yet they are rarely, rarely explored. In a sense, of course, that only adds to their mystique, tempting the adventurer latent in all of us to venture into the unknown. Less a voyage along the BCN, more a voyage to distant galaxies. "It's boating, Jim, but not as we know it."

## Tame Valley Canal

Egressing dolefully eastwards, across a pock-marked landscape populated by ponies and pylons - but little else - the Tame Valley Canal of 1844 offers alternative routes to Brownhills and Birmingham. Twin-towpathed, it crosses the Tame before passing beneath the South Staffordshire Railway, presently being revitalised as part of the West Midlands Metro. The line will link Wednesbury with Brierley Hill; a mouth-watering prospect. Despondent convoys of steam locomotives arrived at John Cashmore's neighbouring scrapyard to be broken up in the 1960s. Illustrious casualties, which would be gold dust in the preservation era, include: 6005 *King George II*, 46256 *Sir William A Stanier FRS* and 60152 *Holyrood*.

A brackeny cutting precedes the massive bulk of James Russell & Sons New Crown Tube Works, erected after the First World War as a replacement for premises partially destroyed in a Zeppelin raid. Russells were patentees and prize-winners in the art of tube making for gas appliances. Part of the Metro system since 1999, the railway bridge adjoining Jones Bridge originally carried the Great Western Railway's main line from London to Merseyside across the canal. Zippy as the trams are, one longs retrospectively to see a 'King' or a 'Western', Paddington bound with a twelve coach express from the shores of Cardigan Bay.

## Walsall Canal

Notwithstanding its proximity to burgeoning housing estates and the dual-carriagewayed Black Country New Road, Tame Valley Junction is one of the loneliest on the BCN, the uninhabited former BW offices serving only to add to the doleful scene. Correspondents tell us you need at least 80ft of hose to reach the water point. Limited secure visitor moorings are

available on the remaining stub of the Ocker Hill Tunnel Branch, opened in 1785 to feed water to the pumping engines at Ocker Hill via an unnavigable tunnel. To the west, another through route has been irretrievably lost. The Tipton Green & Toll End Communication Canal doesn't exactly roll off the tongue, but until 1960 it 'communicated' with the main line at Tipton, easing congestion in the heyday of the BCN when boats were choc-a-bloc at Ryders Green.

Alan Godfrey's reprint of the 1902 Ordnance Survey Map for Great Bridge & Toll End depicts in all its fascinating complexity the stretch of canal between Toll End Junction and Ryders Green Bottom Lock. Here the Danks Branch made its dog-leg connection with the Tame Valley Canal, whilst the aforementioned South Staffordshire Railway spanned the Walsall's main line. Both the Midland and London & North Western railways boasted interchange basins, the latter having been subsumed by the swampy undergrowth abutting the Black Country New Road.

Hempole Lane Bridge is date-stamped MDCCCXXV - the year *Locomotion* debuted on the Stockton & Darlington Railway - the writing was already on the wall for canals. The River Tame passes beneath an aqueduct above the top gate of Lock 8, somewhat anti-socially removed from its seven fellows. At the tail of the lock the Haines Branch, opened in 1833 to serve Pumphouse Brick Works (Map 13), has vanished.

It's fairly safe to say that the Ryders Green 'Eight' are not deemed to be one of the Canal & River Trust's flagship locations. An air of introspection hangs over the flight; as might befit the occupants of a doctor's surgery waiting room. Confidence is in short supply. Ditto, seemingly, water in the short intervening pounds; though with the

⚪ **Key**
A former New Crown Tube Works
B site of Ocker Hill Power Station
C site of Golds Green Colliery
D site of Crown Brick Works
E site of LNW Railway Basin
F site of Midland Railway Basin
G site of Cashmore's scrapyard
H site of GW Railway basin

⚫ **Key**
A Tipton Green & Toll End Communication Canal
B Haines Branch
C Danks Branch
D Balls Hill Branch
E Ridgacre Branch

Birmingham level at your disposal, there is plenty of it on tap, if you get our drift.

Cutting a wedge between a corridor of noisy factories when we first became acquainted with the flight, decades of industrial retreat have deepened its melancholy. Furthermore, the eponymously named Eight Locks public house, which used to reward one with refreshments at the top lock, has pulled its last pint. Liquid solace is thus not easily obtained, unless cadged from the regular coterie of all-day drinkers perched on the balance beams of Lock 7, an affable bunch in our experience, too much victims of life's vicissitudes to pose a threat to passing boaters. Bricked-up arches hint at lost trade. Between locks 6 and 7 a peculiar 'guillotine' gate formerly afforded access to an adjoining works.

*Ryders Green 8*

## Wednesbury 'Old' Canal

Robinson Brothers long established chemical works cast a pungent tang over Ryders Green Junction, meeting place of the Walsall and Wednesbury 'Old' canals. The inverted commas remind us that the Wednesbury Canal wasn't always 'old'. Indeed, it was the earliest section of the Birmingham Canal to be completed, for the promoters were anxious to attract trade at the earliest opportunity, and there were coal pits to tap at Hill Top on the outskirts of Wednesbury. When the canal opened in 1769, America, it will be remembered, was still a British colony.

The WOC doesn't look like a route of some importance now. Ostensibly navigable, a few hundred yards in the reeds and rushes are so dense you'd need a weed-cutter to penetrate them. Thus the winding-hole, provided where the Black Country New Road was allowed to slice across it so contemptuously in 1995 - despite assurances that navigable head-room would be provided - is, to all intents and purposes, obsolete.

Historically the canal continued to Swan Bridge Junction where one arm, which became known as the Balls Hill Branch, wound its circuitous way to Hill Top, terminating amidst colliery shafts beside the Holyhead Road. A second arm, called the Ridgacre Branch - trifurcated into the long forgotten Dartmouth, Halford and Jesson extremities beyond the edge of the map. A former railway interchange basin remains in (shallow) water alongside a pub and travel lodge. Thomas Clayton boats carried tar from Swan Village gasworks to Oldbury until 1966. Part of the Ridgacre Branch was actually restored by Sandwell Council in the 1980s, but subsequently severed by the new road. That's planning for you! Its towpath can, however, be followed for about two thirds of a mile, and Black Lake station on the Metro offers easy access by public transport. The back of beyond, even by BCN standards, inhabited, by herons, coots, and guide book compilers. Anecdotal evidence suggests it is unwise to approach the latter of these species.

**GREETINGS** *from* **GREAT BRIDGE**

51

# 14 BIRMINGHAM CANAL NAVIGATIONS Oldbury 2mls/0lks*/1hr

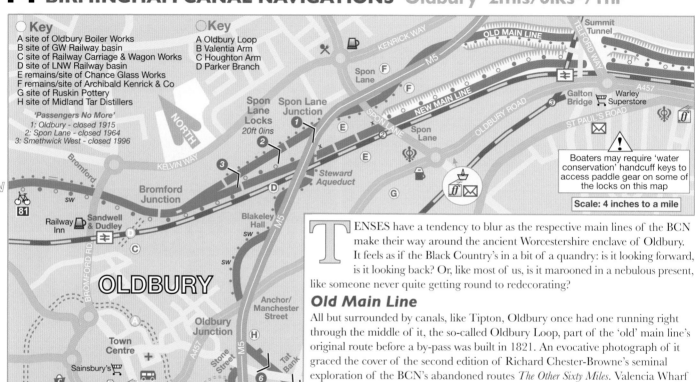

**Key**
A site of Oldbury Boiler Works
B site of GW Railway basin
C site of Railway Carriage & Wagon Works
D site of LNW Railway basin
E remains/site of Chance Glass Works
F remains/site of Archibald Kenrick & Co
G site of Ruskin Pottery
H site of Midland Tar Distillers

*'Passengers No More'*
*1: Oldbury - closed 1915*
*2: Spon Lane - closed 1964*
*3: Smethwick West - closed 1996*

**Key**
A Oldbury Loop
B Valentia Arm
C Houghton Arm
D Parker Branch

Boaters may require 'water conservation' handcuff keys to access paddle gear on some of the locks on this map

Scale: 4 inches to a mile

## Old Main Line

TENSES have a tendency to blur as the respective main lines of the BCN make their way around the ancient Worcestershire enclave of Oldbury. It feels as if the Black Country's in a bit of a quandry: is it looking forward, is it looking back? Or, like most of us, is it marooned in a nebulous present, like someone never quite getting round to redecorating?

### Old Main Line

All but surrounded by canals, like Tipton, Oldbury once had one running right through the middle of it, the so-called Oldbury Loop, part of the 'old' main line's original route before a by-pass was built in 1821. An evocative photograph of it graced the cover of the second edition of Richard Chester-Browne's seminal exploration of the BCN's abandoned routes *The Other Sixty Miles*. Valencia Wharf is a corruption of Valentia Wharf, the name of a nearby colliery, which itself drew inspiration from an island off the coast of County Kerry. Valencia or Valentia, the wharf has become something of a shrine to the owners of the many Allen pleasure boats constructed here down the years. Previously the yard had belonged to T & S Element, well known BCN contractors, who still have a road haulage business based in the town.

Oldbury Junction (egress point of the Titford Canal - see Map 14A) suffers the indignity of being located beneath the M5 motorway. This was the site (between 1935 and 1966) of a boat-yard belonging to another carrying company inseparable from the history of this area's canals. Thomas Clayton specialised in the transport of bulk liquids. With a fleet in excess of eighty boats to maintain, this yard presented a busy scene, a distinctive aspect of which were two mobile slipway shelters which provided some protection from the weather while craft were being re-paired. Clayton's best known long distance traffic was the carriage of oil from Ellesmere Port to Shell's depot at Langley Green on the Titford Canal, a contract which lasted from 1924 until 1955; some of the boats remaining horse-drawn until virtually the end.

Southwards from Oldbury, Clayton boats - with their distinctive decked holds and river names - served gasworks at Oxford, Banbury, Leamington and Solihull, but the bulk of their trade was of a more localised nature, notably the carriage of gas works by-products such as tar. Their last cargo - carried aboard the now preserved motor *Stour* - arrived at Midland Tar Distillers, Oldbury from Walsall Gasworks on 31st March 1966. Faced with diminishing cargoes (brought about largely by the advent of North Sea gas) and the disruption brought about by construction of the elevated section of the M5, Thomas Clayton called it a day. The contemporary face of transportation manifests itself nearby in the shape of DPD's vast road-based distribution hub.

Playing hopscotch with the elevated motorway, the old main line proceeds towards Smethwick. The simple, hump-backed character of Blakeley Hall Bridge contrasts starkly with the overhanging motorway's

*Galton Bridge*

concrete ceiling. In dramatic sequence, the canal passes beneath the Birmingham to Wolver-hampton railway, crosses Telford's route by way of Steward Aqueduct, and meets Brindley's original route to Wednesbury at Spon Lane Junction. The aqueduct's impact is somewhat diluted by the hefty pillars of the motorway towering above it. Interestingly, the iron lattice footbridge immediately south of the railway is numbered as a railway and not canal structure, undoubtedly because it was part of the adjoining interchange basin with the London & North Western Railway.

From Spon Lane Junction a trio of locks leads down to the new main line - see overleaf. Then the canal is swallowed up by the motorway again; in low light you could be forgiven you'd strayed into a cathedral nave. The electric advertising hoardings are there for the dubious benefit of motorists, not boaters. Coal brought down by cable tramway from Jubilee Colliery in Sandwell used to be loaded onto boats via shutes at this point. A regular run from here was to King's Norton (Map 19) with coal for the paper mill's furnaces. Deemed unsafe, the shutes were demolished, and replaced by a hoarding with a photograph of them. Is this the way forward for unwanted buildings? Certainly a cheaper option than restoration.

A blue brick viaduct carries the busy railway line from Snow Hill to Stourbridge over the canal before it plunges into Summit 'tunnel', merely a bridge before the dual-carriageway was built. The 'portal' sprouts buddleia and is dated MDCCXC. 1790 was the year that John Smeaton - better known for his work on the Eddystone Lighthouse - lowered the canal's original summit of 491ft above sea level, eliminating half a dozen locks in the process.

## New Main Line

No BCN junction lacks appeal of one sort or another, but Bromford is one of the most photogenic of all. Three cast iron bridges and the remains of a toll island set the tone, and there's a link with the old main line through the trio of Spon Lane Locks. These locks are quite possibly the oldest working chambers in the country, and enjoy listed status. Here, between 1861 and 1890 the evangelist John Skidmore held weekly, open air revivalist meetings each summer, with attendances peaking at an incredible twenty thousand souls. According to Skidmore's diaries, the throngs assembled on slag heaps bordering the middle lock. 'Thousands worshipped God in the open air ... rich and poor, old and young, well-dressed and ragged, drapers, grocers, butchers, tailors, publicans, ironmasters, clerks, magistrates, puddlers, coalmasters, mine agents, colliers, navvies, boatmen, roadmen, labourers, sweeps, a goodly number of Frenchmen from the Glass House (Chances - see below), the aged and infirm, the lame and the blind, men of all creeds and no creed at all.' Skidmore had been inspired to hold meetings when, whilst out distributing tracts, he had come upon a gathering of colliers and ironworkers at Spon Lane engaged in cockfighting and dog-fighting, gambling and whippet-racing. Through sheer force of personality the then youthful missionary persuaded these rough diamonds to attend an evangelist meeting on the spot the following Sunday. The meetings continued for nearly thirty years until the canal company reclaimed this lawless land. Negotiating the flight now, you need all the imagination you can muster to visualize the al fresco congregation, moved, in turn, to laughter and tears by Skidmore's oratory. There must have been times when they made as much noise as the crowd at West Bromwich Albion's nearby Hawthorns football ground. Nowadays the noise comes from the incessant roar of traffic on the elevated section of the M5 motorway. The top lock is all but engulfed by the road, its tiny, cantilevered, cast iron tail bridge appearing decidedly frail by contrast with the motorway's massive concrete pillars and girders.

Meanwhile Telford's route keeps to the 'Birmingham Level' and passes beneath the M5 and Steward Aqueduct, entering a vast cutting of blue-brick retaining walls between the railway on one side and the crumbling remains of Chance's once mighty glassworks on the other. The works, which in its heyday lined both sides of the canal and railway (hence the linking arches which appear superfluous now) was known world-wide as a manufacturer of, amongst many other things, glass for lighthouses. Formed in 2015, the Chance Glassworks Heritage Trust are manfully attempting to reverse decades of decay, foreseeing a golden future for the works as a business and community hub.*

Another local manufacturer of note was Archibald Kenrick & Sons. A clocktower abutting the elevated motorway is virtually all that remains of their extensive premises either side of the canal. Kenrick's speciality was 'hollow ware': household iron work, door knobs, letter boxes, pots & pans etc. The company still exists, making door and window fittings.

Devotees of television antiques shows will be intrigued to learn that the much revered Ruskin Pottery stood on Oldbury Road, just down the hill from Spon Lane Bridge. Drawing inspiration from John Ruskin's tenets, it was founded in 1898 by Edward R. Taylor head of the Birmingham Municipal School for Arts & Crafts. Subsequently his son, William, developed the pottery's growing reputation for incandescent use of colour and innovative glazing techniques. A sizeable collection of Ruskin Ware can be enjoyed in Wednesbury Museum & Art Gallery ... when it's open.

Galton Bridge should be a shoo-in for a canal system's Greatest Hits compilation. It is one of Thomas Telford's masterpieces; as marvellous, in its own way, as Pontcysyllte, but no World Heritage kudos here. Frankly it deserves a better setting, the setting it originally had, as depicted in mezzotints contemporary with its completion in 1829. All the paraphernalia of modern times does it no favours, least of all the neighbouring dual-carriageway which some bright spark lacked the tact to name Telford Way. It's high time they called the tree surgeons in as well. Every time we pass the bridge becomes a little bit harder to photograph. *An unsafe wall has forced closure of the towpath between the Steward Aqueduct and Spon Lane Bridge for the forseeable future. An easy detour is available via the Old Main Line.

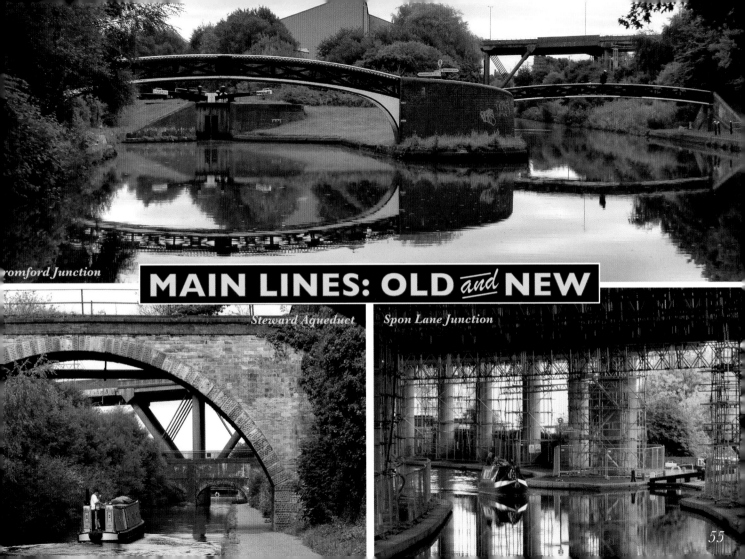

*Bromford Junction*

# MAIN LINES: OLD *and* NEW

*Steward Aqueduct*

*Spon Lane Junction*

DOING 'The Titford' sounds like some sort of dance they might have concocted in the discotheques of Dudley, back when one's flares were as wide as Titford Pools. But until you've done it, you can't really claim to have won your BCN spurs, and it really is one of the canal system's Great Little Adventures.

From the subfusc gloom of Oldbury Junction, a flight of half a dozen locks - nicknamed 'The Crow' after a local industrialist called Jim - raise the canal up to 511ft above sea level, the loftiest pound on the BCN.

Titford Pools were dug in the 1770s to supply the 491ft summit at Smethwick with water. Later an additional feeder was laid to Rotton Park (Edgbaston) Reservoir. The Titford's navigable status dates from 1837, and for over a century it was busy with boats carrying coal, chemicals, and much besides, to and from a hinterland thronged with great industrial partnerships: Chance & Hunt, Accles & Pollock, Albright & Wilson et al.

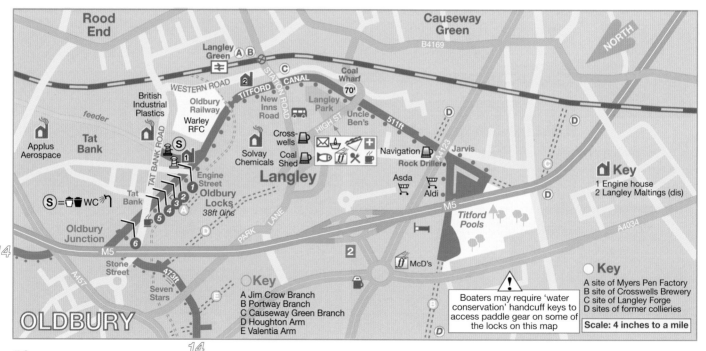

Key
1 Engine house
2 Langley Maltings (dis)

Key
A Jim Crow Branch
B Portway Branch
C Causeway Green Branch
D Houghton Arm
E Valentia Arm

Key
A site of Myers Pen Factory
B site of Crosswells Brewery
C site of Langley Forge
D sites of former collieries

Scale: 4 inches to a mile

Boaters may require 'water conservation' handcuff keys to access paddle gear on some of the locks on this map

Oldbury Locks feature single-leaf gates at both top and tail, and the short intervening pounds boast extended side ponds to increase water capacity: not always to great effect. Manufacturing - an alien concept in many parts of Britain now - clings on hereabouts, and an acrid smell - part chemical, part burnt offering - seems to hang permanently over proceedings. Sadly, the Lucy Truscanian Foundry on Engine Street, part of a group which could trace its origins back to the former Jericho Foundry in Oxford in the 19th century, closed in 2019.

An engine house looms alongside the top lock. Originally it housed a Boulton & Watt beam engine. A second beam engine, manufactured by G & J Davis of Tipton doubled capacity in 1864. Both were eventually replaced by a Tangye internal combustion pump. The engine house was refurbished in 2001 and is now used, most appropriately, as headquarters by the Birmingham Canal Navigations Society, stalwart keepers of the BCN flame, and organizers of annual rallies, challenges and convoys. It stands securely and not a little picturesquely, in the V of a junction with the Tat Bank Branch.

Sandwiched between a noisy aluminium recycling plant and a cement depot, the canal breathes-in to squeeze beneath the rusty girders of the Great Western Railway's Langley Green-Oldbury branchline, closed to passengers as long ago as the First World War. One's senses are rebuffed by the skeletal remains of Langley Maltings, destroyed by fire in 2009. Though Grade II listed, they had ceased being used three years earlier. An iconic Black Country building by any standards, its devastation is nothing short of tragedy. Barley used to be brought in by boat. Across

Langley Maltings

Rock Driller

the cut, Solvay's plant specialises in all manner of chemical products: pharmaceuticals, paint, detergents and fertilizers. Locals still fondly refer to it as Albright & Wilson, a partnership which could trace its history back to the 1850s and the production of phosphorous for match heads.

Uncle Ben's Bridge is said to have got its name from a local pawnbroker, 'uncle' being a euphemisim for pawnbrokers in the past. Slade's Coal Wharf was supplied by boat until 1967. A neat little park (from which the strains of the prize-winning Langley Band are sometimes to be heard) precedes the bifurcation of the Portway and Causeway Green arms at Jarvis Bridge.

The Portway Branch's towpath is graced by Luke Perry's 'Rock Driller' sculpture, erected in 2016 to commemorate the hard toil once associated with coal mining in the vicinity. Intrepid boaters can toy with exploration of the coot-haunted, silt-filled Titford Pools. The BCNS kindly offer a much-prized plaque by way of reward, and valuable advice on how best to boat the Pools can be found on their website.

The Pools, once considered something of a pleasure resort, are not without a murkier past. In 1889 Joseph Harvey and Lizzie Bates tied themselves together and threw themselves in. Their hats were found at the water's edge the next morning. Joseph's watch had stopped at 2.20am. Joseph's suicide note to his father read: 'now you will see what has been done by trying to keep me from Lizzie'. Lizzie's counterpart read: 'he could not have me in life, so I thought he should have me in death'. Poignantly, they wrote each other's notes.

# DOING *the* TITFORD

**B**ACK in the eighteenth and nineteenth centuries big name civil engineers were as interchangeable as football managers today. Increasingly frustrated with Brindley's crumbling legacy - patently a victim of its own initial success - the proprietors of the Birmingham Canal Navigations commissioned Thomas Telford to recommend improvements. He discovered a canal 'little better than a crooked ditch'! The original towing path had deteriorated to the extent that horses frequently slid and staggered into the water, tow lines entangled when boats met, and boatmen quarrelled over precedence at locks. The canny Scot devised a bold improvement plan cutting through the already

lowered Smethwick summit. The work took five years and was completed in 1829. It reduced the distance between Wolverhampton and Birmingham by a third. A contemporary onlooker found the new route "unsurpassed in stupendous magnificence"!

Appreciation of the impact made by Thomas Telford's new main line comes with exploration of the lengthy loops it superseded, and it is difficult to this day not to be impressed by the puissance of Telford's engineering; though just as easy to be beguiled by Brindley's peregrinations. The old loops retained their local traffics, serving works firmly established along their banks, and even when that fizzled out in the 1950s, water supply

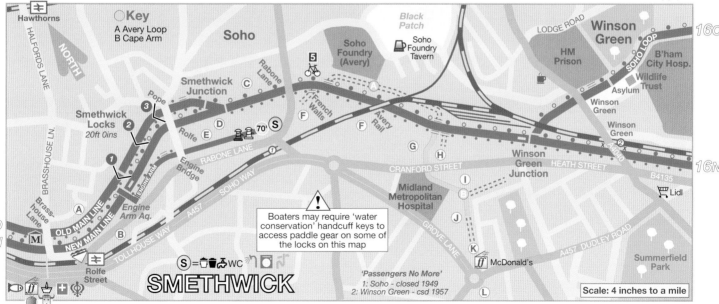

**Key**
A Avery Loop
B Cape Arm

Boaters may require 'water conservation' handcuff keys to access paddle gear on some of the locks on this map

Ⓢ = 🗑🍴🚿 WC

SMETHWICK

*'Passengers No More'*
1: Soho - closed 1949
2: Winson Green - csd 1957

Scale: 4 inches to a mile

**SOJOURN in SMETHWICK**

and drainage ensured their survival into the leisure boating era.

Westwards from Smethwick Junction the old and new main lines forge their separate routes to and from Tipton. The earlier canal ascends through three locks to reach its 473ft summit. Originally its course lay even higher at 491ft, traces of which can be discerned along the embankment above the canal as it proceeds west of Brasshouse Lane Bridge. The Birmingham artist, Edward Richard Taylor, painted this view in all its unsullied glory in 1905: Galton Bridge shimmers in the distance whilst a horsedrawn narrowboat makes its way along the Old Line. On the increasingly rare occasions that budget cuts permit it to be open, the painting can be viewed at Wednesbury Museum & Art Gallery. Nowadays a panoramic view in the opposite direction can be obtained from the footbridge straddling the railway. One cannot help but mourn, however, the disappearance of the Brasshouse Lane Foundry (and particularly the Sikhs amongst its labour force who would habitually cool off in the canal), transformed into housing marred by a sequence of descending terraces which would be more at home at West Bromwich Albion's nearby Hawthorns football ground.

Access to the celebrated Engine Arm is through the tiny arch of a stone side bridge adjacent to Smethwick Top Lock. The arm spans the new main line by way of a wonderfully Gothic iron bridge - as depicted on this book's frontispiece - a real treasure in the context of its industrial setting. Boating is busier on the arm since the provision of moorings, boating facilities and, most pertinently, a winding hole at its far end. The arm was built to serve as a feeder from Edgbaston Reservoir at Ladywood, and if you scale the grassy bank opposite the junction with the Soho Loop at Winson Green you can see the remnants of its narrow brick channel. The Engine Arm derives its name from James Watt's 'Smethwick Engine' of 1779 which was introduced to pump water up the original flight of six locks. Even when three of these were by-passed in 1790 the engine continued its work for another century until the pumping engine at Brasshouse Lane was commissioned.

The 1892 pump house has become distinctly more appropriate for the Galton Valley Canal Museum than the former pub which previously hosted it. West of here the old main line, running along the course engineered by Smeaton penetrates an unexpected oasis of water plantain and rosebay willowherb. For a moment it is possible to make believe you are deep in the countryside, but any rural illusion is shattered by the so-called Summit Tunnel (Map 14), an ugly concrete tube covered by the high embankment of a dual carriageway.

Between Smethwick and Winson Green the old and new main lines are one, sharing the same route through an industrial heartland of foundries and railway sidings. Much of the fun to be had from exploring the BCN derives from piecing together clues to its past. Railway boats would ease out of the Cape Arm's tunnel-like exit with nuts and bolts from GKN destined for the railway basin at Hockley Port; now a centre for residential moorings. Earlier still, near Rabone Lane Bridge, Matthew Boulton and James Watt opened their Soho foundry, the first factory in the world to be lit by gas so that work could continue after darkness had fallen. Visited by Boswell in 1776, Boulton boasted: 'I sell here, sir, what all the world desires to have - power!' Much of the Soho site remains in use by the weighing machine manufacturers, Avery. Nearby lies a parcel of common land known as the Black Patch. Implausible as it might seem, evidence has recently emerged to suggest that Charlie Chaplin was born in a gypsy camp on this site in 1889.

Adjacent to the western junction of the Soho Loop (and again beneath the Engine Arm aqueduct) stand the bases of former toll houses and gauging stops. A replica toll house has been erected alongside Smethwick Top Lock; of necessity recently rebuilt again following an arson attack which destroyed its roof.

## ○ Key

| | |
|---|---|
| A site of District Iron & Steel Works | G site of London Works (GKN) |
| B site of Rolfe Street Public Baths | H site of Imperial Wire Mills |
| C site of Cornwall Engineering Works | I site of Patent Screw Works |
| D site of Kingston Metal Works | J site of Reynolds Tube Works |
| E site of Credenda Cycle Works | K site of Cape Arm Boatage Depot (GW) |
| F site of French Walls (Muntz) Works | L site of Cape Hill Brewery |

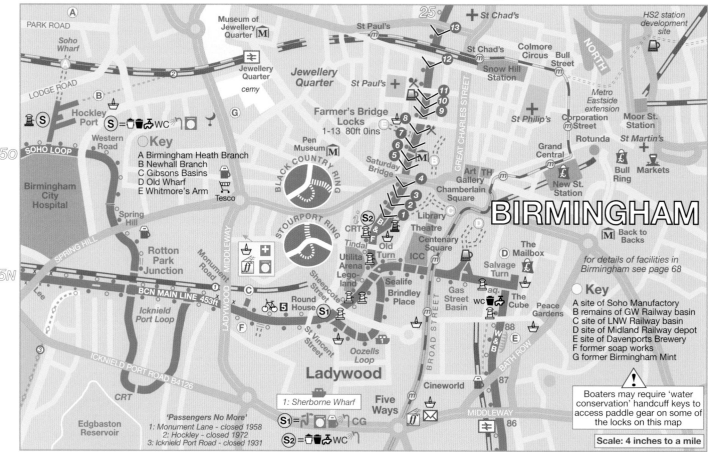

PARK ROAD

Museum of Jewellery Quarter

St Chad's

HS2 station development site

Soho Wharf

25

St Paul's

NORTH

Jewellery Quarter cemy

St Chad's

Colmore Circus

Bull Street

13

Snow Hill Station

LODGE ROAD

12

Jewellery Quarter

Metro Eastside extension

HOCKLEY PORT

St Paul's

St Philip's

Corporation Street

Moor St. Station

Hockley Port

WC

Western Road

○ **Key**
A Birmingham Heath Branch
B Newhall Branch
C Gibsons Basins
D Old Wharf
E Whitmore's Arm

Farmer's Bridge Locks
1-13 80ft 0ins

Rotunda

Grand Central

St Martin's

Bull Ring

Markets

SOHO LOOP

150

Pen Museum

11
10
9

Saturday Bridge

New St. Station

GREAT CHARLES STREET

Birmingham City Hospital

Spring Hill

Tesco

8

7

6
5

M

Art Gallery Chamberlain Square

4

TH

Library Theatre

**BIRMINGHAM**

15N

SPRING HILL

Rotton Park Junction

Monument Road

LADYWOOD MIDDLEWAY

STOURPORT RING

BLACK COUNTRY RING

3

2

1

S2

CRT

Old Turn

Centenary Square

C

M Back to Backs

for details of facilities in Birmingham see page 68

Lee

BCN MAIN LINE 453ft

1

C

Tindal

Utilita Arena Legoland

ICC

The Mailbox

Salvage Turn

○ **Key**
A site of Soho Manufactory
B remains of GW Railway basin
C site of LNW Railway basin
D site of Midland Railway depot
E site of Davenports Brewery
F former soap works
G former Birmingham Mint

Icknield Port Loop

Round House

5

S1

Sheepcote Street

F

Sealife

Brindley Place

Gas Street Basin

WC

The Cube

Peace Gardens

ICKNIELD PORT ROAD B4126

St Vincent Street

Oozells Loop

88

W & B

E

87

CRT

**Ladywood**

*'Passengers No More'*
1: Monument Lane - closed 1958
2: Hockley - closed 1972
3: Icknield Port Road - closed 1931

1: Sherborne Wharf

S1 = CG

S2 = WC

Cineworld

**Five Ways**

MIDDLEWAY

86

BROAD STREET

BATH ROW

⚠ Boaters may require 'water conservation' handcuff keys to access paddle gear on some of the locks on this map

Scale: 4 inches to a mile

Edgbaston Reservoir

*13 locks on B&F Canal (allow 2hrs)

B & F = Birmingham & Fazeley Canal
W & B = Worcester & Birmingham Canal

**F**IST BUMPS BRUM! Nowhere else in Britain has demonstrated quite so conclusively how to rejuvenate and integrate the canals on their doorstep. From St Vincent Street to Saturday Bridge, from Old Turn to Salvage Turn, they've got the ingredients spot on. Water buses and trip-boats mingle with hire and private boaters to create a cavalcade of passing vessels drawing envious looks from land-based onlookers. Could there be a better urban advert for canals as a lifestyle? Restaurants and bars vie for the custom of the passing crowds. For a moment the hackneyed analogy with Venice seems almost restrained, until one shudderingly recalls stretches of canal on the city's edges so dissolute the authorities would be mortified, were their fragile, ivory castle egos remotely cognisant of them.

Brimming with 19th century confidence, the main line marches in and out of central Birmingham with the swagger of a military band. Lee Bridge, dated 1826, soars above the broad canal, but offers no access to or from the outside world. An enigmatic mid-channel pier has long outlasted the removal of the bridge it supported carrying the branch line railway to Harborne; closed to passengers in 1934, but now a cycleway. Much of the railway infrastucture at Monument Lane has vanished too.

*Monument Lane*

*Rotton Park Junction*

The canalside station closed in 1958, the site of the associated engine shed (3E for aficionados) lies beneath Legoland. But a side bridge spanning the basin which served an interchange basin enigmatically survives. By Sheepcote Street Bridge the curious circular building was a Corporation depot and stables dating from 1874. Following a period of disuse it has thankfully been refurbished with Heritage Lottery funding by the CRT & NT in partnership as a visitor hub.

Brindley's old loops are apt to disappear beneath side bridges with the uncertainty of lost souls. Certainly there were plenty of the latter to be found alongside the Soho (or Winson Green) Loop which old maps depict as being bordered by a prison, a lunatic asylum, small pox and fever hospitals, and a workhouse. Perhaps the past is not so rosy-hued after all.

The Soho Loop still affords access to Hockley Port, where the once extensive railway interchange basins have become one of the Canal & River Trust's most sought after residential moorings in Birmingham. Originally, the arm, known as the Birmingham Heath Branch, served

The Roundhouse

handsome buildings which may possibly have been designed by Telford. In the absence of a towpath, one has always had to rely on a boat to explore this particular loop. And in any case its character is changing fundamentally as part of a substantial regeneration scheme. Urban Splash are involved, which usually bodes well. Shortest of the inner city loops, Oozells (rhymes with bells) is invariably chock-a-block with moored boats, but the trip boats invariably manage to squeeze through without losing too much paint in the process.

Old Turn might well be described as the pivotal point of the inland waterways network. Overlooked by Legoland, Arena Birmingham and the National Sea Life Centre, it symbolises the massive changes which have overtaken the canals generally - and those of Birmingham and the Black Country in particular - during the last decade or two. All a far cry from the day, over two centuries ago, when a certain Mr Farmer's land

Sheepcote Street

Matthew Boulton's Soho Works. A pioneer in mass production (of buttons, buckles and varnished ware) the factory was in use between 1766 and 1848, but demolished fifteen years later.

Hockley was the Great Western Railway's principal goods depot in the area, boasting in its heyday over a thousand employees. In order to form a link with the canal, which lay at a higher level, wagons were lifted by hydraulic hoist and shunted about the upper sidings by strategically placed capstans. Regular consignments of bagged nuts and bolts, brought by boat from Guest Keen & Nettlefold's (GKN) works on the Cape Arm, was one of the major traffics at Hockley. The depot also had a two-storey stable block which can still be seen.

A continuation of Brindley's original meandering route at Rotton Park Junction, the Icknield Port Loop skirts the foot of Edgbaston (previously Rotton Park) Reservoir opened in 1826 as part of Telford's improvements. CRT have a maintenance yard at the apex of the loop featuring some was bisected by the new fangled waterway, and an accommodation bridge (long since demolished) erected to preserve his right of way. They rang the church bells all day when the canal reached Birmingham, and wild celebrations continued well into the night. Perhaps they will again when HS2 finally arrives. Perhaps not. During the rest of the 18th Century, Birmingham became a magnet for canal promoters and, in 1794, the Birmingham Canal Navigations were formed, amounting to some 160 miles of waterway, of which 100 miles remain navigable in an area bounded by Wolverhampton, Walsall, Dudley and Tamworth.

A suspension bridge - upon which the footfall is conceivably as unrelenting as any on the canal system - connects Brindley Place with the International Convention Centre and Symphony Hall. Less Venice, more Amsterdam, it crosses your mind. Culture is yours for the taking. Broad

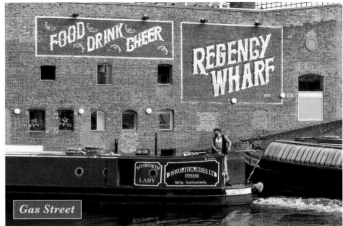

Gas Street

Street Tunnel (renamed Black Sabbath Bridge, after the heavy metal band) separates Brindley Place from Gas Street Basin. A non-conformist church once straddled the canal: baptisms apocryphally via a trap door!

Gas Street had come to symbolise the BCN to such an extent that it is often forgotten that the actual terminal wharf and offices of the Birmingham Canal lay to the east of here. Two arms terminated at the rear of the BCN company's handsomely symmetrical offices on Suffolk Street which, sadly, were demolished in 1928. Demolition controversially took its toll of the Gas Street canalscape in 1975 as well, by which time the planners should have known better, and British Waterways were never forgiven for razing their rich heritage of 18th century waterside warehouses to the ground in a calculated move to sidestep a preservation order.

For a time nothing was done to fill the void. Gas Street might have ceased to exist but for a community of residential boats which lent a splash of colour and humanity to a decaying canalscape. A decade elapsed before the developer's proposals were realised in bricks and mortar, and the biggest irony of all is that the new pubs and offices emerged in a warehouse

Old Turn

*Salvage Turn*

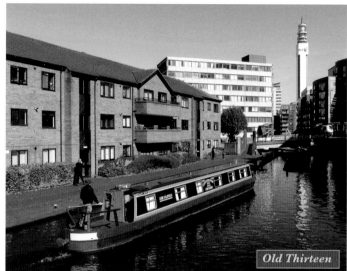

*Old Thirteen*

vernacular style of remarkable similarity to the bulldozed originals. The only post Seventies interloper unsympathetic to the scale of the original Gas Street is the towering, shimmering, slippery, silvered edifice of the Hyatt Hotel. What do its sybaritic guests make of the little boats miles below their air-conditioned eyries? Do they see them as 'local colour', as archaic as the sampans of Hong Kong harbour?

## Worcester & Birmingham Canal

Work began on the Worcester & Birmingham Canal from the Birmingham end in 1794, but it was not until 1815 that the route was completed throughout. Fearful of its water supply disappearing down into the Severn, the Birmingham Canal Company at first refused to be directly linked with the newcomer, and so laborious transhipment of through traffic took place across an infamous divide known as the 'Worcester Bar'. Eventually,

however, a stop lock was provided between the two waterways, affording the BCN some measure of protection, yet enabling passage of boats.

Boaters are largely oblivious to the crossing of Holliday Street by aqueduct, but we can recommend nipping down Gas Street to view its highly decorated western girders. Salvage Turn, named after a Corporation refuse depot, takes the canal through ninety degrees past The Mailbox and its lofty neighbour, The Cube, before it makes a bee-line for the sylvan suburbs of Edgbaston.

## Birmingham & Fazeley Canal

Farmer's Bridge Locks (aka the 'Old Thirteen' - as opposed to Perry Barr locks on the Tame Valley Canal which working boatmen termed the 'New Thirteen') pass dramatically beneath the commercial core of the city. Each time we update, more change has accrued: redeveloping the redeveloped

Snow Hill

Lock 5

The dramatic descent to Aston Junction commences at Lock 1. Replica gas lamps are a reminder that the flight was once so busy with working boats it was used day and night. Saturday Bridge carries Summer Row across the canal, together with a sense of hurrying humanity inexplicably going about its business while you escape from the routine. The bridge is said to have got its name from the custom of boatmen being paid their wages here each Saturday.

Below Lock 7 the towpath rises to cross a former arm. Here stood Birmingham's Museum of Science & Industry before most of its exhibits were moved to Thinktank. Earlier it had been the site of Elkington's huge electro-plating works. Locks 10 and 11 lie in a cavern beneath the soaring BT Tower completed in 1967; just shy of five hundred feet high, it's the city's tallest building (... so far!). Here is access to Ludgate Hill and the calm oasis of St Paul's Square, nicknamed the 'Jeweller's Church' because of its connections with the adjoining Jewellery Quarter, a pocket of the city redolent of an older, perhaps wiser Birmingham.

Between Locks 12 and 13 the canal negotiates a stygian vault under Snow Hill railway station; closed and subsequently demolished at some cost in 1972, but re-opened and rebuilt at more cost (though markedly less flamboyance) just fifteen years later. Poke your head up to street level for a glimpse (to the right) of an astonishingly slender terracotta building squeezed between Constitution Hill and Hampton Street: 'Eclectic Gothic with Spanish touches and an almost oriental dome' is how Andy Foster puts it in the *Pevsner Architectural Guide to Birmingham*, and it's hard not to share his excitement. Lock 13 marks the foot of the flight. Nearby - all but obscured from the canal - stands St Chad's, Pugin's Roman Catholic Cathedral of 1841, the first Catholic cathedral erected in England since the Reformation. The traffic-choked Queensway does it few favours. Time, perhaps, to cross yourself and scurry back to the sanctuary of your boat or the towpath

one might quip. At Cambrian Wharf there are boaters' facilities, whilst the Canal & River Trust's adjacent Information Centre is open between 9.30am and 3pm Monday to Friday, and during those hours will provide patient and friendly answers to even the most inane of enquiries. Nearby, on Kingston Row, a group of period cottages retain their BCN numberplates. The arm adjoining the top lock was once part of the Newhall Branch which, until 1926, extended deeper into the city centre. On the towpath side stands a lock keeper's cottage and toll office. Tower blocks overlook the canal now, but in the 18th century work began on an impressive crescent of town houses imitating Bath. Then, as a bit of a nuisance, the Napoleonic Wars intervened.

# Birmingham

Map 16

Generally speaking, Birmingham is not somewhere that springs immediately to mind when one thinks of cities travellers beat a well-thumbed guide-book accompanied path to for architecture, heritage, and a cultural sense of well-being. Its crass capitulation to the demands of the motor car in the Sixties handicapped it for decades, and whilst lessons have been learned in that respect, and whilst the existence of the humble pedestrian is once again acknowledged - and occasionally even catered for - there remains a suspicion that the city's new buildings are interlopers mistakenly erected from blueprints destined for Dallas or Dubai. Andy Foster, in the latest edition of Pevsner's *Birmingham & The Black Country*, appears pessimistic: 'Not since the 1960s has Birmingham's architectural future seemed so bleak'. And yet there is still much to admire about 'Brum'. Some of its 19th century survivors bowl you over, harking back to an era when architecture manifested itself in an approachable, more human scale. The Town Hall, Art Gallery, Council House, St Philip's and St Paul's, the Jewellery Quarter, the backstreets of Digbeth and Deritend all reward diligent exploration. The Roundhouse, Belmont Works and the original Curzon Street railway station illustrate the benefits of taking a regenerative cue from the past. So one fervently hopes that more of the city's inheritance can be dusted down for new roles, much as its canals were, so effectively, in the 1980s.

## Eating & Drinking

BISTROT PIERRE - Gas Street. Tel: 0121 616 0730. Canalside French restaurant from noon daily. B1 2JT
THE CANAL HOUSE - Bridge Street. Tel: 0121 643 8829. Popular contemporary bar/restaurant overlooking Gas Street Basin. B1 2JR
ITIHAAS - Fleet/Newhall Streets. Tel: 0121 212 3383. Well thought of Indian restaurant overlooking Farmers Bridge Locks. B3 1JL
MEDICINE - The Mailbox. Tel: 0121 616 2952. Artisan bakery, kitchen & cafe. 9am-5pm daily. B1 1RE
NOEL'S - Tel: 0121 389 3896. Waterfront Walk. Mediterranean inspired cuisine overlooking Salvage Turn. Open from noon daily. B1 1SN
PRINCE OF WALES - Cambridge Street. Tel: 0121 413 4180. Famous old pub tastefully regenerated by Black Country Ales. Open from noon. B1 2NP
PURNELL'S - Cornwall Street. Tel: 0121 212 9799. Michelin listed fine dining. B3 2DH
THE WELLINGTON - Bennett's Hill. Tel: 0121 200 3115. Real ale mecca between Colmore Row and New Street. Up to fifteen beers on tap. Plates and cutlery and condiments supplied for you to bring your own food. B2 5SN

## Shopping

Canallers in a hurry - if that's not an oxymoron - will find convenience stores marked on the accompanying maps at various handy points. Otherwise you'll find all the facilities of a major city within easy reach of the canal. The Bull Ring markets (located on Edgbaston Street south-east of New Street station) are a famous focal point of midland merchandising. The Bull Ring Shopping Centre has been redeveloped, the landmark Rotunda having escaped by the skin of its Grade II listed teeth, so that it now rubs shoulders with the likes of Jan Kaplicky's shimmering Selfridges store. Grand Central is the city's latest shopping experience located above its revitalised New Street railway station. The Mailbox - opened at the beginning of the 21st century on the site of a former postal sorting office - is largely devoted to upmarket fashion.

## Things to Do

BACK TO BACKS - Hurst Street. Tel: 0121 622 2442. How Brum's poor used to live. National Trust owned, pre-booking essential. B5 4TE
COFFIN WORKS - Fleet Street. Tel: 0121 233 4790. Tours of Victorian factory embalmed in aspic. B3 1JP
GO BOAT - Water's Edge. Tel: 0203 887 6955. Self-drive open boats for hire, max 8 persons. B1 2HL
LEGOLAND - King Edward's Road. Tel: 0121 794 2386. Canalside visitor attraction. B1 2AA
LIBRARY OF BIRMINGHAM - Centenary Square. Tel: 0121 242 4242. From the Secret Garden on the 7th floor there are bird's eye views over the canals radiating from Old Turn Junction. B1 2ND
MUSEUM & ART GALLERY - Chamberlain Square. Tel: 0121 348 8000. Open daily, admission free. Rivals Manchester in the richness of its Pre-Raphaelite collection. Shop, Edwardian Tea Room. B3 3DH
NATIONAL SEA LIFE CENTRE - Brindley Place. Tel: 0121 794 2386. Turtles, sharks and other non BCN resident maritime species. B1 2HL
PEN MUSEUM - Frederick Street. Tel: 0121 236 9834. Fascinating story of the writing pen trade. B1 3HS
ROUNDHOUSE - Sheepcote Street. Tel: 0121 716 4077. NT/CRT redevelopment of semi-circular municipal depot. Open daily (ex Mon) 9.30am-4.30pm, but beware other 'out of season' closures. B16 8AE
SYMPHONY HALL - Broad Street. Tel: 0121 780 3333. Home to the 'world class' City of Birmingham Symphony Orchestra. B1 2EA
THINKTANK - Curzon Street. Tel: 0121 348 8000. Science for all the family. Contains Watt's Smethwick Engine and Stanier's *City of Birmingham*. B4 7XG

## Connections

METRO - Tel: 0345 835 8181.
TAXIS - TOA (black cabs). Tel: 0121 427 8888.

'CANALS stretch green fingers into towns.' was Robert Aickman's apt description of the Worcester & Birmingham Canal's entrance into Birmingham, a phrase coined aboard his first trip with the Rolt's aboard *Cressy* in April 1946. It's impossible not to share his enthusiasm, for this is a lovely stretch of canal - given its proximity to the city centre - and its towpath is much valued by walkers and cyclists as an alternative to the choked and inherently lethal carriageways of the A38. In cahoots with the Birmingham West Suburban Railway,

opened in 1876, and now nose to tail with suburban and inter-city trains, the canal negotiates Edgbaston Tunnel, whose towpath has recently been widened for the benefit of all those pedestrians and cyclists. Birmingham University is dominated by an Italianate tower affectionately known as 'Old Joe' after the university's main founder and first Chancellor, Joseph Chamberlain. In the absence of designated visitor moorings, boaters are pretty much honour-bound to keep going, but on foot there is every temptation to abandon the canal to its own devices and explore.

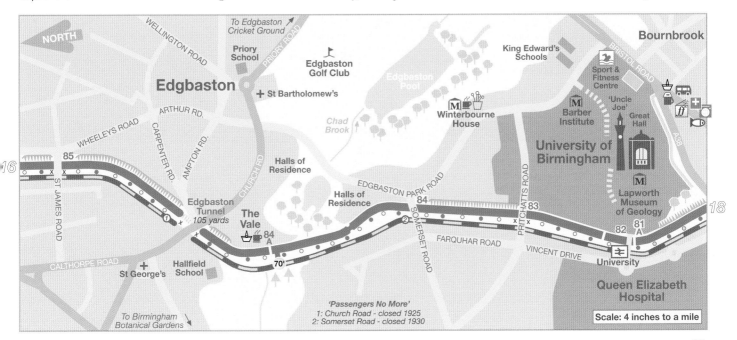

ARIEL Aqueduct, erected in 2011 to span Selly Oak's new by-pass, derives its name from a bicycle and motorcycle factory which once stood nearby. Subsequently the works belonged to Boxfoldia, progenitors of the folding carton. Canal enthusiasts rejoiced in 2020 when the Lapal Canal Trust persuaded developers to provide a new, partially subterranean channel at Battery Retail Park, safeguarding reinstatement of the Dudley No.2 Canal, opened in 1798 to provide a by-pass to Birmingham via Halesowen (Map 39). A new winding hole has been provided to facilitate access immediately north of Bridge 80. But at least there is now a 'ring-fenced' development route through to Selly Oak Park and the original course of the canal.

The substantial blue-brick framework of Bridge 78 conceals the fact that it carries the Elan Valley water main across the canal - see Map 4. The imposing girders and vaulted arches of Bridge 77A tell a different story. They are all that remains of Cadbury's internal railway, a link between the world famous chocolate factory itself - still very much in business on the west bank of the canal - and the east bank of the canal which was lined with warehouses. These were served by Cadbury's own fleet of narrowboats and those of other operators such as Severn & Canal and Fellows Morton & Clayton as well. Wagons were shunted by a fleet of perky tank locomotives painted in a dark red colour inspired by the company's cocoa tins.

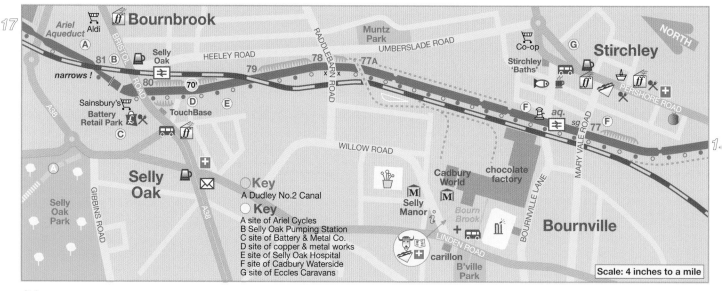

Key
A Dudley No.2 Canal

Key
A site of Ariel Cycles
B Selly Oak Pumping Station
C site of Battery & Metal Co.
D site of copper & metal works
E site of Selly Oak Hospital
F site of Cadbury Waterside
G site of Eccles Caravans

Scale: 4 inches to a mile

## Edgbaston
Map 17

Developed residentially for the well-to-do by the Gough-Calthorpe family from the opening years of the 19th century, Edgbaston is a garden suburb any city in the world would be proud to cuddle up to. Architecturally eclectic, the houses are commonly set in extensive grounds. Some of the more grandiose examples, erected in an era of large families and servants, are no longer sustainable as family homes and have been turned into offices and institutions. Incidentally, the Gough-Calthorpes initially objected to the construction of the Worcester & Birmingham Canal, grudgingly acquiescing on the understanding that there would be no vulgar wharves or warehouses lining the waterway's passage through Edgbaston.

### Things to Do
BARBER INSTITUTE - University of Birmingham. Tel: 0121 414 7333. Art gallery of international repute (featuring works by Cezanne, Gainsborough, Magritte, Monet, Turner, Van Gogh etc) open 10am - 5pm Mon-Fri and 11am-5pm weekends. Admission free. B15 2TS
LAPWORTH MUSEUM OF GEOLOGY - University of Birmingham. Tel: 0121 414 7294. Open 10am-5pm Mon-Fri and 12-5pm weekends. B15 2TT
WINTERBOURNE HOUSE - Edgbaston. Tel: 0121 414 3003. Captivating Arts & Crafts house erected 1903 for the industrialist John Nettlefold of GKN fame. Gardens inspired by Gertrude Jekyll. Open from 10am daily. Shop and tea room. B15 2RT

## Selly Oak
Map 18

Studenty enclave on the A38 with a wide choice of shops and food/drink outlets. Battery Retail Park features a canalside Sainsbury's supermarket. TouchBase Pears, overlooking Bridge 80, is a multi-purpose community centre with an emphasis on the needs of the deaf and blind.

## Bournville
Map 18

Bournville exists in a chocolatey enclave all its own, and which of us wouldn't want to do just that! Perambulating its arboreally nomenclatured streets, one quickly succumbs to the Cadbury vision. Why can't all the world exist so well-adjustedly, so self-contentedly? Use of a CRT 'facilities' Yale key provides access from the secure (if not particularly salubrious) offside moorings opposite Bournville railway station.

### Shopping
Useful row of shops on Sycamore Road opposite The Green: bookshop, butcher, pharmacy and bakery.

### Things to Do
BOURNVILLE CARILLON - Linden Road. Tel: 0798 655 2770. 48 bells erected by George Cadbury in 1906 following an inspirational visit to Bruges. Performances on Saturdays at noon and 3pm throughout the year ex February. B30 1LB
CADBURY WORLD - Linden Road. Tel: 0121 393 6004. Self-guided tours 'choc-full of fun'. B30 2LU
SELLY MANOR - Maple Road. Tel: 0121 472 0199. A pair of medieval half-timbered buildings. Open from 10am daily Jun-Aug, Tue-Fri otherwise. B30 2AE

## Stirchley
Map 18

Bournville Lane leads (past handsome three storey terraced villas with paired names) to Stirchley strung out along Pershore Road; a yang to Bournville's yin. Of note are the library and the public baths, the latter reconfigured as a community hub sans pool.

### Eating & Drinking
ALICIA'S - Pershore Road. Tel: 0121 246 0947. Artisan pizzeria; eat in or take away. Open from 4.30pm Tue-Thur and from 11.30am Fri & Sat. B30 2JR
WILDCAT - Pershore Road. Micropub open weekdays (ex Mon) from 2pm, weekends from noon. B30 2JR

### Shopping
Co-op, Farm Foods and convenience stores. Bakery (and cookery school) called Loaf open Wed-Sat. P. Browell is a traditional tobacconist established 1924.

## Cotteridge
Map 19

Somewhat confusingly the location of King's Norton railway station. Shopping and fast food opportunities. Handsome 'Queen Anne' Fire Station. Cotteridge Wines on Pershore Road are open from noon and retail an exceptional choice of bottled beers. The legendary 11A/11C outer circle buses cross the canal on Bridge 75; two hour odysseys in their own right.

## King's Norton
Map 19

It's only a short uphill walk to the centre, grouped about a pretty green and overlooked by the imposing spire of St Nicolas' Church. Queen Henrietta Maria stopped here overnight on her way to meet Charles I at Edge Hill. Half-timbered 17th century grammar school in churchyard. Lovely little Arts & Crafts library endowed by the Scottish philanthropist Andrew Carnegie in 1906. Extensive park and civic garden dating from the 1920s.

### Eating & Drinking
THE NAVIGATION - Wharf Road (up from Bridge 71). Tel: 0121 458 1652. Wetherspoon revamp of pub which was closed for several years. B30 3LS
MAHFIL - The Green. Tel: 0121 448 5820. Stylish Indian restaurant open from 5pm Mon-Sat and from noon Sun. B38 8RU
MOLLY'S - The Green. Tel: 0121 459 9500. Cheerful cafe, good for breakfasts. B38 8SD

### Shopping
Facilities include: a pharmacy, Co-op convenience store, post office, newsagent and off licence. Farmers Market on The Green second Saturdays.

GIVEN the twenty plus mile lockless pound between Tipton and Tardebigge, steerers are apt to lose concentration if not plied with a regular supply of bacon sandwiches, cakes, teas and coffees; or even something a little stronger if the sun is over the yard-arm. And bear in mind, that due to height restrictions, yard-arms are often very low on the canal system.

Between bridges 75 and 73 the towpath swaps sides. Not on a whim, but because the Midland Railway once operated a transhipment basin on the west bank of the canal. The Birmingham & Gloucester Railway of 1840 crosses Bridge 74. A small aqueduct carries the canal over the River Rea just north of Bridge 72.

At King's Norton the Stratford Canal comes in to join the Worcester & Birmingham, a route described in the *South Midlands* and *Severn & Avon* Canal Companions. Baldwins paper mill formerly overlooked the canal junction and large quantities of coal were brought here by narrowboat from Black Country mines. The increasingly decrepit Junction House is backed by the soaring steeple of St Nicolas, the parish church of King's Norton, where the Rev W. Awdry of *Thomas the Tank Engine* fame was a curate during the Second World War.

At 2,726 yards, Wast Hill Tunnel is the Worcester & Birmingham's longest. It takes around half an hour to pass through and, whilst appearances can be deceptive, rest assured that there *is* room to pass oncoming craft inside its gloomy depths. Like all Worcester & Birmingham tunnels (except Edgbaston), it has no towpath. The lads who led their boat horses across the tunnel top in the past would be flummoxed now to find a housing estate built over much of their route, and a degree of diligence is required of latter-day towpath walkers if they are not to become disorientated. Follow our footprints, and you shouldn't go far wrong! On an historic note, look out for the semicircular brick-lined embrasures in the canal bank at either end of the tunnel - these are the remnants of the turning points for tugs which were once employed to haul unpowered craft through the tunnel.

## Key

A site of Bournville MPD 21B
B former GKN screw works
C site of Lifford Wharf (MR)
D former paper mill
E former guillotine lock
F former tug turning points

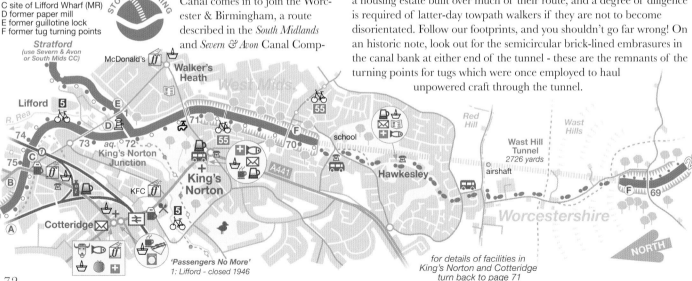

*for details of facilities in King's Norton and Cotteridge turn back to page 71*

**A**LVECHURCH had begun to march relentlessly towards the canal even before Neville Chamberlain incredulously received 'no such undertaking' from the German government on 3rd September 1939: houses, in the words of Louis MacNeice 'climbing tentatively upward on jerry-built beauty' with merely a 'six-inch grip of the racing earth in their concrete claws'. Prior to that invasion, only a brickworks dared to impinge upon the canal's dreamy, lock-less progress above the valley of the River Arrow. There are panoramic views eastwards towards Weatheroak Hill crossed by the Roman's Ryknild Street. A feeder comes in from Upper Bittell Reservoir beside a former canal employee's cottage near Bridge 66. The Lower Reservoir, rich in wildfowl, lies alongside the canal and is given a gorgeous wooded backdrop by the Lickey Hills.

Only the Upper Reservoir feeds the canal, the Lower was provided to compensate millers whose water supplies from the Arrow had been detrimentally affected by construction of the canal. A short section of the canal was re-routed in 1985 to accommodate the M42. Bridge 62 carries the electrified commuter line from Redditch through Birmingham to Lichfield. A seventy-five minute train journey ... three days by boat to the nearest canal settlement at Fradley Junction. But time is an irrelevance on the canals, so relax and savour the charms of Shortwood Tunnel, its approach cuttings so suffocated by the odour of wild garlic that you feel as if you are being embraced by an over enthusiastic Frenchman.

As with all other Worcester & Birmingham tunnels (Edgbaston excepted) the towpath isn't subterranean, but the old horse-path across the top remains well-defined, and it is pleasant to wander across the top, fantasising that you've a horse to lead while your boat is hauled through the earth beneath your feet by one of the erstwhile tunnel tugs.

1: Alvechurch Marina ABC Boat Hire

Shortwood Tunnel 613 yards tunnel spoil tip

Cobley Hill

Withybed Moorings

River Arrow

Upper Bittell Reservoir

Lower Bittell Res.

Hopwood Park Motorway Services

Hopwood

Alvechurch

A441 to Redditch

A441 to Birmingham

B4120 to Barnt Green

Towpath quality varies between good and adequate on this section. A popular five mile walk is that between Alvechurch and Bromsgrove railway stations (both linked by frequent trains to/from Birmingham) which includes Robert Aickman's route to his historic meeting with Tom Rolt at Tardebigge in 1945 (see Map 21).

for details of facilities at Hopwood and Alvechurch jump to page 74

**Key** A site of brick works

## Hopwood
Map 20

HOPWOOD HOUSE INN - canalside Bridge 67. Tel: 0121 445 1716. Comfortably furnished Marston's 'Rotisserie' pub/restaurant open from noon. B48 7AB. *Petrol station with convenience store to south of Bridge 67. Small garden centre nearby. Buses to/from Birmingham.*

## Alvechurch
Map 20

Bloated Worcestershire village hugely expanded from its original core. Alan Smith, the ex Arsenal forward and Sky Sports pundit, played for the local football team. In the 1950s Dellow sports cars were made here. The church was much rebuilt by Butterfield.

### Eating & Drinking

THE CROWN - canalside Bridge 61. Tel: 0121 445 2300. A refurbished canalside pub. B48 7PN
NEW DILSHAD - Red Lion Street. Tel: 0121 445 5660. Village centre Indian restaurant open from 5-11pm daily. B48 7LF
THE WEIGHBRIDGE - canalside Bridge 60. Tel: 0121 445 5111. ABC owned pub housed in 'weighbridge' for local coal wharf in days gone by. Spring and Autumn beer festivals. Food served from noon throughout Thur-Sun. Bar only Mon-Wed. B48 7SQ
*Plus Chinese take-away and fish & chips in village centre.*

### Shopping

Co-op (with ATM), pharmacy, *two* butchers, and a nice deli called Gin & Pickles (Tel: 0121 445 6769).

### Connections

TRAINS - handy canalside station: West Midlands 20 minute frequency service (half-hourly Sun) to/from Redditch and Birmingham. Tel: 0345 748 4950.

## Tardebigge
Map 21

'No village in the proper sense of the word', in Rolt's opinion seventy years ago, and nothing (as yet!)

has occurred to alter that perception. To the south-east stands Hewell Grange, a late Victorian mansion, acquired by the government after the Second World War in lieu of death duties and subsequently used as a rather palatial prison.

### Eating & Drinking

THE TARDEBIGGE - Hewell Lane. Tel: 01527 546724. Refurbished pub in what was long ago the village hall. Food from 11am daily (noon Mon). B97 6QZ

### Connections

BUSES - Diamond services 42/3 operate hourly Mon-Sat (plus limited Sunday service) from stops above the southern tunnel mouth to/from Kidderminster (via Bromsgrove) and Redditch. Tel: 0871 200 2233.

## Aston Fields
Map 21

A suburb of Bromsgrove surprisingly well endowed with facilities, notably Banners deli and hot food outlet established as long ago as 1906 (Tel: 01527 872581 - B60 2DZ) and they operate a cafe/restaurant as well (Tel: 01527 872889) open from 8am daily and providing evening meals Wed-Sat. Alternative eating-out opportunities include Fuso, an Italian restaurant (Tel: 01527 877789); Ascott's 'Strret Food' bar & kitchen (Tel: 0157 833318); Zinga an Indian (Tel: 01527 871187); and 3A, a coffee & gin bar (Tel: 01527 874139). The Co-op convenience store contains a post office counter. Aston Fields is easily reached from Tardebigge by bus. Bromsgrove's recently enlarged and electrified railway station is here too, for taxis telephone Gold & Black on 01527 570707.

## The Stokes
Map 21

A quintet - Heath, Pound, Prior, Wharf and Works - of scattered settlements in the vicinity of the canal.

### Eating & Drinking

QUEEN'S HEAD - Sugarbrook Lane, Stoke Pound (Bridge 48). Tel: 01527 557007. Open daily from 11am.

One of eight 'Lovely Pubs' in Warwickshire and Worcestershire. Full menu served 12-2.30pm and 5.30-9.00pm Mon-Sat, 12-7.30pm Sun. B60 3AU
NAVIGATION - Hanbury Road, Stoke Wharf (adjacent Bridge 44). Tel: 01527 837992. Comfortably refurbished pub. Food served from noon daily ex Mon. B60 4LB

### Things to Do

AVONCROFT - Stoke Heath (a mile west of Bridge 48). Tel: 01527 831363. Marvellous outdoor collection of reassembled buildings. Tea room & shop. B60 4JR

## Stoke Works
Map 22

BOAT & RAILWAY - Shaw Lane, Stoke Works (Bridge 42). Tel: 01527 575597. Marston's/Banks's pub with a canalside terrace and skittle alley. Food from noon daily but not Sunday evenings. B60 4EQ
BOWLING GREEN - Shaw Lane (5 mins west of Bridge 41). Tel: 01527 861291. Lunch and dinner (from 6pm) Mon-Sat. B60 4BH

## Hanbury Wharf
Map 22

EAGLE & SUN - Hanbury Road (Bridge 35). Tel: 01905 799266. Canalside pub serving food Mon-Sat 12-8.30pm and Sundays 12-7pm. WR9 7DX

## Dunhampstead
Map 23

FORGE STUDIO - Bridge 30. Tel: 0751 796 1569. Andy Edwards hand paints canalware and sells gifts and guides as well as coffee and ice cream. WR9 7JX
FIR TREE FARM SHOP & CAFE - Trench Lane. Tel: 01905 774094. Previously a pub. Open 9am-4pm Tue-Sat. WR9 7JX

## Tibberton
Map 23

BRIDGE INN - Plough Road (canalside Bridge 25). Tel: 01905 345135. Food served daily throughout from noon. WR9 7NQ
SPEED THE PLOUGH - Plough Road. Tel: 01905 344900. Village local. WR9 7NQ

Tardebigge  Dunhampstead

# TUNNELS GALORE!

Edgbaston  Wast Hill

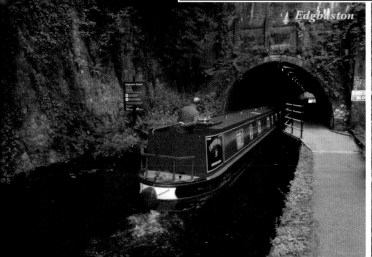

75

# 21 WORCESTER & BIRMINGHAM CANAL Tardebigge 4mls/36lks/7hrs

TARDEBIGGE represents a boater's Rite of Passage. Once you have tackled this flight which, coupled with the neighbouring six at Stoke, amount to thirty-six locks in four miles, other groups of locks, however fiendish, however formidable, pale into insignificance. The thirty chambers of the Tardebigge flight raise the canal over two hundred feet, the top lock - somewhat removed from the rest - replaced a lift dysfunctionally prone to recalcitrance and water wastage.

Well maintained and surrounded by fine countryside, with wonderful views to the Malvern Hills, Tardebigge Locks are there to be enjoyed, not dreaded. And in the summer months you'll have plenty of fellow travellers to share the experience with, never mind the work. Tardebigge's 18th century church, with its slender 135ft spire, is an inspirational landmark: 'belatedly baroque' in the words of James Lees-Milne in his pithy 1964 *Shell Guide to Worcestershire*. Another spire to look out for - on the western horizon - is that of Bromsgrove's parish church, St John the Baptist.

Tardebigge holds a special place in the story of the inland waterways movement. It was to here that Robert Aickman and his wife made their way from Bromsgrove railway station to meet Tom and Angela Rolt aboard their narrowboat home *Cressy* which had been moored above the top lock throughout the Second World War. As a direct result of their meeting the Inland Waterways Association was formed. A plinth adjacent to the lock tells the story, along with a supplementary plaque correcting the date to 1945 - as Pearsons had averred all along!

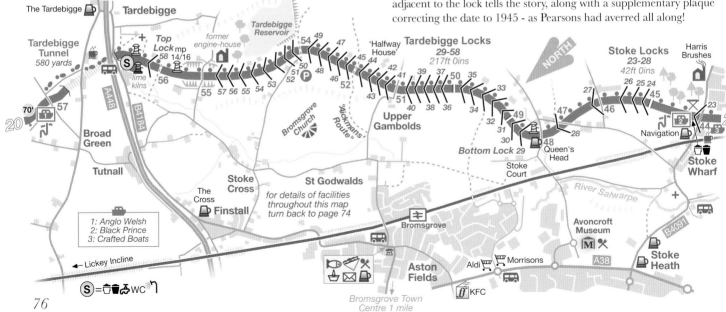

76

The former engine house by Lock 57 ceased being used around the time of the First World War. In the 1950s it was used as a jazz club; the scene, by all accounts, of some riotous nights. The cottage by Lock 53 featured in Pat Warner's delightful book *A Lock Keeper's Daughter*. Don't be in too much of a hurry to miss climbing the rim of the reservoir at Bridge 54 for some spellbinding views. The old farm adjoining Lock 43 was at one time licensed and known as The Halfway House.

The picturesque lock-keeper's cottage between locks 31 and 32 is available for holiday lets from the Landmark Trust, a body devoted to the rescue and refurbishment of worthwhile buildings in all shapes and sizes. A wheelbarrow is at the disposal of guests for the conveyance of luggage along the towpath. It was the demolition of the junction house

*The Queen's Head*

at Hurleston, on the Shropshire Union Canal, which 'maddened' the Trust's founder, John Smith, into creating this laudable organisation in 1965.

Only the briefest of pounds separates the Tardebigge and Stoke flights. Room enough, just, for half a dozen boats to moor for a breather and/or refreshments at the Queen's Head. Stoke Wharf plays host to a busy hire fleet. Nearby stands the factory of Harris Brushes whose pig bristle paint brushes are apparently much revered by the Royal Family.

*Tardebigge Locks*

*Lock 57*

# 22 WORCESTER & BIRMINGHAM CANAL Hanbury 4mls/6lks/2½hrs

NOWADAYS, Britain's salt industry is largely confined to Cheshire but, as the name Droitwich suggests, this part of Worcestershire was once a centre of salt making too. The salt obsessed Romans built a special road between Droitwich and Alcester to carry this valuable commodity. Similarly, the Worcester & Birmingham built the short Droitwich Junction Canal from Hanbury Wharf to carry the same cargo. Abandoned in 1939, it has become one of the success stories of the canal restoration movement, finally re-opening in 2011 and forming, along with the Droitwich Barge Canal what has become a hugely popular circular route - the Mid-Worcestershire Ring. Full coverage can be found in *Pearson's Severn & Avon Canal & River Companion*. If you're remaining loyal to the W& B's 'main line', it would be churlish not at least to stroll down the first three locks as far as Gateway Park, offering fulsome thanks as you go to those who steadfastly kept the faith with regard to the canal's second coming.

At the end of the 18th century, John Corbett, son of a local boatman, discovered large deposits of brine at Stoke Prior and developed one of the largest saltworks in the world on the site. It made his fortune. He met an Irish woman in Paris, married her and erected a replica French chateau for her on the outskirts of

Droitwich, a town he transformed from one of industrial squalor into a fashionable spa. In its heyday the canalside works at Stoke was producing 200,000 tons of salt a year. The company had a fleet of fifty narrowboats and hundreds of railway wagons. Corbett died in 1901 and is buried at the pretty little church of St Michael's, Stoke Prior (Map 21). The 'John Corbett Way', a seven and a half mile waymarked trail, has been developed between Stoke Heath and Droitwich.

Attractive countryside returns at Astwood Locks, as canal and railway drift lazily through lush farmland overlooked by the wooded slopes of Summer Hill to the east. Westward views encompass Abberley and Woodbury hills beyond the River Severn. Closer at hand are the twin 700ft high masts of Wychbold radio transmitting station. Opened in 1934, its call sign "Droitwich Calling" became known throughout Britain and in many parts of Europe. During the Second World War Droitwich's long range transmitter broadcast the 'voice of freedom' throughout occupied Europe.

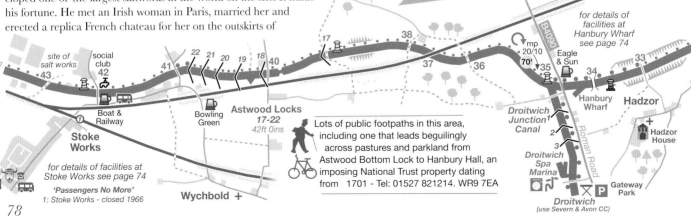

Hanbury Hall (NT)

for details of facilities at Hanbury Wharf see page 74

mp 20/10 70'

Eagle & Sun

site of salt works

social club 42

Boat & Railway

Stoke Works

for details of facilities at Stoke Works see page 74

'Passengers No More'
1: Stoke Works - closed 1966

Bowling Green

Astwood Locks 17-22
42ft 0ins

Wychbold

Lots of public footpaths in this area, including one that leads beguilingly across pastures and parkland from Astwood Bottom Lock to Hanbury Hall, an imposing National Trust property dating from 1701 - Tel: 01527 821214. WR9 7EA

Hanbury Wharf

Hadzor

Hadzor House

Droitwich Junction Canal

Droitwich Spa Marina

Gateway Park

Droitwich
(use Severn & Avon CC)

**S**KIRTING the mellow settlements of Shernal Green, Dunhampstead, Oddingley and Tibberton, the canal luxuriates in a sense of remoteness. High clumps of sedge border the canal, swaying with the passage of each boat emphasising the loneliness of the landscape. At Shernal Green the Wychavon Way - a 42-mile long distance footpath running from Holt Fleet on the River Severn to Winchcombe in Gloucestershire - makes its way over the canal.

Dunhampstead Tunnel is tiny compared to the 'big three' to the north, but like them it has no towpath, forcing walkers to take to the old horse-path through deciduous woodland above. A hire base adds traffic to the canal at this point, whilst a canal shop and a country pub provide an excuse to break your journey. Four Scots pine strike a pose in a neighbouring field like a boy band at a photo-shoot.

Oddingley consists of little more than an ancient manor house, a tiny church, and a level-crossing. Murder was done here in 1806. Visit the Fir Tree Inn, or the church for the gory details. More murderous goings on occurred here in Andy Griffee's authentically inland waterway-based thriller *Canal Pushers*. Tibberton is a long straggling village of mostly modern housing. Well-piled visitor moorings are provided west of Bridge 25. A deep cutting and the M5 motorway precede Offerton Locks where, southbound the Worcester & Birmingham recommences its descent to the Severn. Boating northwards you can take a breather. Worcester's industrial fringe makes its presence felt. Worcester Warriors rugby club, who played at Sixways Stadium, sadly went out of business in 2022.

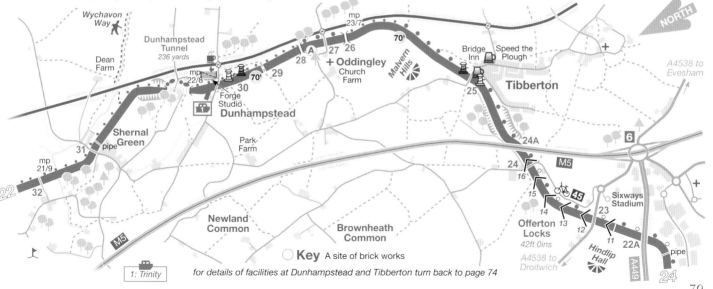

Key ○ A site of brick works

*for details of facilities at Dunhampstead and Tibberton turn back to page 74*

WORCESTER'S suburbs extend a warm welcome to incoming canallers - perfect hosts, they are not too intrusive - but there remains the little matter of ten locks to negotiate before you reach the running waters of the Severn. A large munitions factory was built at Blackpole during the First World War; specialising in bullets for both the British and *Russian* armies! After the war the works was purchased by Cadbury and concentrated on making cakes instead of cartridges. Cadbury employed water transport a good deal as we have already seen at Bournville (Map 18), and their wharf survives, albeit occupied by a cement plant now. A leisure centre and municipal golf course border the

canal above Bilford Upper Lock. Worcester City FC sold their St George's Lane ground by Bridge 12 to property developers in 2013, and, after a period of playing their home games in Kidderminster have moved to Bromsgrove; their fan-base are entitled to feel disenfranchised. The properties erected are, however, not entirely unpleasing, and one admires the use of balconies and weatherboarding. A mural in a nearby bridge-hole recalls humble City's elimination of mighty Liverpool from the FA Cup on 15th January 1959.

By Bridge 11 the charmingly named Flagge Meadow playing fields of Worcester's ancient Royal Grammar School are overlooked by a handsome pavilion. Sir Edward Leader Williams, engineer of the

for details of facilities in Worcester turn to page 83

**Canal Locks**
1/2 Diglis Canal Locks 18ft 0ins
3 Sidbury Lock 11ft 0ins
4 Blockhouse Lock 11ft 0ins
5/6 Gregory's Mill Locks 14ft 0ins
7/8 Bilford Locks 14ft 0ins
9 Black Pole Lock 7ft 0ins
10 Tolladine Lock 7ft 0ins

(S) = 🗑🚮♿WC

Diglis River Locks (duplicated)
7ft 11ins
Tel: 01905 354280

1: Worcester Marina
ABC Boat Hire
2: Diglis Marina

note overlap and 180° spin with Map 1

*figures refer to canal only

Lowesmoor

Sidbury Lock

Manchester Ship Canal, was a pupil, as indeed was his brother Benjamin Williams Leader (sic) the landscape artist. Another knighted Edward, Elgar, lived at Marl Bank on Rainbow Hill until his death in 1934. Controversially the property was demolished in 1969.

A shapely railway bridge (10) spans the canal by Lowesmoor Wharf. It has a hole cut out of it, presumably in order to lessen the weight of the structure as opposed to considerations of aesthetic virtue. Lowesmoor Wharf (aka Worcester Marina) is a good spot to moor securely close to the city centre - just slip beneath the roving bridge and make yourself known at the office.

For a cathedral city, Worcester attracted a surprisingly large amount of industry; spurred on, one imagines by the connectivity provided by the river, canal and railway. The Italianate clock tower peeping over the canal by Bridge 8, belongs to the Shrub Hill Engineering Works of 1864. McKenzie & Holland's railway signalling works extended both sides of the canal. Hill, Evans & Co.'s Vinegar Works has been replaced by a shopping precinct, but was once served by a branch line railway which crossed the canal alongside Bridge 6. The lengthy saw-toothed building on the towpath side is a Firstbus garage; previously, and somewhat more illustriously, Midland Red. On the offside, above Blockhouse Lock, on a site now occupied by Smiths News and Magnet, stood Hardy & Padmore's foundry, makers of all manner of cast iron items, such as the decorative dual lamp posts which still grace Worcester Bridge and

## ◯ Key

A former Munitions/Cadbury factory
B site of Railway Works
C site of Gas Works
D Shrub Hill Engineering Works
E sites of McKenzie & Holland Signal Works
F site of Vinegar Works
G site of Hardy & Padmore Foundry
H site of Glove Works (Fownes Hotel)
I  site of Porcelain Works
J  former Flour Mill

⚠ Two broad locks separate the basins from the river. They are closed overnight, re-opening at eight in the morning. Entering or leaving the river can pose problems, especially if the current is flowing quickly, and getting your crew on or off for the locks needs careful consideration. See Map 1 for further advice.

*Diglis Basins*

*Diglis Canal Locks*

Cavaliers. The elevated fort is a pleasant park now, easily reached from the Commandery moorings. A panoramic plaque identifies major incidents of the Battle of Worcester and the gardens offer a marvellous view over the city and its multitudinous churches. Bridge 3 carries amusing sculptures of Civil War pikestaffs, shields and helmets.

Burgeoning apartment blocks usher the canal down to Diglis Basins. Townsend's Mill (by Bridge 2), once an intensive user of water transport, has been incorporated into these developments: ditto Royal Worcester's porcelain works; thus, rather sadly, one is no longer subjected to what we described in earlier editions as the erstwhile workforce's 'distinctly earthy sense of humour'. Nowadays, the 'brand' belongs to the Portmeirion Group and output is centred on Stoke-on-Trent, or even further afield. A bane on brands! Products should stay true to their roots or bow gracefully out.

Diglis Basins opened in the 19th century to facilitate transhipment of cargoes between river and canal. One would have relished being here in their working heyday, marvelling at the constant comings and goings of boats of all shapes and sizes. When the river was in flood, river craft would ignore the locks and sail straight into the basins. Don't seek to emulate them! Rebranded now as Diglis Water, the massed ranks of apartments offer - to the amazement and incomprehension, one imagines, of the spirits of boatmen and dock workers who presumably haunt the place - 'a whole new environment for living and working in the modern world'. Are any of the present occupants cognisant of Henry Webb & Co, manufacturers of 'High-Class Chemical Manures' and processors of horse hair whose noxious works - topped by a 150ft high chimney - once occupied the site?

the decorative cast iron railway bridge on Foregate Street. Interestingly, they also made barge stoves.

Blockhouse and Sidbury locks lower the canal towards the Severn. Between them, on the offside, Fownes Hotel was formerly a glove factory. Virtually opposite stands the Commandery, which Charles II used as his headquarters during the Civil War Battle of Worcester in 1651, though it was originally a hospital and dates from as early as the 15th century. There is space here for half a dozen boats to moor overnight within euphonious earshot of the cathedral bells.

Sidbury Lock lies near the site of a gate in the city wall where a thousand Royalist troops are said to have been killed. Cromwell's men had captured the nearby fort and turned its canons on the escaping

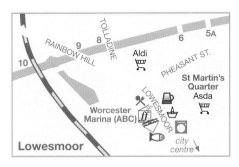

**Lowesmoor**

# Worcester

Maps 1 & 24

Descending from Birmingham to Worcester, the West Midlands are left intuitively behind, and you find yourself in streets where the patois has a distinct West Country burr. 'Royal' Worcester suffered more than most at the hands of the developers during the philistine Sixties (Ian Nairn, the late architectural writer and broadcaster, was incensed, and James Lees-Milne got into hot water for permitting his *Shell Guide to Worcestershire* to be too critical) but much making of amends has been done in recent years to enhance the city's fabric. The Cathedral, gazing devoutly over the Severn and containing the tomb of King John shares, with Gloucester and Hereford, Europe's oldest music festival, 'The Three Choirs'. From the deep well of Worcester's history you can draw inspiration from almost any era that captures your imagination. This was the 'faithful city' of the Civil War from which Charles II escaped following the final defeat of the Cavaliers. It was the home, for much of his life, of Sir Edward Elgar. Home too of that ensign of the empire, Lea & Perrins sauce - still produced on Midland Road. And here lies one of the loveliest cricketing venues, in England - Worcestershire's New Road ground.

## Eating & Drinking

THE ANCHOR - Diglis. Tel: 01905 351094. Marston's local alongside Diglis Basins. Breakfasts from 9.30am. Skittle alley and canalside patio. WR5 3BW
BENEDICTO'S - Sidbury. Tel: 01905 21444. Italian on the Cathedral side of Sidbury Lock. WR1 2HZ
BROWNS AT THE QUAY - Quay Street. Tel: 01905 25800. Fine dining in former riverside mill. WR1 2JN
CENTENARY LOUNGE - The Cross. Tel: 01905 724242. Echoes of the old Great Western Railway and Jazz Age define this charming establishment. WR1 3PZ
COTE - High Street. Tel: 01905 676177. Invariably a reliable Pearson favourite. WR1 2HW
DIGLIS HOUSE HOTEL - Severn Street. Tel: 01905 353518. Bar and restaurant food, open to non-residents throughout the day. Riverbank setting, former home of Benjamin Williams Leader. WR1 2NF
FIREFLY BEER HAUS - Lowesmoor. Tel: 01905 616996. Vibrant pub, from 3pm (noon Sat & Sun). WR1 2SE

## Shopping

The Shambles, Friar Street and New Street feature numerous fascinating little shops and small businesses. Crown Gate is the main shopping precinct with adjoining street markets on Tue-Sat. An Asda supermarket in the St Martin's Quarter on Lowesmoor is easily accessible from bridge 9 and/or Worcester Marina. Also handy on Lowesmoor are east European convenience stores, a bakery and a launderette. The Post Office is housed in W. H. Smith on High Street.

## Things to Do

TOURIST INFORMATION CENTRE - The Guildhall, High Street. Tel: 01905 726311. Well stocked and welcomingly staffed! Closed Sundays. WR1 2EY
THE COMMANDERY - canalside by Sidbury Lock. Tel: 01905 361821. Civil War history. WR1 2HU

CITY MUSEUM & ART GALLERY - Foregate Street. Tel: 01902 25371. Admission free. One or two works by Benjamin Williams Leader (brother of the canal engineer Edward Leader Williams) best known for *February Fill Dyke* which hangs in Birmingham Art Gallery if you're going that way. WR1 1DT
GREYFRIARS - Friar Street. Tel: 01905 23571. National Trust 15th century timber framed house. WR1 2LZ
TUDOR HOUSE - Friar Street. Tel: 01905 612309. Local history displays in five hunded year old half-timbered house. Admission free. WR1 2NA
MUSEUM OF ROYAL WORCESTER - Severn Street. Tel: 01905 21247. Open daily from 10am. WR1 2ND

## Connections

TRAINS - stations at Foregate Street and Shrub Hill. Services to/from the Malverns (and on through the hop-yards to Hereford) Droitwich, Kidderminster, Birmingham etc. Good service also to and from London Paddington. Tel: 0345 748 4950.
BUSES - links throughout the area, but of particular note is Diamond's service 296 connecting Worcester with Stourport half a dozen times per day (ex Sun) facilitating one- way walks along the Severn Way. Tel: 01562 561220.
TAXIS - Cathedral Cars. Tel: 01905 767400.

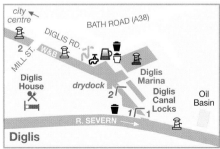

**Diglis**

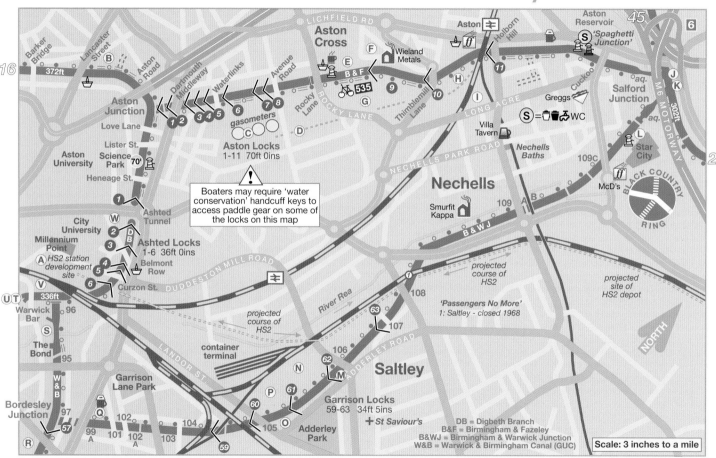

# 25 BIRMINGHAM & FAZELEY CANAL Aston & Saltley 2mls/11lks/3hrs

LICHFIELD RD

Aston Cross

Aston Reservoir

'Spaghetti Junction'

45

6

16

Barker Bridge

Lancaster Street

372ft

Aston Road

Dartmouth Middleway

Waterlinks

Avenue Road

Wieland Metals

Aston

Holborn Hill

Aston Junction

Love Lane

Lister St.

Science Park

70'

Aston University

Heneage St.

gasometers

Rocky Lane

ROCKY LANE

B & F

535

Thimblemill Lane

LONG ACRE

Cuckoo

Greggs

Salford Junction

aq.

J

K

M6 MOTORWAY

20

Aston Locks
1-11 70ft 0ins

**Boaters may require 'water conservation' handcuff keys to access paddle gear on some of the locks on this map**

Villa Tavern

Nechells Baths

S = 🚻 WC

109C

Star City

McD's

BLACK COUNTRY RING

City University

Millennium Point

HS2 station development site

Ashted Tunnel

Ashted Locks
1-6 36ft 0ins

Belmont Row

Curzon St.

NECHELLS PARK ROAD

Nechells

Smurfit Kappa

109

A B

B & WJ

Warwick Bar

336ft

96

The Bond

95

DUDDESTON MILL ROAD

projected course of HS2

River Rea

projected course of HS2

108

63

107

106

'Passengers No More'
1: Saltley - closed 1968

projected site of HS2 depot

NORTH

Bordesley Junction

97

57

Garrison Lane Park

102

99 101 102
103

104

105

LANDOR ST.

container terminal

59

62

M

61

60

O

P

Saltley

Garrison Locks
59-63 34ft 5ins

✝ St Saviour's

Adderley Park

ADDERLEY ROAD

DB = Digbeth Branch
B&F = Birmingham & Fazeley
B&WJ = Birmingham & Warwick Junction
W&B = Warwick & Birmingham Canal (GUC)

Scale: 3 inches to a mile

84 GU Canal
(use South Mids CC)

**F**ROM Snow Hill (Map 16) to Aston the Birmingham & Fazeley Canal, clear of locks for a welcome respite, widens and is less claustrophobically engulfed by the high canyons of commerce. Barker Bridge - a graceful span of cast iron supported by brick piers and abutments dating from 1842 - got its name from a Staffordshire ironmaster. Nearby stood the city's original General Hospital opened in 1779. Beyond Lancaster Street - overlooked by new student accommodation blocks - a switchback sequence of side bridges formerly gave access to wharves serving a Corporation depot and various engineering works.

## Aston Locks

Atmospherically a subtle change overtakes the B&F as it proceeds eastwards from Aston Junction; Birmingham's commercial core has been left astern and an industrial zone takes over. A Horseley Iron Works cast iron roving bridge marks the junction of the main line with the Digbeth Branch; its elegance, amounting almost to a misleading fragility, is in marked contrast to the overpowering concrete edifice of the adjacent Expressway. Time and time again exploration of Birmingham's canal network emphasises the great gulf in aesthetic achievement between the civil engineering of the nineteenth century and the twentieth. Time alters perception, but it does seem inconceivable that any age will ever be able to indentify beauty in the Aston Expressway ... though you never know!

Like old school friends, Aston's eleven locks grow farther apart as they descend towards Salford Junction. In the short pound between locks 4 and 5 once stood the Armstrong Umbrella Works. We trust you won't need one on the day of your travels. Going down the flight aboard the (now preserved) Thomas Clayton tar boat *Towy* as Birmingham was waking up one morning in 1952, Vivian Bird revealed in *By Lock & Pound* that on average only a dozen working boats were using the locks on a daily basis, whereas in the 1920s the figure would have been in the seventies ... both ways! Bird went on to imply that the boatmen had nicknamed the flight the 'Lousy 'Leven'; adding humorously that the epithet might equally have applied to Aston Villa. A good joke, but the term is generally considered

to refer to the combined chambers of the Garrison and Camp Hill flights, which were even more deserving of the pejorative.

The colourfully painted framework of a trio of gasholders mark the site of Windsor Street Gas Works opened by the Birmingham Gas, Light & Coke Co. but later taken over by Birmingham Corporation. Once there were ten of them. This whole area was filled with so many intriguing factories that those depicted, almost randomly, on the accompanying map barely scratch the surface. By Rocky Lane Bridge are offside visitor moorings and access to a small convenience store and take-away.

Access to and from the canal is provided at Holborn Hill Bridge. No excuse, then, for not using Aston railway station as a staging post on a five minute train ride out from New Street followed by a healthy, and rarely less than fascinating hour's walk back along the towpath to the city centre. The outward leg would carry you along one of the earliest main line railways. Opened in 1838, only fifty years after the canal, the Grand Junction linked Birmingham with the north-west. Moorings and boating facilities are provided by Cuckoo Bridge.

## Salford Junction

Barely a tiny fraction of the stressed-out motorists, fighting their way around the confusion of Gravelly Hill Interchange (aka Spaghetti Junction) are aware of the older, less frenzied meeting and parting of ways entombed in the concrete gloom below. But such is Salford Junction, where the Birmingham & Warwick Junction (later Grand Union) Canal and Tame

### ○ Key

A Curzon Street railway terminus
B site of Corporation Wharf
C former Corporation Gas Works
D site of Windsor Street Goods Depot
E site of Eagle Range Foundry
F site of Button Works
G site of Aston Paper Mills
H site of Essex (cooker) Works
I site of Aston MPD (3D)
J site of T & S Element Boatyard
K site of Spencer Abbott Boatyard
L site of Nechells Power Station
M site of FMC Saltley Dock/Park Wharf
N site of Saltley MPD (21A/2E)
O site of Union Paper Mills
P site of Midland Railway C&W Works
Q former Colmore Bedstead Works
R site of Adderley St. Gas Works
S former FMC Warehouses
T former Digbeth Basins
U former Typhoo Tea Factory
V Gun Barrel Proof House
W Belmont Works

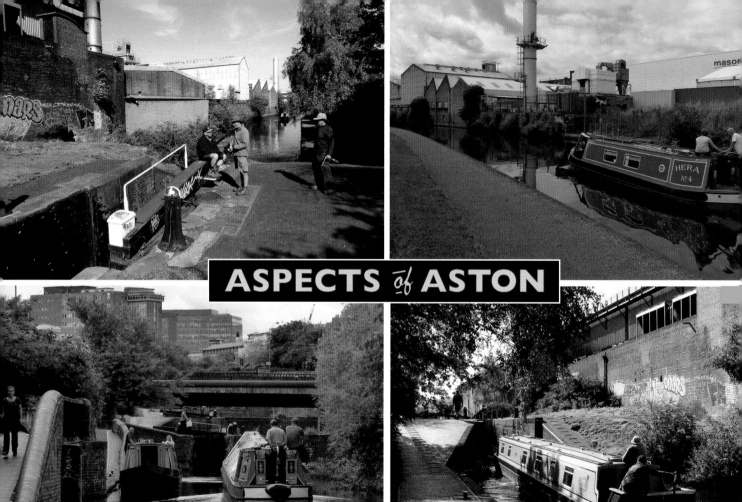

ASPECTS of ASTON

Valley Canal (Map 45) - both dating from 1844 - form a canal crossroads with the Birmingham & Fazeley Canal. It is a sobering spot for contemplating Man's contribution to the landscape. Monstrously compromised, the River Tame churns despondently through artificial channels beneath successive generations of roads like a slave in chains. But nature rolls with the punches, and yellow wagtails search assiduously for their next meal in the shallow margins of the river.

## Digbeth Branch

The most expedient route out of and into Birmingham is via the Birmingham & Fazeley Canal, but you may well enjoy exploring the other canals depicted on Map 25. The Digbeth Branch was opened in 1799 and descends through the six locks of the Ashted flight to a junction with the Warwick & Birmingham Canal, later part of the Grand Union. This part of Birmingham is undergoing so much regeneration that it is difficult to describe the Digbeth Branch in the present tense. Forty years ago Aston Science Park seemed futuristic, now it feels rather forlorn and overlooked.

There are visitor moorings and a winding hole between Lister Street and Heneage Street bridges, but little in the way of nearby amenities to prolong a stay. Below the top lock the canal plunges immediately into Ashted Tunnel before emerging into the brave new world of Eastside and the burgeoning campus of Birmingham City University. Dwarfed by interlopers, Belmont Row Works is a Victorian survivor redeveloped as an enterprise hub called the Steam House. In the past it has enjoyed various uses including the manufacture of bicycles, rubber goods, underwear, pianos and bedsteads. By Belmont Row Bridge a BCN cottage has also escaped demolition. Beyond the bottom lock, the canal enters a curving tunnel beneath a series of railway lines to which HS2, on the approach to its Curzon Street terminus, is in the process of being added.

Once your eyes have grown reaccustomed to daylight - or what passes for it on the BCN - the canal has reached Warwick Bar and its T-shaped junction with the Warwick & Birmingham Canal. Self-effacingly hidden behind a brick wall on the opposite bank to the towpath is one of the city's

least known but most remarkable buildings, the Gun Barrel Proof House, dating from 1813, and still fulfilling its original purpose two centuries on.

It remains to be seen if the rejuvenation of Eastside will impact beneficially on Warwick Bar. From time to time sundry initiatives have attempted to smarten it up, but it always seems to revert back to a rather shabby default setting ... shabby, that is, without the chic. It is tedious to moralize, but improvements are futile if not succeeded by regular maintenance.

## Warwick & Birmingham Canal

The stop lock (whose cosmetically reinstated gates are left permanently open) was constructed to separate the valuable waters of the Birmingham & Fazeley (later BCN) and Warwick & Birmingham canal companies. Alongside the remains of the stop lock stands a warehouse with an awning supported by cast-iron pillars over an arm lying parallel to the narrows. At one time it was leased by Geest the fruit importers and earned the sobriquet 'Banana Warehouse'. There are plans - as part of BBC's regeneration of the neighbouring Typhoo tea factory - for it to be refurbished as a television studio. Beyond lies New Warwick Wharf, marked by the tall curved wall of Fellows, Morton & Clayton's warehouse built in 1935 in belated response to modernisation of the canal from London. This confident 'Art Deco' style of architecture - emblazoned with the company's name along Fazeley Street, as pictured overleaf - was not rewarded by a significant increase in trade, and, having been for a number of years used by HP Sauce, it now houses a conglomeration of small businesses.

Crossing the River Rea - an unsung (and, in central Birmingham, much culverted) tributary of the Tame - the canal encounters more FMC warehousing built of alternate courses of red and blue brick, and equipped with weather-boarded elevators and an attractive saw-tooth valanced canopy over a side arm. Known now as 'The Bond', it has become a centre for graphic art based businesses. Directly opposite the towpath rises and falls over a side bridge spanning an arm which once led into one of the City of Birmingham's Salvage Department basins. Horsedrawn rubbish boats operated between here and the Small Heath destructor until 1965. By Great Barr Street (Br. 95) Duddeston Viaduct spans the canal, a railway bridge, erected out of rivalry, which never carried trains.

The ripples of redevelopment may, or may not, lap Warwick Bar, but it's difficult to imagine them ever transforming the perpetual gloom that is Bordesley Junction. Welcome to Birmingham's bowels, the sort of scene Heironymous Bosch would have relished employing as a backdrop to some fairly harrowing earthly tortures. Goodness knows what the occupants of the boats negotiating the popular 'Warwickshire Ring' make of this interlude in their predominantly scenic itinerary. Some, doubtless, will look back on this part of their voyage fondly; others, scarred for life.

## Birmingham & Warwick Junction (Saltley Cut)

Even the working boatmen of the dim and distant past recoiled at the thought of the Birmingham & Warwick Junction Canal: alias 'Saltley Cut'; alias 'The Bottom Road'. Had they been better educated - had they been educated at all - some mordant wit amongst them might have nicknamed it 'The Alimentary Canal'; demonstrably it carried a good deal of waste in its noxious waters. 'Grease oozed blackly from the lock chambers as we dropped. A sort of foul, black patina settled on brass and paintwork,' was how David Blagrove described it in *Bread Upon The Waters*. But that was back when gas works, goods yards, engine sheds and electricity generating plants lined its banks. Post-industrially the abiding atmosphere is of emptiness. Rarely do you encounter any other human beings. The graffiti - and there is plenty of it - must appear, like crop-circles, extra-terrestrially.

The B&WJC was a latecomer in the Canal Age. It opened in 1844 as a by-pass between Bordesley and Salford junctions to ease the congestion on other routes into and out of Birmingham. In an odd sort of way it fulfils the same function now, enabling Warwickshire Ringers, and others for whom central Birmingham is not necessarily a goal (let alone anathema) to avoid a good deal of time-consuming lockage.

Overlooked by the Liverpool Street Bus Depot of 1936 ('Birmingham

Bordesley

Corporation Tramway & Omnibus Dept.' remains engraved above the entrance), the B&WJC leaves Bordesley Junction beneath a graceful roving bridge cast by Lloyds & Fosters and immediately plunges beneath a factory. Beyond Middleway - Birmingham's 'ring road'- an impressive building on the towpath side was formerly Colmore Bedstead Works, one of a number in the area whose slumberous product lines were conveyed by boat to the capital. There ensues a lengthy straight through the regenerated housing zone of Heartlands, spanned by a succession of brick overbridges as in some Salvador Dalian dream of diminishing perspective. The towpath burgeons with poppies, cranesbill, dog rose and daisies: a fecundity derived from generations of boat horse dung perhaps.

Garrison Locks are criss-crossed by railway lines and hemmed in by factory walls. Nip up onto Garrison Street by the top lock (No.59) for an

- was a hectic transhipment point between boats and trains: 'a supreme example of rail-canal co-operation' according to Tom Foxon, working boatman turned canal historian. Loading boats at Saltley was a popular informal occupation, it being practical to earn in a couple of hours of casual hard graft the equivalent of a formally employed worker's daily wage.

A short detour from Bridge 109 is worth making to admire - but alas no longer to swim in - Nechells Baths, a Grade II extravagancy dating from 1910. The once gigantic, but now vanished, Nechells power station was served by its own loop canal. Here tugs would bring in 'trains' of up to four coal-carrying boats to be speedily unloaded by electric grabs. An entertainments complex called Star City has risen phoenix-like from the power station's ashes. Nominally secure visitor moorings are provided on an offside pontoon. Treat yourself to the latest zombie movie and the horrors of the Saltley Cut will be placed comfortably in perspective.

Garrison Locks

Backstreet 'Brum'

unexpected backstreet encounter with the Birmingham Accordion Centre. Indeed, it would be remiss of you not to abandon the canal to its own devices from time to time: something interesting and/or quixotic can nearly always be found in the streets bordering it.

By Bridge 106 stood Park Wharf where Fellows, Morton & Clayton had a boat dock. Some of their most famous boats were built here, like the steamer *President*, now fully restored and often to be seen at boat rallies and museum events. On the towpath side stood the Midland Railway's Saltley engine sheds; symbolically replaced by a scrap yard.

Gas works and electricity generating plants demanded a constant supply of coal brought in by 'Joey-boats' from the collieries of Cannock and North Warwickshire. Chemical by-products were taken away in Thomas Clayton tanker boats. 'Saltley Sidings' - now occupied by inscrutable industrial units

LIKE someone painstakingly negotiating a release clause, the Birmingham & Fazeley seems to take forever to extricate itself from the city's sub-claused, codicilled contract. A couple of hours, and these nebulous suburbs have more than outstayed their welcome. And yet, as always, there is something inherent in the pace of canal travel - on foot or afloat - that makes you delve deeper, that evinces responses, that engenders 'negotiations and love songs'. So what can you relate to here?

Forging east from Salford Junction, two overbridges called Troutpool (might be a character in a Terence Rattigan play) recall the pre-industrial landscape which predated the B&F's late 18th century completion. Between Troutpool and Erdington Hall bridges the canal glides claustrophobically beneath an overhanging works once belonging to Birlec, manufacturers of electric arc furnaces. Bromford Bridge (aka Birmingham) Race Course held meetings from 1894 to 1965. In 1915 the grandstand was set on fire by sufragettes. Lester Piggott rode two winners at the final meeting.

At Wood Lane Bridge there are BCN concrete posts, and beyond Brace Factory Bridge glimpses south to Fort Dunlop, the massive tyre factory dating from 1916. To transport the workforce to and from this new plant, the company operated a small fleet of passenger carrying narrowboats between Aston and Bromford until the neighbouring Tyburn Road was laid with tram tracks. Apparently the two and a half mile, lock-free journey took around half an hour and each boat could seat a hundred passengers.

Fort Dunlop is enjoying a new lease of life as an hotel and office space. Not so fortunate, though of equal architectural value, the Art Deco Cincinnati Machine Company's premises below Minworth Top Lock have been demolished and replaced by new housing. It is difficult to comprehend why the imposing facade could not have been incorporated in this development like the Ovaltine factory at Kings Langley on the Grand Union Canal. Another casualty is the Drome Cafe, a once reliable fry-

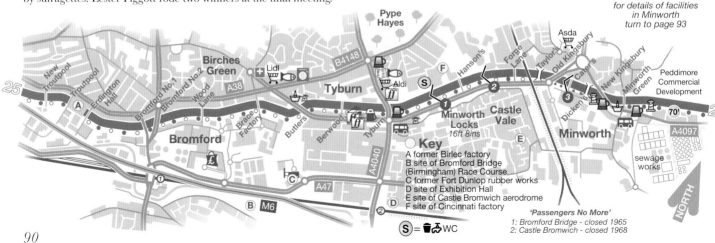

for details of facilities
in Minworth
turn to page 93

Key
A former Birlec factory
B site of Bromford Bridge
(Birmingham) Race Course
C former Fort Dunlop rubber works
D site of Exhibition Hall
E site of Castle Bromwich aerodrome
F site of Cincinnati factory

S = 🗑🚻 WC

'Passengers No More'
1: Bromford Bridge - closed 1965
2: Castle Bromwich - closed 1968

up and fish & chip pit stop whose name harked back to Castle Bromwich's aerodrome. In 1938, as Britain was belatedly arming for war, fields in the vicinity were occupied by a 'shadow' munition factory. During the next seven years over eleven thousand Spitfires were built at the plant. In the 1960s a housing zone called Castle Vale replaced the factory and adjoining aerodrome. Five thousand homes in blocks of flats rising to sixteen floors, housing the population of a medium-sized town. Streets on the new estate were named after RAF aerodromes.

The trio of locks at Minworth lie alongside the busy A38 dual-carriageway. Goods trains rumble across the canal on a line linking Castle Bromwich with Walsall which lost its passenger services in 1965, though there are periodical calls for them to be reinstated, and not merely by passengers who missed the last train. Castle Bromwich was the location

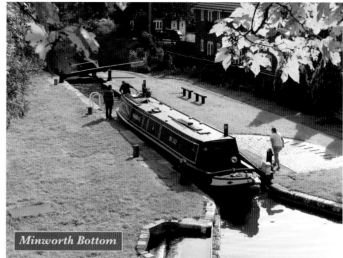

Minworth Bottom

Minworth Top

of the British Industries Exhibition Hall, a forerunner of the NEC. The BI Fair was held over a fortnight, annually from 1920-60, and was quite something in its heyday, all the movers and shakers of the day attended. *YouTube* carries a Pathe Newsreel of the Prince of Wales attending the fair in 1932, four years before he briefly became King Edward VIII. Accompanied by fawning courtiers, he scarcely conceals his ennui watching a demonstration of a crane and drag-line depositing rubble in dumper wagons shunted by a Hunslet diesel locomotive.

Minworth Sewage Works is Severn Trent's largest treatment plant and disposes of the waste of over one and a half million West Midlanders. Narrowboats unloaded ash in the arm to the east of Minworth Green Bridge for use in the plant's filter beds. A 2ft gauge railway was employed in transporting dried sewage around the site. And, yes, the plant is the source of that whiff in the air, so you don't necessarily need a pump-out.

A S if to celebrate leaving the West Midlands for Warwickshire, the towpath promptly deteriorates, becoming narrower and muddier; though just about cyclable. Not the most charismatic of canals, the Birmingham & Fazeley nevertheless evinces a sort of sullen charm, though you sense its relative popularity lies in its importance as a link between the east and west midlands, together with the fact that it is part of two popular cruising rings.

Couched in a wooded cutting, a short tunnel at Curdworth precedes a flight of eleven locks, single-gated top and tail, as per BCN custom,

with which the B&F merged in 1794. Construction of the M6 Toll road necessitated repositioning of the top lock and replacement of the lock-keeper's house at Dunton Wharf. A spanking new winding hole was dug as well, and it's not often you can say that! Lorry contractors, Freeman & Sons of Dunton Wharf, celebrated their centenary in 2008.

Locks 2-5 come in a cluster, otherwise they are of sufficient distance apart to make indolent lock-workers think twice about walking between them. The western route of HS2, northwards from Birmingham to who

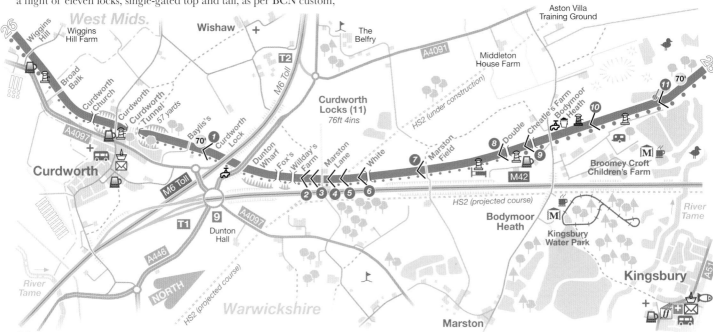

knows where, is being built to cross the canal between locks 3 and 4. The eastern route will head, initially, to East Midlands Parkway. Their trains will travel sixty-four times faster than your narrowboat; but who will be journeying, in the words of Robert Louis Stevenson, more hopefully?

Not far north from Dunton Wharf, along the A446 is the Belfry Hotel and its famous golf course, scene of many a nail-biting Ryder Cup denouement. Another sporting association belongs to Bodymoor Heath where Aston Villa, the illustrious Birmingham football club, have their impressive training ground.

The bottom lock of the Curdworth flight is overlooked by a quartet of canal cottages. Life must be pleasant here if, as one supposes, the inhabitants find the isolation conducive. Skeins of geese rise into the wide skies from flooded gravel workings. Gravel has been extracted from the valley of the Tame since the 1930s. Originally by dredger, later by dragline. Nowadays conveyor belts carry the minerals to screening and washing plants where they are sorted into varying types of aggregates. The landscape might have been irrevocably scarred by such activities were it not for the imaginative creation of Kingsbury Water Park out of the abandoned gravel workings. Moorings are available above the bottom lock and it's but a short walk to the park's visitor centre.

## Minworth    Map 26

### Eating & Drinking
BOAT INN - Old Kingsbury Road. Tel: 0121 240 7790. Canalside pub open from noon. Food lunch and evening Tue-Sat and Sun lunch. B76 9AE

### Shopping
Convenience stores. Asda supermarket to NW.

### Connections
BUSES - X4 hourly to/from Birmingham from stop at Asda. Tel: 0871 200 2233.

## Curdworth    Map 27

Curdworth is one of the oldest settlements in this part of the world and derives its name from Crida, the first King of Mercia.

### Eating & Drinking
CUTTLE BRIDGE INN - Kingsbury Road. Tel: 01675 475626. Modern canalside pub and hotel. Breakfasts followed by food throughout from noon. B76 9DP
WHITE HORSE - Kingsbury Road (adjacent Curdworth Bridge). Tel: 01675 470227. 'Vintage Inn'. Open from noon, food served throughout. B76 9DS

### Shopping
Post Office stores in village on far side of A4097.

Echills Wood Railway

### Connections
BUSES - Diamond 75 to/from Sutton Coldfield/NEC.

## Bodymoor Heath    Map 27

Despite proximity of M42 (and impending HS2), still a remote community to east of Sutton Coldfield.

### Eating & Drinking
DOG & DOUBLET - Dog Lane (canalside Cheatle's Farm Bridge). Tel: 01827 873907. Rambling old Georgian pub. Food lunch & evening Mon-Thur, and from noon throughout Fri-Sun. B76 9JD
OLD BARN CAFE - Kingsbury Water Park. Tel: 01827 874823. Open daily (from 10.30am) for breakfasts, coffees, lunches and afternoon tea. B76 9JB

### Things to Do
BROOMEY CROFT CHILDREN'S FARM - Bodymoor Heath Lane. Tel: 01827 873844. Not so much a genetically-modified approach to child-rearing, more a fun day out for the family. Tractor rides, tea rooms and gift shop. Weekends and school holidays. B76 0EE
KINGSBURY WATER PARK - Bodymoor Heath Lane. Tel: 01827 872660. Over six hundred acres of waterside and woodland walks. Charming rides on Echills Wood Miniature Railway. Cycle hire, cafe and gift shop, Moorings above Bottom Lock. B76 9JB

WARWICKSHIRE gives way to Staffordshire as the Birmingham & Fazeley Canal, done with locks, ambles absent-mindedly towards its junction with the Coventry Canal at Fazeley. A leafy half-mile's walk west of the canal from Fisher's Mill Bridge, Middleton Hall was the home of two eminent naturalists, Francis Willoughby and John Ray. Queen Elizabeth stayed here in 1567, her retinue lustily eating their way through sixty-nine beef cattle, one hundred and twenty-eight sheep, and two thousand chickens during the course of a week. In recent years the property has been painstakingly restored by the Middleton Hall Trust.

On the opposite bank of the canal, the Royal Society for the Protection of Birds acquired a large area of worked out gravel workings in 2007 and opened a nature reserve to human visitors four years later. These Middleton Lakes, as they have become known, play host to an increasingly wide range of flora and fauna. Bitterns are not unknown, and murmurations of up to ten thousand starlings have been sighted (and counted).

Now and again on a canal journey, one encounters an object decorated extravagantly beyond the usual tenets - however gracious - of 18th and 19th century civil engineering. Drayton Foot Bridge is one such example, and consists of two crenellated towers (encasing spiral staircases) which support a slender iron span: the kind of eccentric structure where the inner child feels compelled to engage in swashbuckling acts. The structure took its cue from neighbouring Drayton Manor. No, not the contemporary theme park, but the 18th century mansion designed for the Prime Minister Robert Peel by Robert Smirke, the celebrated Greek Revival architect responsible for the British Museum and Covent Garden Theatre. Demolished in 1929, the house's last occupants were Peel's great grandson and his wife, Beatrice Lillie, a comedy actress once widely considered 'the funniest

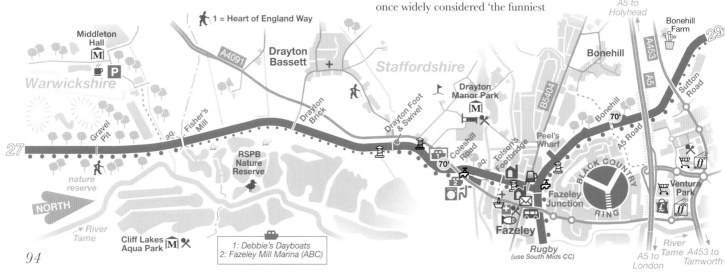

woman in the world'. The grounds were later used for speedway and greyhound racing before being acquired by the Bryan family in 1949, and transformed into the 'fifth most popular theme park' in the UK.

Fazeley Junction exudes a certain grubby grandeur, lent added gravitas by a big old textile mill which quite plausibly might have escaped from Oldham or Rochdale. The Birmingham & Fazeley reached here in 1789 and the following year Sir Robert Peel (father of the Prime Minister) opened a mill for cotton spinning and calico printing. A second mill, of five towering storeys, erected in 1883 for the weaving of haberdashery; corset ribbons and lingerie straps, has been repurposed of late as a mix of apartments and town houses. Gould's sawmill, complete with lofty crane, creates an additional landmark at the junction. The handsome junction house - numbered 261 in the BCN sequence - presides over the meeting of the B&F and Coventry canals.

# Fazeley
Map 28

Motorists on their lengthy journey along the A5 from Marble Arch to Holyhead must have barely batted an eyelid on reaching Fazeley, but in its heyday this was a busy little place. Two mills set the tone, aided and abetted by a lugubrious supporting cast: the United Methodist Free Church of 1884; the terracotta Parish Hall of 1897; workers' terraces, and a timber yard. Back in the day there were monthly cattle fairs; Samuel Barlow provided suitably cleaned out coal boats for Sunday School jaunts; and Tolsons, proprietors of the five storey mill, ran a dance band punningly known as The Music Weavers.

## Eating & Drinking
FAZELEY FISH BAR - Coleshill Street. Tel: 01827 284940. Fish & chips etc. B78 3RB
FAZELEY PARK - Atherstone Street. Tel: 01827 261718. Indian restaurant open from 5pm. B78 3RF
IVORY TUSK - Coleshill Street. Tel: 01827 285777. A *second* Indian restaurant, open from 5pm. B78 3RG
KUDOS - Coleshill Street. Tel: 01827 254777. A *third* Indian restaurant, open from 5.30pm. B78 3RB
PENINSULAR - Coleshill Street. Tel: 01827 288151. Chinese restaurant open from 5pm. B78 3RB
THREE TUNS - Lichfield Street. Tel: 01827 918725. Homely Watling Street pub backing onto the canal with offside moorings for customers. B78 3QS
*Plus two other pubs and two Chinese take-aways.*

Drayton Foot Bridge

## Shopping
There's a Tesco Express (with cash machine), pharmacy and post office (in the petrol station) in the village centre. From Bonehill Bridge a footpath leads under the A5 to Ventura Park featuring Asda and Sainsbury's supermarkets, John Lewis, M&S et al, plus Nando's, Pizza Express, KFC, Costa, and McDonalds.

## Things to Do
DRAYTON MANOR PARK - open daily Easter to October. Admission charge. Access on A4091 adjacent to Drayton footbridge. Tel: 01827 287979. Family theme park, 'Thomas Land', amusements, zoo, farm park, nature trail and woodland walk. B78 3TW
MIDDLETON HALL - Middleton (access from Fisher's Mill Bridge) Tel: 01827 283095. Open Sun-Thur 11am-4pm April to mid September. Plus quirky retail outlets in converted Victorian stable block Wed-Sun. Coffee Shop open daily 9.30am-4.30pm. B78 2AE
MIDDLETON LAKES - Bodymoor Heath (access from the towpath at Fisher's Mill Bridge). Tel: 01827 259454. A Royal Society for the Protection of Birds reserve open daily dawn to dusk. Signposted woodland, wetland and meadow trails. B78 2AE

## Connections
BUSES - Arriva 'Sapphire' 110 runs every 15 mins (30 mins Sun) to/from Tamworth, Sutton Coldfield and Birmingham. Additional services (16, 115/6) also run to/from Tamworth. Tel: 0871 200 2233.

**N**OT generally thought of as a beautiful canal, the Coventry nevertheless becomes almost picturesque in its wandering between Fazeley and Huddlesford; particularly as it glides through the brackeny woodlands of Hopwas, where red flags warn of military manoeuvres. Glibly we call this the Coventry Canal, but actually - and by now the presence of nameplates and not numbers on the bridges should have quickened your suspicions - the canal between Fazeley and Whittington was built by the Birmingham & Fazeley company.

The Coventry Canal received its Act of Parliament in 1768, but seventeen years later it was nowhere near completion; primarily through periodic bouts of what we would now call cash-flow difficulties but also,

historians suspect, because some of its directors with investments in the Warwickshire coalfield were niggled by the thought that their through route, were it to be finished, would boost trade from the North Staffordshire pits at the expense of their own. In frustration the Trent & Mersey and Birmingham & Fazeley companies undertook to jointly build the canal between Fazeley and Fradley. The two met at Whittington Brook in 1790.

The canal curves endearingly through Hopwas, with visitor moorings and pubs either side of Lichfield Road Bridge commending an extended stay. To the west looms a tall transmitting mast at Hints, erected as long ago as 1956 to broadcast the then fledgeling ITV Channel to the west midlands. A relatively new section of the A5 carves its way through the adjoining

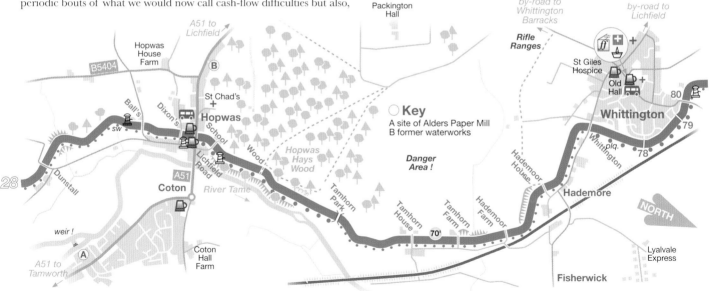

*Hopwas Wood*

escarpment with scant consideration for the equilibrium of this otherwise rural locality. Follow the by-road west from Ball's Bridge, and you'll arrive (having crossed the B5404) on a hillside known enigmatically as 'The Devil's Dressing Room'. The story goes that stone from the hill was quarried during the construction of Lichfield Cathedral, and that devil-faced gargoyles were 'dressed' on site by stonemasons, hence the name. If nothing else, you'll enjoy an invigorating walk, and be rewarded by a fine view of the cathedral in all its three-spired glory.

Skirting Hopwas Wood, 400 acres of ancient woodland, the canal becomes so pretty that you could be forgiven thinking you were on the Monmouth & Brecon and that was the Usk glinting below you. The sound of rapid gunfire may bring you back to earth with a thud, for the woods are part of a military firing range, nearby Whittington Barracks being the headquarters of the British Army's medical services, who obviously require casualties to practise on. There are public footpaths and cycle tracks through the woods, but you would be best advised to check firing days on the *Friends of Hopwas Wood* website before running the gauntlet.

Pleasant scenery, Packington pigs and polytunnels mingle as you negotiate the lower valley of the Tame; passing Hademore, where the houses face the canal in Dutch fashion, rather than turning their backs on it as is more often the case in England. An ornate and enigmatic pair of gateposts stand alongside the telephone kiosk adjacent to Hademoor House Bridge. They formed one of the entrances to Fisherwick Hall, a mansion once couched in a Capability Brown landscape, but demolished as long ago as 1818 to pay off the gambling debts of its owner, the Marquess of Donegal. When the West Coast Main Line was quadrupled the level crossing at Hademoor was replaced by an overbridge. Equestrians are obliged to dismount in case the trains, rushing beneath at a hundred and twenty-five miles an hour, scare their steeds, so mounting-blocks are thoughtfully provided. In steam days, the line at Hademore, being level, was provided with troughs between the rails so that passing locomotives could replenish their water supply without stopping. Enigmatic underground bunkers, on farmland to the north, belong to Lyalvale Express, manufacturers of shotgun cartridges.

# 30 COVENTRY CANAL Fradley & Huddlesford 4½ mls/0lks/1½ hrs

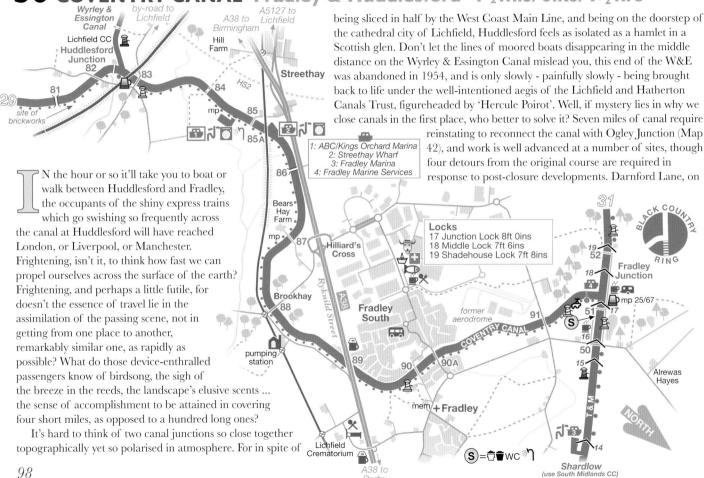

being sliced in half by the West Coast Main Line, and being on the doorstep of the cathedral city of Lichfield, Huddlesford feels as isolated as a hamlet in a Scottish glen. Don't let the lines of moored boats disappearing in the middle distance on the Wyrley & Essington Canal mislead you, this end of the W&E was abandoned in 1954, and is only slowly - painfully slowly - being brought back to life under the well-intentioned aegis of the Lichfield and Hatherton Canals Trust, figureheaded by 'Hercule Poirot'. Well, if mystery lies in why we close canals in the first place, who better to solve it? Seven miles of canal require reinstating to reconnect the canal with Ogley Junction (Map 42), and work is well advanced at a number of sites, though four detours from the original course are required in response to post-closure developments. Darnford Lane, on

I N the hour or so it'll take you to boat or walk between Huddlesford and Fradley, the occupants of the shiny express trains which go swishing so frequently across the canal at Huddlesford will have reached London, or Liverpool, or Manchester. Frightening, isn't it, to think how fast we can propel ourselves across the surface of the earth? Frightening, and perhaps a little futile, for doesn't the essence of travel lie in the assimilation of the passing scene, not in getting from one place to another, remarkably similar one, as rapidly as possible? What do those device-enthralled passengers know of birdsong, the sigh of the breeze in the reeds, the landscape's elusive scents ... the sense of accomplishment to be attained in covering four short miles, as opposed to a hundred long ones?

It's hard to think of two canal junctions so close together topographically yet so polarised in atmosphere. For in spite of

1: ABC/Kings Orchard Marina
2: Streethay Wharf
3: Fradley Marina
4: Fradley Marine Services

**Locks**
17 Junction Lock 8ft 0ins
18 Middle Lock 7ft 6ins
19 Shadehouse Lock 7ft 8ins

(S) = 🚽🗑 WC

98

the southern outskirts of Lichfield, demonstrates the benefits that snowball from canal restoration. It's just a pity that the purse-string holders don't chip in more enthusiastically. Nevertheless, we look forward to the day when sufficient progress has been made to include the course of the W&E in this guide. Fictionalised as the 'Ogley & Huddlesford Canal', it takes centre stage in the crime writer Stephen Booth's novel *Drowned Lives*, a page-turning mystery entwining the canal's restoration with its shadowy past.

**Huddlesford Junction**

the lonely waterway which reputedly inspired Elizabeth Jane Howard to write her haunting story *Three Miles Up* over seventy years ago. Some discerned the warring characters of Aickman and Rolt between the lines, as the ghostly tale's two male protagonists become increasingly at loggerheads, though the author laughingly dismissed the notion in an interview given prior to a reprint in 2003.

The Second World War aerodrome bordering the canal comes replete with its own ghosts. Originally opened for bomber maintenance and acceptance trials in 1939, RAF Lichfield soon developed into an Operational Training Unit, being especially associated with young flyers from the Commonwealth, who must have found the mist-bound purlieus of the Trent Valley something of a culture shock. Crews from Lichfield took part in Thousand-Bomber Raids over Germany. Extant 'blister' hangars evoke their own resonances, which the burgeoning housing developments of Fradley South (whose roads are named after aircrew that failed to return) cannot entirely dispel. A headless airman is reputed to haunt the old runways. Conceivably, it could be the ghost of K. H. Hewitt of the Royal Australian Air Force who died accidentally on 15th April 1943. Cleared for take-off, he discovered he had left his code book in the mess and distractedly walked into the flailing path of one of the plane's propellers on the way to retrieve it. His simple war grave can be seen in St Stephen's churchyard a short stroll north-east of Bridge 90.

HS2 is being built is the vicinity of Bridge 84, part of its extension from the West Midlands to the north-west; though how far it will eventually go is open to conjecture. Occupants of its trains will be going even faster! The South Staffordshire Railway - encountered on a number of occasions in this guide en route to Dudley - crosses the canal at Streethay where there is a busy boatyard. Old maps show that the wharf buildings were originally maltings. By Bridge 87 a stone milepost quotes three miles from Whittington and two and a half to Fradley.

Near Bridge 88 stands Fradley Pumping Station, a handsome assemblage of boiler houses and quaint employees' cottages with half-timbered gables belonging to the South Staffordshire Waterworks Company and dating from 1891. Did coal to fire the pumps come in by boat or train? Old maps show neither a dock, nor a siding off the adjoining railway, so perhaps it was simply shovelled ashore and carted across the road. Bridge 89 carries Ryknild Street across the canal, and one can't help wondering what the Romans would have made of the modern A38 and the distribution hubs of Fradley Park which feed a constant stream of juggernauts onto it. The growth of canalside housing has exorcised this section of the Coventry Canal's formerly fey atmosphere. Thus, it's difficult now, to equate it with

Where Huddlesford is shy and retiring, Fradley is as gregarious as canal junctions get. And yet canals invariably have a knack of absorbing hordes of humanity without losing face. We've always maintained that it's Fradley's simplicity which appeals, a canal community in microcosm, the Swan Inn its cynosure, and a well earned pint at the end of a long day's canalling.

## Hopwas
Map 29

18th century river bridge, 19th century church (in Arts & Crafts style) and ornate waterworks.

### Eating & Drinking
TAME OTTER - Lichfield Road. Tel: 01827 53361. Canalside (on towpath side) 'Vintage Inn' with an entertaining pun to its name. Open from noon daily, food served throughout. B78 3AF

RED LION - Lichfield Road Bridge. Tel: 01827 62514. Homely canalside (offside) pub with large garden and children's play area. Open daily from 10am for breakfasts and food throughout the day. B78 3AF

### Connections
BUSES - Arriva service 765 runs hourly, daily to/from Lichfield and Tamworth. X65 provides an additional half-hourly service Mon-Sat. Tel: 0871 200 2233.

## Whittington
Map 29

Whittington History Society's website is exemplary. From it we gleaned that Thomas Spencer, co-founder of M&S, lies buried in St Giles churchyard, having retired comparatively early from retailing and bought a farm in the neighbourhood. Another significant resident was the architect Samuel Lipscomb Seckham, developer of Park Town, Oxford, and erstwhile owner of Bletchley Park, Buckinghamshire, the WWII code-breaking centre, who dwelt at the Old Hall.

### Eating & Drinking
BELL INN - Main Street. Tel: 01543 432377. Beamy village pub. Food lunchtimes and evenings. Draught Bass, Pedigree etc. WS14 9JR

DOG INN - Main Street. Tel: 01543 433091. Comfortable pub offering accommodation. Good choice of food Tue-Sat lunchtimes and evenings from 5pm. Sun 12-5pm. Black Sheep, GK Abbot. WS14 9JU

WHITTINGTON CANTONESE - Main Street. Tel: 01543 433397. Chinese takeaway. WS14 9JU

### Shopping
Co-op store, newsagent and pharmacy. Food/craft market 3rd Saturday monthly.

### Things to Do
STAFFORDSHIRE REGIMENT MUSEUM - Whittington Barracks, Tamworth Road. Tel: 01543 434394. History of the Staffordshire Regiment from its formation in 1705 up to current incorporation in Mercian Regiment. Open daily 10am-4pm. Most easily accessed by catching 765 bus from village. WS14 9PY

### Connections
BUSES - Arriva service 765 runs hourly Mon-Sat to/from Lichfield and Tamworth. Tel: 0871 200 2233.

## Huddlesford
Map 30

### Eating & Drinking
THE PLOUGH - Huddlesford Lane. Tel: 01543 432369. Comfortably furnished canalside pub open from 11am daily with food throughout. WS13 8PY

## Lichfield
(Map 30)

Those three spires on the horizon are difficult to resist, and this small cathedral city lies just a bus, taxi or bicycle ride away from various points of the Coventry and Trent & Mersey canals. Moreover, there's the lure of Dr Johnson - and his sidekick, Boswell - both of whom are remembered by statues in the market square. So it would be remiss not to make a conscious detour to soak up Lichfield's atmosphere.

### Eating & Drinking
EGO - Bird Street. Tel: 01543 258234. Mediterranean restaurant and bar ovelooking the Minster Pool with views to the cathedral beyond. Open from 11am daily. WS13 6PW

### Shopping
Markets Tue, Fri & Sat; Farmers' & Crafts 1st Thursday.

### Things to Do
TOURIST INFORMATION - St Mary's, Market Square. Tel: 01543 308924.

SAMUEL JOHNSON BIRTHPLACE - Breadmarket Street. Tel: 01543 264972. WS13 6LG

ERASMUS DARWIN HOUSE - Beacon Street. Tel: 01543 306260. Home of Charles Darwin's grandfather and friend of Josiah Wedgwood. WS13 7AD

### Connections
BUSES - Midland Classic 812 operates hourly Mon-Sat to Lichfield from Fradley Park (stop adjacent Bridge 90A). X12 operates hourly Mon-Fri from Streethay to Lichfield. Tel: 01283 500228.

TRAINS - stations at Trent Valley (for Birmingham, London and the North) and City (for Birmingham). TAXIS - VIP. Tel: 01543 547979.

## Fradley Junction
Map 30

### Eating & Drinking
THE SWAN - canalside, Fradley Junction. Tel: 01283 790330. This well known former boatmen's pub plays a leading role in the social life of Fradley Junction. Open from 11am, food lunch & evening daily. Everard's & guest ales. DE13 7DN

LAUGHING DUCK - cafe located in part of the former maintenance yard buildings. Outdoor waterside tables. Tel: 01283 792508. DE13 7DN

CANALSIDE CAFE BISTRO - cafe connected to holiday park. Tel: 01283 792919. DE13 7DN

FRADLEY FRYER - Tye Road. Tel: 01543 449291. New build fish & chip shop to SW of Bridge 90A. Lunch and evening (from 4.45pm) daily ex Sun. WS13 8ST

BILASH SPICE - Tye Road. Tel: 01543 444637. Balti & Tandoori restaurant/take-away. WS13 8ST

### Shopping
Well-stocked Co-op, butcher and pharmacy 10 mins walk south-west of Bridge 90.

**M**ILEPOST 26/66 marks the southernmost tip of the Trent & Mersey Canal's 92-mile odyssey from Preston Brook near Runcorn to Shardlow near Derby. Doing the Black Country Ring, you keep it company for a mere 13 miles. But largely agreeable miles they are, predominantly rural, and downright beautiful by the time you get to the forested flanks of Cannock Chase.

HS2's extension from the Midlands to Manchester is earmarked to cross the canal around the corner from Woodend Lock. As initially surveyed, it would have crossed three times in quick succession, but interventions from various inland waterway bodies happily saw this reduced more sensibly to one.

North-westwards from Woodend the canal winds through a village-less tract of country, comprehensively agricultural now, but betraying signs of the wild heathland it must once have been in its sandy soil, gorse, bracken and gnarled oaks.

From Bridge 58 it's but a short stroll to the old High

Bridge across the Trent. Rendered obsolete by a contemporary concrete span entirely without aesthetic value, the older structure's contrastingly graceful cast iron span was made at Coalbrookdale in 1830. We're not convinced, however, that the bridge's current livery of dull maroon and green does it full justice. Nevertheless, it's pleasant to stand on the old bridge for a while, watching the Trent flowing below, whilst idly wondering what's for tea.

Armitage and Shanks are synonymous with toilet plumbing, their trade marks are emblazoned on public conveniences throughout the world; though inevitably more focussed on by males. Once they were separate firms - they merged in 1969 - but the site alongside the canal at Armitage dates back to 1817. Sanitaryware became a speciality in the 19th century under the management of Edward Johns - the origin of the Americanism 'going to the John'. Today the works is part of the Ideal Standard group, though the days when raw materials came in by boat and finished sanitaryware went out are a distant memory.

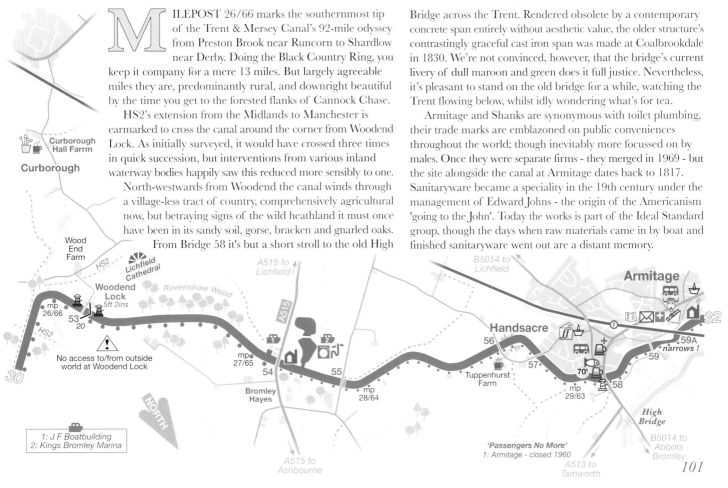

A tempting path leaves the towpath between bridges 60 and 61. It tunnels beneath the railway, thence over the Trent on a slender iron footbridge dated 1866. A field away lies the isolated settlement of Mavesyn Ridware which gained the first part of its name from the Norman lords of the manor, the Malvoisin family, and the second part from the Anglo-Saxon for 'river people'. All Mavesyn has to offer is peace and calm, but sometimes - as with your nearest and dearest - you just feel an urge to turn your back on the canal. Of note are a 17th century timber-framed barn, a gatehouse, and the half stone, half brick (entirely locked) church of St Nicholas with a Victorian postbox in its perimeter wall. If Wikipedia can be relied upon, Henry Fourdrinier the notable paper maker, passed his last years at the Old Rectory. Neighbouring Ridwares rejoice in the euphonious prefixes: Pipe, Hill and Hamstall.

Squeezing beneath the A513, the canal negotiates a rocky cutting. One-way working is the order of the day. This was formerly the site of Armitage (or "Plum Pudding") Tunnel, a dramatic, unlined bore through the rock face. An evocative painting of it by Brian Collings adorned the first edition of Tom Foxon's working boatman memoir *No.1*. Subsidence, brought about by coal mining, necessitated opening out of the tunnel (in 1971) and raising of the canal banks. Note how high the canal is now above the Plum Pudding inn with which it was once level.

Emerging from the cutting, the exotic outlines of Hawkesyard Hall present themselves for your appraisal. It once belonged to Josiah Spode, a member of the North Staffordshire pottery dynasty. Following his death it passed to a Dominican Order in 1893 and the monks proceeded to build a priory in the grounds. The buildings now house, somewhat less piously, a conference centre.

⚠ One-way working through Armitage 'tunnel'.
Ensure way ahead clear before proceeding.

## ○ Key
A site of Lea Hall Colliery
B site of Brereton Colliery basin
C site of Brereton Brewery
D former Trent & Mersey flour mill
E site of Phoenix Tannery
F site of Colton Mill (cement/paint)
G site of Rugeley Power Station

Lea Hall Colliery (1960-1990) stood canalside and was, initially, a showcase pit for the NCB, much of its output making the shortest of journeys to an adjacent power station, closed itself in 2016; its four cooling towers spectacularly demolished on 6th June 2021. 'No carbon emissions here, chum!' An industrial estate has replaced the colliery, Amazon a notable occupant. Bridge 65B carries the 'Chase Line' railway across the canal. It's led a chequered career. Opened in 1859, it was a victim of the Beeching axe in 1965, only to re-open in 1997. In 2019 it was electrified; a year and a half behind schedule and three times over budget. Reflect, then, how much Beeching's 'savings' must have cost in the longer term.

Rugeley gets a bad press from most guide-books which condescend to mention it at all, but we have always had a soft spot for this down to earth little town, formerly known for its tanneries; as the home of the notorious Victorian poisoner, William Palmer; and as the scene, in 1839, of the canal murder of Christina Collins. In the churchyard of St Augustine's (adjacent Bridge 67) an isolated gravestone marks her last resting place, noting that 'having been most barbarously treated was found dead in the Canal in this parish on 17th June 1839'. The story behind her misadventure - for which two boatmen were hung publicly at Stafford Gaol - inspired Colin Dexter's Inspector Morse story *The Wench is Dead*.

At Brindley Bank the canal suddenly stops running parallel to the Trent and turns sharply to cross it. Once there was a wharf here where flint was swapped between canal and river vessels for the short run down to Colton Mill by Trent Valley railway station. By Bridge 68 a short reedy arm adjacent to the railway provides a useful turning point for lengthy craft. It occurs to us that this may have been used as a transhipment basin in the fledgling days of the railway, perhaps for the conveyance of building materials.

## Handsacre
Map 31

Difficult to know where Handsacre begins and Armitage ends, let alone to care, but the facilities are undoubtedly useful and there's High Bridge to admire.

### Eating & Drinking
MICHAEL'S - The Green. Tel: 01543 491314. Lengthy queues for great ('Italian') fish & chips. WS15 4DT
TUPPENHURST FARM CAFE - Tuppenhurst Lane (Bridge 56). Tel: 01543 491955. Open Wed-Sun, 10am-3pm. B&B and machinery museum. WS15 4HJ
*Plus two pubs: The Crown Inn (Tel: 01543 318164) and The Olde Peculiar (Tel: 01543 491891) and a Chinese take-away on Tuppenhurst Lane (Tel: 01543 493123)..*

### Shopping
Convenience store on Tuppenhurst Lane, four minutes walk from Bridge 58.

## Armitage
Map 31

Offside moorings provide access via an alleyway to a goodly number of shops on the main road.

### Eating & Drinking
PLUM PUDDING INN - Rugeley Road (Bridge 61A). Tel: 01543 490330. Canalside pub (previously an Italian restaurant) open from noon daily. WS15 4AZ
ASH TREE - canalside Bridge 62. Tel: 01889 578314. Marston's 'Two for One' pub/restaurant. WS15 1PF

### Shopping
Butcher/baker, post office, pharmacy, convenience store and fishing tackle shop.

### Connections
BUSES - Chaserider services 826/8 as per Rugeley.

## Rugeley
Map 32

Stoic little town which is often, undeservedly, cold-shouldered by canallers. The high-spired Catholic church is by Hansom, inventor of the horse-drawn cab. Miners statues on Globe traffic island.

### Eating & Drinking
COLLIERS - Power Station Road. Tel: 01889 503951. TableTable pub/restaurant. Breakfast from 6.30am (7am at weekends) and for all day food after 11.30am. Access from canal near Bridge 65A. WS15 1LX
PLAZA - Horsefair. Tel: 01889 586831. Wetherspoons characterfully housed in old cinema. Local beers. Open from 8am. WS15 2EJ
TERRAZZA - Lichfield Street. Tel: 01889 570630. Homely and welcoming Italian restaurant open Tue-Sat from 6pm. WS15 2EH

### Shopping
Moor either side of Bridge 66 for access to town centre: Morrisons, Tesco and Aldi supermarkets. Market Hall and outdoor markets Tue, Thur, Fri & Sat.

### Connections
BUSES - Chaserider services 826/8 (half-hourly) to/from Stafford and Lichfield. Tel: 0871 200 2233.
TRAINS - useful hourly London Northwestern service along the Trent Valley and half-hourly from Town or Trent Valley stations to Walsall and Birmingham. Tel: 0345 748 4950.
TAXIS - AJ. Tel: 01889 585858.

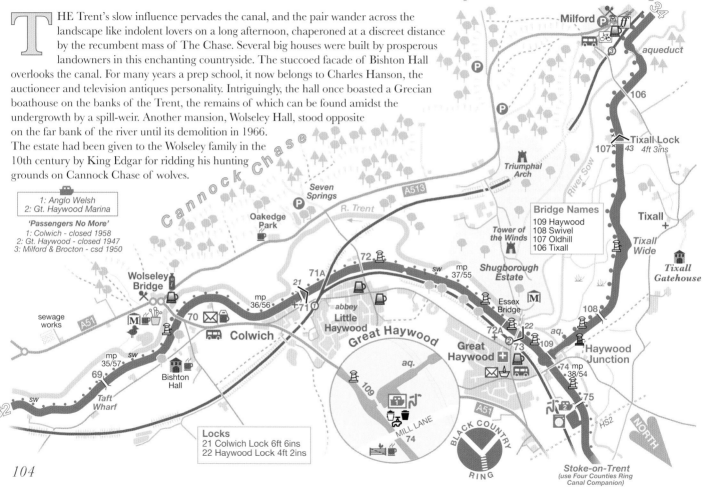

THE Trent's slow influence pervades the canal, and the pair wander across the landscape like indolent lovers on a long afternoon, chaperoned at a discreet distance by the recumbent mass of The Chase. Several big houses were built by prosperous landowners in this enchanting countryside. The stuccoed facade of Bishton Hall overlooks the canal. For many years a prep school, it now belongs to Charles Hanson, the auctioneer and television antiques personality. Intriguingly, the hall once boasted a Grecian boathouse on the banks of the Trent, the remains of which can be found amidst the undergrowth by a spill-weir. Another mansion, Wolseley Hall, stood opposite on the far bank of the river until its demolition in 1966. The estate had been given to the Wolseley family in the 10th century by King Edgar for ridding his hunting grounds on Cannock Chase of wolves.

**Cannock Chase**

1: Anglo Welsh
2: Gt. Haywood Marina

**'Passengers No More'**
1: Colwich - closed 1958
2: Gt. Haywood - closed 1947
3: Milford & Brocton - csd 1950

Milford

aqueduct

106

Tixall Lock
43  4ft 3ins

107

Triumphal Arch

River Sow

Tixall

Tixall Wide

Tixall Gatehouse

Seven Springs

Oakedge Park

R. Trent

Tower of the Winds

Shugborough Estate

**Bridge Names**
109 Haywood
108 Swivel
107 Oldhill
106 Tixall

72

71A

mp 37/55

sw

108

Wolseley Bridge

21

71

mp 36/56

abbey

Essex Bridge

72A

22

109

aq.

Haywood Junction

sewage works

70

mp 35/57

sw

Colwich

Little Haywood

Great Haywood

73

74  mp 38/54

75

69

Bishton Hall

Taft Wharf

sw

aq.

109

Great Haywood

MILL LANE
74

A51

HS2

NORTH

**Locks**
21 Colwich Lock 6ft 6ins
22 Haywood Lock 4ft 2ins

BLACK COUNTRY RING

Stoke-on-Trent
(use Four Counties Ring
Canal Companion)

Colwich Lock

Great Haywood

The 11th Baronet, Sir Charles Wolseley, attempted to transform the grounds into a Garden Park in the 1990s, but was bankrupted in the process. His home, Park House, was seized by those paragons of fiscal probity, the Royal Bank of Scotland, and sold to pay off his debts. As one observer caustically observed, 'the baronet had failed to keep the wolves from his door'. After the failure of the garden park project, Staffordshire Wildlife Trust acquired the grounds as their headquarters and a visitor centre. Sir Charles died a pauper, though far from friendless, in 2018.

Wolseley Bridge has graced the Trent since 1800. It was designed by John Rennie, best known in canal circles for his work on the Kennet & Avon. The Staffordshire Way joins the towpath at Bridge 68 and follows the canal as far as Great Haywood, before disappearing off into the grounds of Shugborough on its way to the southernmost tip of the county at Kinver Edge (Map 5). On foot, Kinver is thus approximately forty miles and about fifteen hours away; by boat the respective figures are a not dissimilar thirty-six miles and eighteen hours. Race you!

Colwich Lock lies in an attractive setting between the village church, a picturesque farm, and a bend in the river. From Bridge 72 you can take an idyllic walk to Severn Springs, a wonderful springboard for exploring Cannock Chase. Between frequent trains roaring across the bifurcation of the main lines to Manchester and Scotland, bells ring out from St Mary's abbey, occupied by Benedictine nuns who can trace their origins back to 17th century Flanders. They've been in Colwich since 1836, residents of a gothic pile built by an 18th century member of the Trubshaw architectural dynasty. Solely six nuns and a dog inhabit the abbey now, but it's somehow inspiring to encounter so tiny an enclosed community existing devoutly out of kilter with the cut and thrust of the modern world.

Between Colwich and Great Haywood the Trent & Mersey is arguably at its most bewitchingly beautiful as it skirts the boundary of Shugborough. On one bank beechwoods tumble down to the water's edge. On the other, across the Trent, there are glimpses of the statues, antiquities and follies which pepper the grounds of this famous property.

Tixall Wide

Sow Aqueduct, Milford

Brindley invariably found it simpler to follow river valleys, and Great Haywood was an obvious choice of location for a canal junction designed to establish his scheme for a 'Grand Cross' of man made waterways linking the four great English estuaries: Humber, Thames, Severn and Mersey. With the completion of the Staffordshire & Worcestershire Canal in 1772, and the Trent & Mersey five years later, Haywood became a canal junction of major importance, as significant to transport in the 18th century as any motorway interchange today. One is only left to marvel at the simplicity of it all - two quiet ribbons of water meeting beneath a bridge of exquisite beauty - and compare it wistfully with transport interchanges of the 21st century, acres of concrete, noise and pollution. Where did we go wrong? History may have taken some wrong turnings, but there is little chance for the canal traveller to make a mistake, for a prominent fingerpost directs one concisely enough to "Wolverhampton", "The Trent", or "The Potteries". If the latter is for you, turn to the Four Counties Ring Canal Companion.

## Staffordshire & Worcestershire Canal

Through the charming arch of Bridge 109 the Staffordshire & Worcestershire Canal commences its 46 mile journey down to the Severn at Stourport. Presently, the canal casts off its inhibitions and widens into a broad lake of quite un-canal-like proportions, bordered by thick reedbeds inhabited by a gorgeous array of wildfowl. Boaters will find their craft looping the loop out of sheer exuberance. This is Tixall Wide or Broadwater and there are two theories for its surprising existence. Some maintain that the canal was widened into an artificial lake to placate the owner of Tixall Hall. Others that the expanse of water predates the canal, that it was naturally formed, and that Izaak Walton learnt to fish here. Whichever explanation suits you, don't miss the extraordinary Elizabethan gatehouse which overlooks the Wide. The hall itself, where Mary Queen of Scots was imprisoned for a fortnight in 1586, was demolished long ago. The gatehouse is let for holidays by the Landmark

Trust who specialise in restoring and holiday-letting properties worth saving from neglect or demolition.

West of Tixall's solitary lock the canal meanders enchantingly through the valley of the Sow, bridging the river by way of a low-slung Brindley masonry aqueduct. Southbound trains on the neighbouring railway are gobbled up by the decorated portal of Shugborough Tunnel. Those of a railway bent may be intrigued to learn that Francis William Webb, the great locomotive engineer of the London & North Western Railway, hailed from Tixall, where his father was Rector for over half a century.

## Wolseley Bridge — Map 33

An eclectic community centred on a pair of busy roundabouts. A reconstructed barn houses an antiques outlet and there's a cluster of other rescued buildings and artefacts: dovecot, RAC patrolman's hut, and a William Foster threshing machine bearing the Lincoln agricultural machinery firm's WWI tank trademark.

### Eating & Drinking

WOLSELEY ARMS - far side of river bridge. Tel: 01889 883179. Vintage Inns establishment, once the meeting place for the canal's promoters. Food served daily throughout from noon. ST17 0XS

SHIMLA PALACE - far side of river bridge by roundabout. Tel: 01889 881325. Indian restaurant, eat in or takeaway. Open from 5.30pm daily. ST17 0XS

### Things to Do

BISHTON HALL - Wolseley Bridge. Tel: 01889 882397. Antique auctions and valuation days. Tea room (ex Mon) and courtyard shopping. ST17 0XN

THE WOLSELEY CENTRE - far side of river bridge beyond roundabout. Tel: 01889 880100. Staffordshire Wildlife Trust headquarters set in revitalised garden park: paths, hides and sensory garden. ST17 0WT

### Connections

BUSES - Chaserider services 826/8 provide a half-hourly link Mon-Sat with Rugeley (and Lichfield) and Stafford. Tel: 0871 200 2233.

## The Haywoods — Map 33

The villages of Great and Little Haywood are separated by a long, high 'make-work' wall. Dormitory housing has significantly expanded both populations, but the centres remain peaceful and largely unspoilt; especially so in the charming lane leading from Great Haywood, under the railway and over the canal, to the Essex Bridge, one of the finest examples of a packhorse bridge imaginable. Tolkien convalesced in Great Haywood after catching trench fever during the Battle of the Somme, and it is thinly disguised as 'Tavrobel' in *The Tale of The Sun and The Moon*. It is further suggested that the rivers Gruir and Afros, which feature in that story, were inspired by the Trent and Sow.

### Eating & Drinking

CANALSIDE CAFE - Mill Lane (Bridge 74). Tel: 01889 881747. Open 9am-5pm daily. Nicely furnished and airy waterside premises. Coffees, teas and lunches etc. ST18 0RQ

CLIFFORD ARMS - Main Road. Tel: 01889 881321. Open daily from noon. Bar food lunchtimes and evenings from 6pm. Restaurant open for dinner Mon-Fri and lunch Sat & Sun. ST18 0SR.

*Two pubs in Little Haywood: Lamb & Flag (Tel: 01889 881501) and Red Lion (Tel: 01889 881314).*

### Shopping

Great Haywood has a Spar convenience store with Post Office counter, a pharmacy and a superbly-stocked farm shop (with butchery and pick your own fruit opportunities) alongside the junction. Laundry facilities are available for resident and overnight moorers at Great Haywood Marina quarter of a mile north of the junction.

### Things to Do

SHUGBOROUGH - access from canal via Haywood Lock and Essex Bridge. Extensive estate and National Trust property associated with the seafaring Anson family. Open daily throughout the year, but some restrictions on access to house. Admission charge. Tel: 01889 880160. ST17 0XA

### Connections

BUSES - Chaserider service 828 operates hourly Mon-Sat to Stafford and Lichfield via Rugeley. Tel: 0871 200 2233.

## Milford — Maps 33/34

Motorist's gateway to The Chase. Canallers' access via partially unpavemented Holidiford Road from Bridge 106. (Path from 105 is *not* a right of way!)

### Eating & Drinking

BARLEY MOW - Main Road. Tel: 01785 665230. Greene King 'Eating-Inn' pub/restaurant open from 9am daily with food served throughout. ST17 0UW

*There is also an Indian restaurant/take-away (Tel: 01785 663239), Wimpy fast food outlet and ceramic cafe.*

### Things to Do

RUN & RIDE - Main Road. Tel: 01785 662769. Substantial bike shop for hire/repair etc. ST17 0UW

### Connections

BUSES - Chaserider service 826 operates hourly (ex Sun) to/from Stafford and Lichfield. Tel: 0871 200 2233.

# 34 STAFFS & WORCS CANAL Stafford 4mls/11k/1½hrs

THE canal cold-shoulders the county town. Nothing personal, it would have incurred a great deal of extra work on Brindley's part to take the canal across the marshy valleys of the Sow and Penk. But later - in 1816, to be precise - the Sow was made navigable into the centre of Stafford, and remained so up until the 1920s. J. Ian Langford, in *Towpath Guide No. 1*, recalls that Ernie Thomas, a renowned boatman, carried a cargo of swedes and mangels down the branch just before the Great War. A group known as the Stafford Riverway Link are actively promoting restoration of navigability into the centre of town, a thoroughly worthwhile cause. Meanwhile you can walk there (half an hour at a brisk pace) along the riverbank past the

cleared site of English Electric's engineering works in the process of being redeveloped as housing.

Baswich church stands aloof above housing estates like a shy vicar impelled to attend a noisy children's party. Note the spelling of the village's name with a 'k' on Bridge 100. There was a substantial wharf by Radford Bridge, but its site is now somewhat less interestingly occupied by a car showroom following demolition of the original warehouses in the Philistine seventies.

Stafford Boat Club - with their impressive club house and warm welcome to visiting boaters - occupy a former brickworks arm near Hazelstrine Bridge. Most of the works' output was despatched by canal. Bridge 97 has disappeared completely, there being not even any tell-tale narrowing in the canal's channel where it once must have stood.

Radford Meadows form part of the River Penk's floodplain and are now administered by the Staffordshire Wildlife Trust as a nature reserve. Public access is restricted to special events, but the towpath offers fine views and interpretive boards.

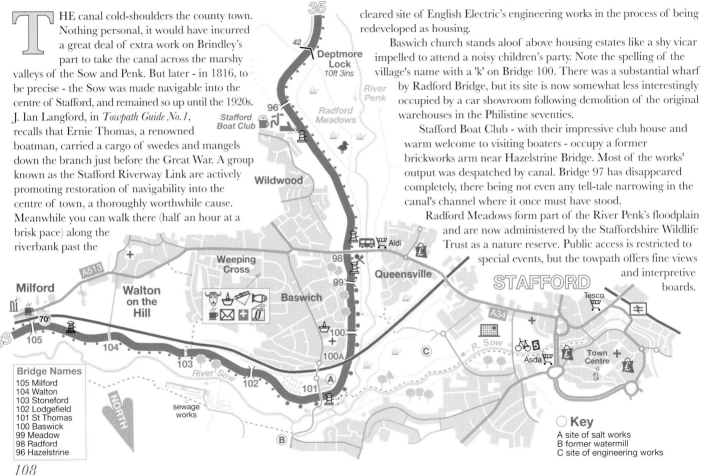

Bridge Names
105 Milford
104 Walton
103 Stoneford
102 Lodgefield
101 St Thomas
100 Baswick
99 Meadow
98 Radford
96 Hazelstrine

Key
A site of salt works
B former watermill
C site of engineering works

# Stafford
Map 34

A rather attractive county town on closer acquaintance. Frustratingly for canal folk, however, the centre lies over a mile from Radford Bridge. But there are frequent buses, and those with time at their disposal will find Stafford a rewarding place to visit. First stop should be the Ancient High House in Greengate Street. Dating from 1595, it is thought to be the largest timber-framed town house remaining in England. Inside there's a heritage exhibition tracing Stafford's history since 913 when Ethelfleda, daughter of Alfred the Great, fortified the settlement against marauding Danish invaders. King Charles I stayed at High House in 1642, and in later years Izaak Walton visited relatives who owned it. An alleyway beguiles you off Greengate Street to discover the town's large parish church of St Mary, much restored by Gilbert Scott in the 1840s and containing a bust of Izaak Walton. Another delightful church worth visiting is St Chad's on Greengate Street. Some impressive buildings reflect the town's administrative importance and lend it an almost metropolitan air.

## Eating & Drinking
RADFORD BANK - canalside Bridge 98. Tel: 01785 242825. Stonehouse pizza and carvery restaurant open from 9am daily. ST17 4PG
THE SOUP KITCHEN - Church Lane. Tel: 01785 254775. Open 9am-4.30pm Mon-Sat. Quaint, sprawling eatery with attentive staff serving coffees, lunches and teas. Rooftop garden. ST16 2AW
*Nandos, Frankie & Benny and Zizzi restaurants at Riverside retail park beside the Sow.*

## Shopping
Comprehensive shopping centre featuring all the well known 'high street' names plus many attractive individual shops tucked away down twisting side streets. Large Asda and Tesco supermarkets. Indoor market (Earl Street) Tue, Thur, Fri & Sat. Farmers' Market on the second Saturday in the month. Aldi 5 minutes west of Bridge 98. Good range of suburban shops on Bodmin Avenue in Baswich about 15 minutes walk east of Bridge 99.

## Things to Do
TOURIST INFORMATION - Gatehouse Theatre, Market Street. Tel: 01785 619619. ST16 2LT
ANCIENT HIGH HOUSE - Greengate Street. Tel: 01785 619131. Local history and gifts. ST16 2JA
STAFFORD CASTLE - Tel: 01785 257698. Preserved Norman remains on western outskirts. ST16 1DJ

## Connections
BUSES - services 6 and 826/7 run from Radford (Bridge 98) at frequent intervals to/from the town centre. Tel: 0871 200 2233.
TAXIS - Stafford Taxis. Tel: 01785 500123.
TRAINS - Important railhead with wide variety of services. Tel: 0345 748 4950. Useful links with Penkridge and Rugeley for clued-up towpath walkers.

# Acton Trussell
Map 35

THE MOAT HOUSE - canalside Bridge 92. Tel: 01785 712217. Four star hotel in former moated farmhouse: restaurant and bars, lovely gardens. Lunches and dinners (from 6.30pm weekdays, 7pm Sat). Food served noon-5.30pm on Sundays. ST17 0RG

# Penkridge
Map 35

A congenial little town in which to break your journey on the northern section of the Staffs & Worcs. Five minutes walk from the wharf will take you to the narrow main street, a pleasant spot to shop and saunter. At its foot stands St Michael's, an impressive church of sandstone, and formerly a collegiate church, considered second only to a cathedral in status.

## Eating & Drinking
BOAT INN - Cannock Road (Bridge 86). Tel: 01785 715170. Greene King canalside pub offering lunches and evening meals (from 5.30pm) Mon-Fri and from noon throughout at weekends. ST19 5DT
CROSS KEYS - Filance Lane (Bridge 84). Tel: 01785 712826. A once isolated pub, described by Rolt in *Narrow Boat*, but now surrounded by a housing estate. Opens 11am, food throughout. ST19 5HJ
FLAMES - Mill Street. Tel: 01785 712955. Contemporary Eastern cuisine housed in one of Penkridge's most historic buildings. ST19 5AY

## Shopping
Convenience shops near bridges 84 and 86. The town centre, with its Co-op supermarket and other retailers, is 5 minutes walk from the canal. Butcher on A449. Down by the river, the outdoor market operates on Wednesdays and Saturdays 8am-3pm.

## Connections
BUSES - NatEX service 54 runs hourly ex Sun to Wolverhampton and Stafford. Tel: 0871 200 2233.
TRAINS - half-hourly London Northwestern services to Wolverhampton and Stafford. Tel: 0345 748 4950.
TAXIS - Corkys. Tel: 01543 505058.

# Coven
Maps 36/37

Coven's village centre is less than ten minutes walk from Bridge 71, but do take care crossing the A449.

## Eating & Drinking
ANCHOR INN - canalside north of Bridge 71. Tel: 01902 798786. Vintage Inns establishment offering food throughout from 11am daily. WV10 7PW
*Fish & chip shop, pub and cafe in the village centre.*

## Shopping
Co-op foodstore, butcher (on the road in) bakery, pharmacy, and post office.

# 35 STAFFS & WORCS CANAL Penkridge 4mls/5lks/2½hrs

CLIMBING steadily towards its summit, the Staffs & Worcs for the most part sustains its inherent rurality, which even the proximity of the M6 motorway can't impair. Acton Trussell - which you'd expect with such a name to be a picture book English village - fails to live up to expectations with its banal 1960s architecture. The solitary building on the towpath side used to be a boatman's pub. Present day boaters, however, slake their thirst in the old moated house by Bridge 92, now well-established as a bar, restaurant and hotel set in charming grounds. It is said that Brindley actually used the old house's moat for a few yards when building the canal: anything to save a few bob. The towpath between bridges 90 and 86 is 'hi-jacked' by the "Staffordshire Way" which seems forever to be bumping into canals and appropriating towpaths in the course of its 92 mile journey from Mow Cop

to Kinver Edge. Its route has come down off The Chase and crossed Teddesley Park. Teddesley Hall was the seat of Sir Edward Littleton, one of the chief promoters of the Staffordshire & Worcestershire Canal. Indeed, the family remained involved with the canal company until its nationalisation in 1947. The hall itself was demolished by the army in the mid Fifties (having been used as a prison camp for German officers during the Second World War) but the estate farm remains, hidden from the canal by some woodland known as Wellington Belt in commemoration of a visit to the hall by the Iron Duke. Bridge 89 once had ornate balustrades commensurate with its importance as the gateway to the hall, but, irresponsibly and unforgivably, these have been infilled by ugly brickwork. Penkridge's built-up outskirts can counter-intuitively come as a bit of a relief after all that open countryside. Trees are alright in their place, but nothing beats a good bungalow when you feel like being nosy.

**Bridge Names**
94 Roseford
93 Acton
92 Acton Moat
91 Shutt Hill
90 Park Gate
89 Teddesley Park
88 Longford
87A Woodbank Lane
87 Broom
86 Penkridge
85 Princefield
84 Filance
83A Cross Keys

**Locks**
41 Shutt Hill Lock 6ft 0ins
40 Park Gate Lock 7ft 6ins
39 Longford Lock 10ft 0ins
38 Penkridge Lock 9ft 3ins
37 Filance Lock 10ft 3ins

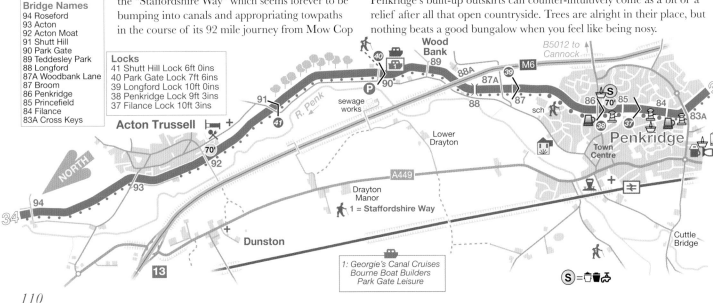

1: Georgie's Canal Cruises
Bourne Boat Builders
Park Gate Leisure

1 = Staffordshire Way

POSTCARD *from* PENKRIDGE

111

# 36 STAFFS & WORCS CANAL Gailey & Hatherton 6mls/5lks/3hrs

REACHING its summit - 340ft 6ins above sea level - at Gailey, the S&W has climbed a hundred feet from its junction with the T&M at Great Haywood: understandably, ordnance datum achieves more significance when travelling by canal than other modes of transport; if you've been doing the locks, every inch is personal!

The heron-grey girders of Bridge 80A carried the colliery railway to Littleton pit across the canal. In the early years of the Canal Companions it was still in use. But the mine closed in 1993, the last in the Cannock coalfield. As a nostalgic gesture a pair of steam saddle tanks, *Whiston* and *Wimblebury*, were employed to haul loaded wagons from the pit head to the

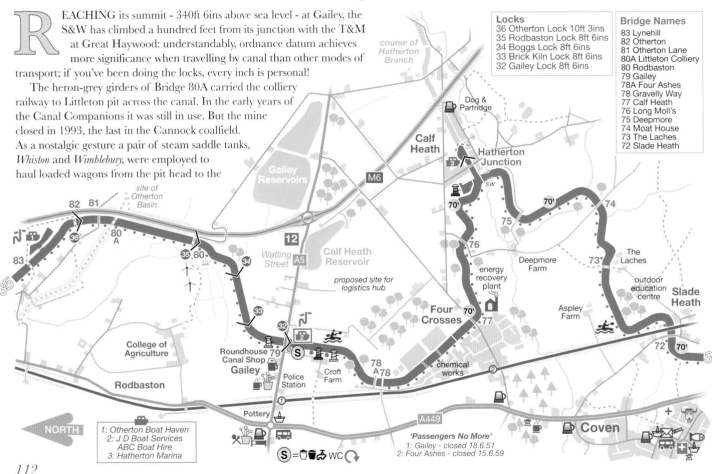

course of Hatherton Branch

**Locks**
36 Otherton Lock 10ft 3ins
35 Rodbaston Lock 8ft 6ins
34 Boggs Lock 8ft 6ins
33 Brick Kiln Lock 8ft 6ins
32 Gailey Lock 8ft 6ins

**Bridge Names**
83 Lynehill
82 Otherton
81 Otherton Lane
80A Littleton Colliery
80 Rodbaston
79 Gailey
78A Four Ashes
78 Gravelly Way
77 Calf Heath
76 Long Moll's
75 Deepmore
74 Moat House
73 The Laches
72 Slade Heath

Dog & Partridge

Calf Heath

Hatherton Junction

Gailey Reservoirs

M6

site of Otherton Basin

Watling Street

Calf Heath Reservoir

proposed site for logistics hub

College of Agriculture

Rodbaston

Roundhouse Canal Shop
Gailey

Police Station

Croft Farm

energy recovery plant

Deepmore Farm

Four Crosses

chemical works

The Laches

outdoor education centre

Slade Heath

Aspley Farm

Pottery

A449

Coven

1: Otherton Boat Haven
2: J D Boat Services
   ABC Boat Hire
3: Hatherton Marina

NORTH

**'Passengers No More'**
1: Gailey - closed 18.6.51
2: Four Ashes - closed 15.6.59

(S) = 🗑🍴♿ WC ↻

*112*

exchange sidings on the main line. There was also a huge basin, long since covered by the motorway, where boats were loaded by gravity from a raised pier. The chief traffic flow for Littleton coal in later years was to Stourport Power Station. Littleton featured in Chris Arnot's beautifully illustrated book *Britain's Lost Mines*, a bittersweet paean to lost endeavours, as were his companion volumes covering breweries and cricket grounds.

Rodbaston Lock boasted a keeper until the noise from the newly constructed motorway drove him out. With no one mad enough to live there, the cottage was subsequently demolished. West of the canal, pinpointed by twin wind turbines, stands Rodbaston Hall. The house dates from 1834 and once belonged to a Wolverhampton ironmaster. It's a wedding venue now, of course - isn't everywhere - but the extensive grounds play host to South Staffordshire College's agricultural and horticultural campus. A feeder from Gailey Reservoirs enters the canal at the tail of Boggs Lock. Divided by a dam, the upper pool is fished, the lower sailed; both are birdwatched.

Conquest of the summit comes at Gailey where the A5 - or, for those

Gailey Roundhouse

of a more romantic disposition, Watling Street - crosses the canal. If you're circumnavigating the 'Black Country Ring' you will also encounter it at Fazeley (Map 28). If you're destined for the wilds of the Wyrley & Essington you will rub shoulders with it at the extremities of the Cannock Extension Canal and Anglesey Branch (Map 42). By our calculations - yours may differ - the A5 crossed nineteen canal bridges on its way from London's Marble Arch to Holyhead on Anglesey.

A notable landmark for canallers and motorists alike, Gailey Roundhouse dates from the year of Trafalgar and may well have been inspired by the Martello towers of the Napoleonic wars. For many years it has been run as a delightful little canal shop by mother and daughter team Eileen and Karen Lester, but in updating this guide we learned, with considerable sadness, that Eileen at passed away in 2022. It goes without saying that she will be missed greatly, but Karen reassures us that she intends to keep the shop going. A busy hire base adds to Gailey Wharf's purposeful air,

Otherton Lock

*Meadowsweet & Poplars*

*Autherley Junction*

and canoeing takes place on the summit pound to boot.

Forgive us if we have remarked before - forty years of guidebook compilation invites repetition - on the remarkable ability of the English landscape - and its Celtic appurtenances - to change appearance in the blink of an eye. Not for us the monotony of the Pripyat Marshes or the Tarim Basin, England reinvents itself every other mile. It only seems five minutes ago that you were lolling about in the lush farmland of the upper Penk valley ... now you're traversing a strangely isolated tract of country known as Calf Heath, pancake flat and reminiscent of the sullen potato fields Van Gogh used to paint before he was blinded by the light of Arles.

Briefly the canal encounters an industrial zone: giant warehousing for automotive products, a chemical works (don't panic if the sirens wail) and an energy recovery plant - we could all do with one of those. The presence of an overbridge named Schenectady harks back to a period of American ownership. Otters are not unknown in this unpromising environment. Cannock Chase broods in the distance. Time to put the kettle on.

A youthful John Liley (*Journeys of the Swan*, *The Trouble With Canals* etc) and his family ventured up the Hatherton Branch in 1952, a fortnight after its abandonment; though no one had thought to erect a signboard to that effect. Photographs show them marooned in a sargasso sea of silt and weeds. Liley, like Aickman before him, was hooked by the air of dereliction, as many diehards are. Freud would have a theory.

The branch was opened in 1841 to tap the fruits of the Cannock coalfield. At Churchbridge (one of those nineteen canal crossings of the A5) a flight of thirteen locks connected with the Cannock Extension of the Wyrley & Essington Canal. The Lichfield & Hatherton Canals Trust have ambitions to reconnect the two, though a different route will need to be dug in the process - see Map 42. Meanwhile, the bottom lock at Hatherton Junction survives, providing access to moorings.

The classical stone abutments of the railway bridge at Slade Heath date back to the opening of the Grand Junction Railway in 1837, linking Birmingham with the north-west, a feat it still performs today, albeit with somewhat different rolling stock.

VISITOR moorings, either side of the Anchor Inn at Cross Green, make this a popular point to moor overnight, either before or after tackling the ladder of twenty-one locks which lead to or from the centre of Wolverhampton. Coven's shops (and fish & chips) lie less than ten minutes walk to the north-west, but take care crossing the A449, the road connects Newport in South Wales with Stafford, and many of its users seem determined to get there as quickly as possible.

Boaters tend not to pay much heed to fishing beat signage any more than motorists do manhole covers, but often the societies involved evoke lost industries and enterprises. Hereabouts one is reminded of Goodyear, the tyre makers, who once had a massive plant on the northern outskirts of Wolverhampton.

If it's your nose that's afflicted by the fruity aromas which emanate from the sewage works by Bridge 69, it's your ears which take the brunt of the M54, opened between the M6 and Telford in 1983. As you pass beneath the motorway you are crossing the county boundary between Staffordshire and something, invented by Ted Heath in 1974, inspirationally known as West Midlands.

i54 ('driving jobs, attracting business') is a 240 acre technology-based business park amongst whose blue-chip occupants Jaguar Land Rover are probably the best known. Employees use the towpath as a short cut to Morrisons for their take-away lunches. South of the motorway bridge on the towpath side there's access to a marshy nature reserve by way of a beguiling boardwalk.

In the vicinity of bridges 68 and 67, Pendeford 'Rockin' is the old boatmen's name for a shallow, but tellingly narrow cutting hewn by Brindley's navvies through a solid belt of sandstone which breaks through the clay strata at this point. There are, however, one or two passing places - as on a single lane road - where oncoming boats can be successfully negotiated without losing one's temper. Autherley and Aldersley junctions are often confused. The former provides access to the lovely Shropshire Union Canal, a 66 mile odyssey via Nantwich and Chester to Ellesmere Port on the banks of the River Mersey. The latter the inimitable BCN, of which more on Map 9.

**Bridge Names**
71 Cross Green
70 Brinsford
69 Coven Heath
68A M54
68 Forster
67 Marsh Lane
66 Blaydon Road
65 Oxley Moor

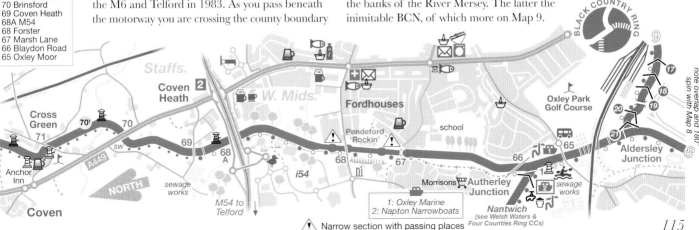

1: Oxley Marine
2: Napton Narrowboats

Nantwich
(see Welsh Waters &
Four Counties Ring CCs)

⚠ Narrow section with passing places

note overlap and 180° spin with Map 8

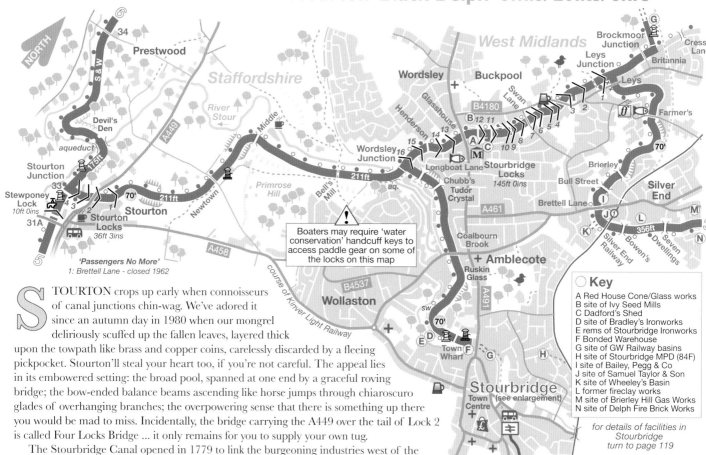

# 38 STOURBRIDGE CANAL  Stourton-Black Delph  5mls/20lks/6hrs

**West Midlands**

Brockmoor Junction

Cresse Lane

Britannia

Leys Junction

Leys

Prestwood

*Staffordshire*

Wordsley

Buckpool

34

S & W

Devil's Den

*aqueduct*

175ft

River Stour

Middle

Glasshouse

Swan Lane

B4180

Henderson

14 13

15

Wordsley Junction

16

Longboat Lane

211ft

Chubb's Tudor Crystal

B 12 11

A C

10 9 8

7 6 5 4

3 2 1

ff

Farmer's

70'

Brierley

Bull Street

Stourbridge Locks
145ft 0ins

Brettell Lane

Silver End

Stourton Junction

33

Stewponey Lock
10ft 0ins

31A

4 3 2 1

70'

211ft

Stourton

Newtown

Primrose Hill

Bell's Mill

aq.

A461

I

J

K

L

Bowen's
Silver End Railway

M

N

356ft

Seven Dwellings

3

Stourton Locks
36ft 3ins

!  Boaters may require 'water conservation' handcuff keys to access paddle gear on some of the locks on this map

Coalbourn Brook

A458

*'Passengers No More'*
1: Brettell Lane - closed 1962

A449

B4537

*course of Kinver Light Railway*

**Wollaston**

+ Amblecote

Ruskin Glass

A491

sw

70'

E D

Town Wharf

F

G

H

## Key

A Red House Cone/Glass works
B site of Ivy Seed Mills
C Dadford's Shed
D site of Bradley's Ironworks
E rems of Stourbridge Ironworks
F Bonded Warehouse
G site of GW Railway basins
H site of Stourbridge MPD (84F)
I site of Bailey, Pegg & Co
J site of Samuel Taylor & Son
K site of Wheeley's Basin
L former fireclay works
M site of Brierley Hill Gas Works
N site of Delph Fire Brick Works

**Stourbridge**
Town Centre

**Stourbridge** (see enlargement)

*for details of facilities in Stourbridge turn to page 119*

STOURTON crops up early when connoisseurs of canal junctions chin-wag. We've adored it since an autumn day in 1980 when our mongrel deliriously scuffed up the fallen leaves, layered thick upon the towpath like brass and copper coins, carelessly discarded by a fleeing pickpocket. Stourton'll steal your heart too, if you're not careful. The appeal lies in its embowered setting: the broad pool, spanned at one end by a graceful roving bridge; the bow-ended balance beams ascending like horse jumps through chiaroscuro glades of overhanging branches; the overpowering sense that there is something up there you would be mad to miss. Incidentally, the bridge carrying the A449 over the tail of Lock 2 is called Four Locks Bridge ... it only remains for you to supply your own tug.

The Stourbridge Canal opened in 1779 to link the burgeoning industries west of the

Rowley Hills with the Staffordshire & Worcestershire Canal, and thence the Severn. Its first two or three miles, however, give little hint of industry, past or present. And frankly, there is a precarious beauty about the canal's progress between the pony-grazed heights of Primrose Hill and the deep scoured valley of the Stour which brings to mind another of Staffordshire's well kept canal secrets, the Leek Arm of the Caldon Canal.

## Stourbridge Arm

Wordsley Junction provides the opportunity - not to be trifled with - for a detour to Stourbridge Town Wharf, though as summer gets into its stride, arrowhead and lilies lay claim to the margins; and not always merely the margins! New houses crowd in on surviving factories like teenagers jostling pensioners. Keep your eyes peeled for the old Dial glassworks by Chubbs Bridge (where a visit can be made to the Tudor Crystal Factory shop); Coalbourn Brook Bridge which used to carry the Kinver Light Railway (where a visit can be made to Ruskin Glass); and the remains of Stourbridge Iron Works where the first steam locomotive to operate in the USA was built. Named *Stourbridge Lion*, it puffed its way through Pennsylvania in 1829. The works had been founded by John Bradley in 1798. His name appears on the southernmost roving bridge, a diminutive structure of cast iron construction dated 1873. The arm terminates abruptly at the foot of Stourbridge High Street (though it used to run a short distance beyond to a railway transhipment basin) beside a handsomely restored bonded warehouse where secure visitor moorings, along with lavish boating facilities (pump-out, Elsan, water, gas, coal, canalia etc) are provided by the Stourbridge Navigation Trust.

## Stourbridge Sixteen

The flight is characterised by side ponds aiding and abetting water supply, though some are so reedy you wonder at their efficacy. The need for 'water conservation' T keys seems random: sometimes top paddles, sometimes bottom paddles, sometimes none at all; at least it keeps the vandals guessing. Evidence of the long deceased industries, whose trade made the Stourbridge Canal so prosperous in its heyday, is mostly confined to old

Stourton Locks

maps and the odd, heavily graffitied, intepretive board. But two classic survivors remain in the form of 'Dadford's Shed', a former transhipment warehouse built of timber and now partially used by a boatbuilder; and the massive Red House Cone (or kiln) which dates from the end of the 18th Century and which is now incorporated into a glass-making heritage centre. One enterprise sadly gone from the district was Ivy Mills, home of Webb's seed works, propagators of such sterling varieties as Wordsley Wonder peas and Stourbridge Glory potatoes.

Our most recent visit coincided with the progress up the flight of the Holt Abbott cruiser *Jemima*, built in Stourport in 1964. Holt Abbott was a pioneer of boatbuilding on the canals for pleasure use, and it was rewarding to see this historic vessel - a veteran of the Wash, the Broads and the Severn - making her stately way past Dadford's Shed. Doubly so when we learned that it was being crewed by her builder's daughter and

Lock 12

widely in the Crimean and Boer campaigns. In contrast, between Brettell Lane Bridge and Silver End Railway Bridge were Samuel Taylor & Son's chain and anchor works whose products could be found aboard those two great Cunarders: *Queen Mary* and *Queen Elizabeth*.

Also adjacent to the railway lay Wheeley's Basin, the subject of much acrimony between the canal and railway authorities in the 1850s, the former arguing that the latter were surreptitiously transhipping goods without paying tolls. In 1903 the bed of the basin caved in, flooding mine workings below. Remnants of some of the fire clay works which flourished hereabouts still manifest themselves beside the canal, before Brierley Hill's high-rises take their place. At Black Delph Junction the Stourbridge Canal makes an unheralded and imperceptible end-on junction with the Dudley No.1 Canal, and the next part of your journey is covered by Map 39.

son-in-law! Locks 9 and 10 are telescoped together like a mini-Bratch, and were similarly once a true staircase. The Bottle & Glass, which used to stand by Lock 3, now pulls pints in the Black Country Living Museum.

## Leys Junction - Black Delph

Leys Junction may not be much to look at now, but it is effectively the custom post to the lost worlds of the Fens Branch and Stourbridge Extension Canal. The SEC was opened in 1840, enjoying six brief years of independence before being absorbed by the Oxford, Worcester & Wolverhampton Railway. Its goal was the coal and ironstone deposits at Shut End, two miles to the north-west. Navigation is feasible as far as Brockmoor, where secure offside visitor moorings have been installed. But the setting is lugubrious to say the least, and one imagines that walkers will derive most pleasure from exploring these forgotten routes.

Between Bull Street and Brettell Lane bridges stood Bailey, Pegg & Company's ironworks. Primarily gunmakers, their weapons were used

Lock 8

# Stourbridge

Map 38

From the canal wharf, it's but a short walk through the underpass beneath the ring-road (which encircles the glass-making town of Stourbridge like a boa-constrictor) to the town centre. And how unexpected! For Stourbridge is not yet another Black Country throwback, but an independent market town with a profusion of shops and some not uninteresting architecture. Ascending Lower High Street one's eyes are drawn firstly to the elegant town house 'Stourhurst', secondly the Unitarian Chapel of 1788 and thirdly to the former Grammar School which even Nikolaus Pevsner (Teutonically predisposed to understatement) was moved to label 'picturesque'. At the top of the climb stands the town clock; imposing, fluted-columned, cast in the local iron works in 1857, and equipped with a match-striking plate (a typical piece of Victorian ingenuity) for passers by. On Market Street stands the Town Hall of 1887, red-bricked and high-towered. Further along is the Anglican church of St Thomas, dating from 1727: 'misses being a beautiful early Georgian church' thought James Lees-Milne, somewhat cuttingly.

## Eating & Drinking

CAFE DE PARIS - Foster Street. Tel: 01384 394026. Independent French restaurant: lunch Fri-Sun; dinner Wed-Sat from 6pm. DY8 1EL

CELLARS - Lower High Street. Tel: 01384 444829. Well appointed Indian restaurant within easy reach of the basin, open from 6pm daily. DY8 1TT

MITRE - Lower High Street. Tel: 01384 395374. Town centre 'Brewers Tudor' pub open from noon daily. Up to five real ales on tap. DY8 1TS

OLD WHARF INN - High Street. Tel: 01384 378798. Re-opened pub adjacent canal basin. From 4pm Mon & Tue and 10am Wed-Sun. Does food. DY8 4LY

Stourbridge FC

Bonded Warehouse

pedestrian subway

Stourbridge
1 Cellars
2 Old Wharf Inn
3 Royal Exchange
4 Cafe de Paris
5 Mitre

Greggs
Costa
KFC
McDonald's

ST JOHN'S ROAD

LOWER HIGH ST.

ENVILLE STREET

Nickolls & Perks

Tesco

Town Hall

BATH ROAD

MARKET STREET

HIGH STREET

Aldi

NEW ROAD

ROYAL EXCHANGE - Enville Street. Tel: 01384 396726. Batham's tied house offering only cobs and pork pies to support the serious business of downing this wonderful Black Country brew. DY8 1EX

SAMSON & LION - canalside Lock 4 of Stourbridge flight. Tel: 01384 480257. Banks's and Marston's beers, good food and a friendly atmosphere. DY8 5SP *A Chinese takeaway called 'White Rose' abuts the basin.*

## Shopping

There's a Tesco supermarket in the Crown Shopping Centre and a Waitrose supermarket in the Ryemarket Shopping Centre, whilst Aldi have a supermarket on New Road. Nickolls & Perks (established 1797) are wine merchants at the top of Lower High Street.

## Things to Do

RED HOUSE GLASS CONE - adjacent Lock 12 of Stourbridge flight. Tel: 01384 812750. Self guided audio tours, including ascent of spiral staircase within the vertigo-inducing hundred foot high cone itself. Crafts, gifts, refreshments etc. Open daily, free admission, offside moorings for boating visitors. DY8 4AZ Other glass makers include Tudor Crystal (Tel: 01384 392525) and Ruskin (Tel: 01384 399419). STOURBRIDGE NAVIGATION TRUST - Canal Street. Tel: 01384 395216. Administrators of town wharf and bonded warehouse. Pump-outs available 10.30am - 2.30pm Mon-Fri. DY8 4LU

## Connections

BUSES - services throughout the area from bus station at top of High Street. Select 242 runs hourly Mon-Sat to/from Kinver via Stewponey. Tel: 0871 200 2233. TRAINS - a pod-like 'people-mover' runs on Britain's shortest branch line between Stourbridge Town and Stourbridge Junction for connections to Birmingham and Worcester. One of the world's great *little* railway journeys. Tel: 0345 748 4950.

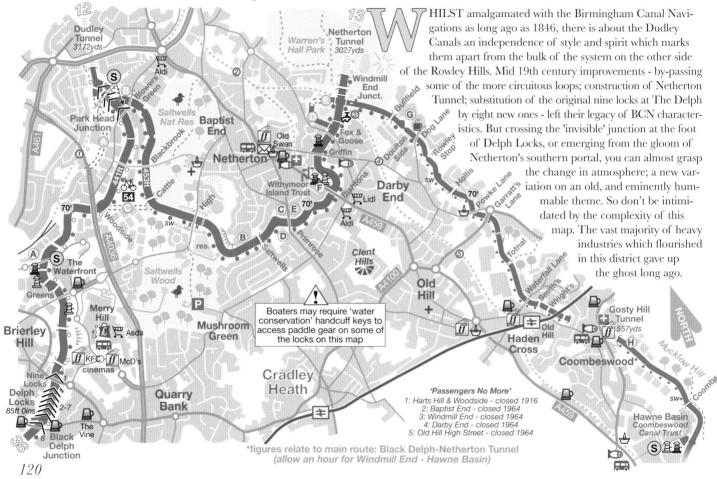

# 39 DUDLEY CANAL  Delph-Parkhead-Windmill End  5mls/9lks/3hrs*

WHILST amalgamated with the Birmingham Canal Navigations as long ago as 1846, there is about the Dudley Canals an independence of style and spirit which marks them apart from the bulk of the system on the other side of the Rowley Hills. Mid 19th century improvements - by-passing some of the more circuitous loops; construction of Netherton Tunnel; substitution of the original nine locks at The Delph by eight new ones - left their legacy of BCN characteristics. But crossing the 'invisible' junction at the foot of Delph Locks, or emerging from the gloom of Netherton's southern portal, you can almost grasp the change in atmosphere; a new variation on an old, and eminently hummable theme. So don't be intimidated by the complexity of this map. The vast majority of heavy industries which flourished in this district gave up the ghost long ago.

Boaters may require 'water conservation' handcuff keys to access paddle gear on some of the locks on this map

'Passengers No More'
1: Harts Hill & Woodside - closed 1916
2: Baptist End - closed 1964
3: Windmill End - closed 1964
4: Darby End - closed 1964
5: Old Hill High Street - closed 1964

*figures relate to main route: Black Delph-Netherton Tunnel
(allow an hour for Windmill End - Hawne Basin)

## Dudley No.1 Canal

The Delph was known in the 19th century as 'Black Delph' because of the proliferation of collieries in the vicinity. Nowadays 'Green' would be a more appropriate sobriquet. Delph Locks consist of eight chambers, of which six are in close proximity, carrying the canal from the 356ft level of the Stourbridge Canal to the 441ft contour of the Dudley No.1 Canal. The flight is one of the most spectacular anywhere on the canal system, but because of its location on the esoteric BCN it tends to be less celebrated than the likes of Bingley, Foxton and Devizes. On the off-side of the locks a series of overflow weirs cascade spectacularly when water levels are high. When the canal opened in 1779 there were nine locks. The top and bottom are originals, but in 1858 the present central six were built to replace seven earlier locks, traces of which can be explored to the east. A Horseley Iron Works roving bridge spans the original course of the canal below the top lock. In the middle of the flight a former block of canal horse stables is leased to the BCN Society and is occasionally open to the public.

Having acclimatized yourself to the 19th century environs of Black Delph, the next bend in the canal opens out to reveal the 21st century vista of Merry Hill, one of the out of town shopping developments akin to Sheffield's Meadowhall or the Metro Centre at Gateshead which we gladly seem to have grown out of; or perhaps simply can't afford to build anymore. The canal has been slightly rerouted and one benefit of this work is the provision of mooring rings for boaters intending to visit the centre; though many of you will doubtless have taken to the water to escape such manifestations of contemporary life.

The Waterfront, a billion pound development mixing commerce with leisure, occupies the site of the once vast Round Oak steel works. Aesthetically it is barely an improvement on the past: arguably the most satisfying building of the development is the pub, a pastiched cross between an East Anglian watermill and a Black Country foundry with plenty of mock weatherboarding and reconditioned brick; there must be a moral in that somewhere. Pre-book pontoon 'pay moorings' with electricity and water laid on are available if you're so inclined, a facility more likely to appeal to private boaters rather than hirers - telephone 01384 487911/2.

Passing the former junction of the Two Locks Line at Woodside Junction, the canal reaches the 12 feet deep Blower's Green Lock and Park Head Junction. Here the two Dudley Canals met, the No.1 Canal proceeding up the Park Head flight to the portal of Dudley Tunnel. The Dudley Canal Trust provide a tug service to haul boats through their Aladdin's Cave of a tunnel; though stringent size limitations apply. The Trust can be contacted (Tel: 0121 557 6265) for advice and further details, and the more advance warning they get of your intended passage the better. It is rewarding, however, to visit Park Head, if only to admire the handsome pump house - which the Trust have developed as an educational centre - and to take in the canal scene as a whole, and we can recommend mooring here and strolling up to view, not only the southern portal of Dudley Tunnel, but the interesting remains of the Pensnett Canal and Grazebrook Arm as well. Incidentally, the blue brick viaduct spanning the flight, last crossed by a train in 1993, will come back into use with the completion of the West Midlands Metro extension from Wednesbury through Dudley to Brierley Hill.

## Park Head - Windmill End

The Dudley No.2 Canal once totalled eleven route miles, linking the Dudley No.1 Canal at Park Head with the Worcester & Birmingham Canal at Selly Oak (Map 18). It was completed in 1798 and included Britain's fourth longest canal tunnel at Lapal (3795 yards), a daunting towpath-less bore subject to a unique system of operation whereby a steam

### ◯ Key
A site of Round Oak Steelworks
B site of chain and anchor works
C remains of Proving House
D former LNWR 'boatage' depot
E site of Hingley's Iron Works
F site of GWR Withymoor Basin
G site of Doulton's Pottery
H site of Coombeswood Tube Works

### ◉ Key
A Pensnett Canal
B Grazebrook Arm
C Two Locks Line
D Bumble Hole Arm
E Boshboil Arm

pumping engine produced an artificial bi-directional current through the tunnel to aid the momentum of boats passing through.

Between Park Head and Windmill End the canal describes a wide arc, clinging to the 453ft contour at the foot of Netherton Hill. Once upon a time industry congregated beside its banks: collieries, claypits, furnaces, limekilns and ironworks. But now this is coot country and the reeds seem as abundant as on any Broadland river. At Blackbrook Junction the other end of the Two Locks Line is still evident through its roving bridge, even if subsidence caused it to be abandoned in 1909. Clothed in gorse and hawthorn, Netherton Hill stands behind the erstwhile junction, climbing to a 600ft summit topped by St Andrew's church where cholera victims are buried in unmarked common graves in the churchyard. The surrounding environs offer generous views over towards the distant wooded tops of the Clent Hills rising to a thousand feet southwards beyond Halesowen.

A housing estate occupies the site of Doulton's once extensive clay pit

Park Head

linked to the canal by a tramway incline. Boats would carry this clay along the Dudley Canal to the firm's works at Darby End. High Bridge spans a rocky cutting where originally the canal builders built a short-lived tunnel. Nowadays the exhaust from your boat reverberates and rebounds between the sheer sandstone slopes of the cutting. No wonder the old boatmen nicknamed this 'Sounding Bridge'. Lodge Farm reservoir, used for watersports, gleams like antimony in its cup of land between the canal and Saltwells Nature Reserve.

We have seen elsewhere on the BCN how the railways developed a network of interchange basins and boatage depots. Two examples of this are encountered hereabouts. Primrose Boatage Depot provided the LMS Railway (and its antecedents) with water access to an area otherwise dominated by GWR lines. LMS boats traded between here and the company's interchange basins at Bloomfield (Map 12) and Albion (Map 13). Half a mile away, by Bishtons Bridge, the Great Western Railway's Withymoor Basin was one of the most extensive interchange points between rail and canal in its heyday. Withymoor opened in 1878 and closed in 1965. Its last regular transhipment cargo was chain from Lloyds Proving House by Primrose Bridge. Sadly (for who would not relish witnessing a Pannier tank noisily shunting wagons around its sidings?) its transhipment sheds and canopies have been demolished, but its arm survives in water, providing useful boating facilities (including pump-out on the main line) and residential moorings for the Withymoor Island Trust.

Mention of chain recalls that there was a tradition of chain and anchor making in this landlocked corner of the Black Country. Hard to credit, but *Titanic's* three anchors were assembled here at Noah Hingley's works in Netherton. On 30th April 1911 a team of twenty horses hauled the largest anchor to Dudley railway station at the beginning of its lengthy journey to Belfast. In 2010, a replica of the ill-fated White Star liner's largest anchor was installed on a triangle of green space at the top end of the High Street. Hingley's, incidentally, were instrumental in the establishment of Midlands & Coast Canal Carriers following the demise of the Shropshire Union fleet in 1921.

*Windmill End*

Windmill End is arguably the epitome of the Black Country canal scene, and given its location at the centre of the inland waterways system, together with the public open space which lines its canal banks, it's not surprising that it serves from time to time as an ideal venue for boat rallies. The gaunt outline of Cobb's engine house, silhouetted against the Rowley Hills, above a profusion of Toll End Works roving bridges, forms one of the Black Country's most potent post-industrial images. If only the 'Bumble Hole' push & pull train still steamed back and forth between Dudley and Old Hill. Windmill End station was immortalised in Flanders & Swann's haunting elegy *Slow Train*. On Christmas Eve 1914 - when, goodness knows, there was already enough suffering in the world - three young people drowned in the canal, having apparently lost their way in darkness, snow and fog between the station and their homes.

Cobb's engine house contained a stationary steam engine which pumped excess water from coal mines in the vicinity and discharged it into the canal. Built in 1831, the engine kept the pits dry and the cut wet for well-nigh a century, until the local collieries were all worked out. The engine subsequently went for scrap, but the engine house remains, adorning the landscape as if somehow transmuted from a Cornish cliff top. The old colliery precincts surrounding Windmill End are now known as Warren's Hall Park; a haunted countryside to saunter in, to go roaming in the gloaming in, imagining the pandemonium of its industrial past.

Three cast iron roving bridges span the waterways radiating from Windmill End Junction. Originally the Dudley No.2 Canal ran east to west here, following the course of what became quaintly known as the 'Boshboil' and 'Bumble Hole' arms after the loop was cut off by the improvements of 1858 associated with the opening of Netherton Tunnel. The tunnel's southern portal stands to the north of the junction through the arch of a blue-brick overbridge which carried a colliery tramway.

Netherton Tunnel provokes piquant contrast with Dudley Tunnel's ancient confines. High, wide and equipped with twin towpaths*, it now lacks only the lighting once generated by a turbine fed from the high level old main line at Tividale (Map 13). It takes roughly half an hour to walk (advisably with a torch) or boat through this monument to the last fling of the canal age. We counted seven airshafts providing 'air-raids' of rainwater, but we've met wetter tunnels on our canal travels.

*Though only the easternmost is currently in use.

Coombeswood

## Windmill End - Hawne Basin

Lapal Tunnel's closure in 1917 severed the Dudley No.2 Canal's route between Windmill End and Selly Oak, but this end of the canal remained in commercial use right up until 1969 to serve the giant Stewart & Lloyds tube making works at Coombeswood on the far side of Gosty Hill Tunnel. Thereafter the canal might easily have deteriorated but for the emergence of the Coombeswood Canal Trust (Tel: 0121 550 1355) who developed the railway interchange basin at Hawne, on the outskirts of Halesowen, into a flourishing centre of Black Country leisure boating.

The journey down to Hawne is seldom less than engrossing, hinting here and there at past endeavours. A sequence of interpretive sculptures elaborates further. By Powke Lane stands the substantial Rowley Regis crematorium, and suburban Blackheath occupies much of the adjacent hillside. At Old Hill a series of overbridges pass in quick succession as the canal approaches the stygian delights of Gosty Hill Tunnel. In the early years of the 20th century the BCN operated a tug service through the tunnel and the remains of its dock can be seen beside the northern portal. At either end the tunnel's confined, towpathless bore feels claustrophobic, but in the middle it opens out into a high vault, like a gloomy church with a lofty nave. Working boatmen were apparently in the habit of abandoning the tiller to its own devices, spending the time it took to pass through the 557 yards long tunnel ensconced in their cabins, whilst, as snugly as a piston in a cylinder, the boat made its own way from one end to the other.

You used to emerge from Gosty Hill Tunnel into the eerie precincts of the aforementioned tube works. The canal traversed a canyon of sheer brick walls and passed beneath a sequence of mysterious corrugated iron clad overbridges and pipes whispering sibilantly with escaping steam. All this has vanished and been redeveloped into a trading estate of soulless units, inscrutable behind their ubiquitous cladding and characterless trading names. The canal ignores them, skirting the foot of Mucklow Hill, a pleasant open landscape threaded by public footpaths, before abruptly reaching the old transhipment basin at Hawne. Visiting boaters are welcomed (there is an excellent range of facilities, including laundry) and this is definitely one Black Country mooring where the spectre of vandalism won't disturb your slumbers. The preserved pair of working boats *Atlas* and *Malus* are based here. As for the remainder of the Dudley No.2's route, its future lies in the warm embrace of the Lapal Canal Trust.

END OF NAVIGATION

**The Waterfront**

# Merry Hill Map 39

Of course intu Merry Hill is really Brierley Hill, but so much does the massive retail complex dominate the vicinity now, that it seems more appropriate to refer to it thus. Like Marmite, you either love this sort of thing or loathe it. "Over 200 shops and stores" shrieks the publicity blurb: "two and a half miles of marbled halls - a uniquely enjoyable experience" - much like the BCN itself you might justifiably retort!

## Eating & Drinking

The Waterfront features a Wetherspoons and a Marston's pub, but real ale devotees will want to visit: THE VINE - Delph Road. Tel: 01384 78293. Better known as the 'Bull & Bladder', Batham's brewery tap is one of the great Black Country pubs. It stands on Delph Road 6 minutes walk east from the foot of Delph Locks. Food available at lunchtimes, and Batham's beer which the family have been brewing for five generations. The Vine, one of only ten tied houses, has a Shakespearean quotation emblazoned across its frontage at roof level. DY5 2TN

## Shopping

If the prospect of Merry Hill's two hundred plus shops

is more than you can bear, then head in the opposite direction for Brierley Hill's beleaguered but traditional High Street. An Odeon multi-screen cinema complex stands adjacent to the canal south of Green's Bridge. Launderette on Dudley Road west of Burger King.

## Connections

BUSES - will take you back to reality with a - "did I *really* spend all that" - bump. Tel: 0871 200 2233.
TAXIS - Newline Taxis. Tel: 01384 384384.

# Netherton Map 39

Once of Worcestershire, shorn of its traditional industries, Netherton nevertheless remains a quintessentially Black Country community worthy of close inspection. After many a fruitless pilgrimage down the years, we finally got to see inside the Commissioner's church of St Andrew's, serendipitously finding ourselves in Netherton just as a Sunday service was drawing to a close. There was no anticlimax. The stained glass was impressive, but the galleries beguiled us most, especially on being informed that they are regularly filled with up to three hundred school children. The graveyard is extensive, and includes Noah Hingley's memorial.

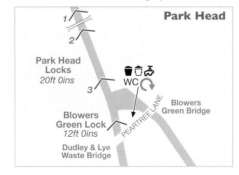

**Park Head**

**Windmill End**

## Eating & Drinking

THE OLD SWAN - Halesowen Road. Tel: 01384 253075). Older regulars still lovingly call it 'Ma Pardoe's' after a former landlady. They brew on the premises and a lovely pale, fruity beer the bitter is too. Additionally a wide choice of food is available lunchtimes and evenings. DY2 9PY
*Ethnic take-aways and fish & chip shop as well.*

## Shopping

Netherton's shops evince character and courtesy with Black Country wit never far from the surface. Allan's discount store remains difficult to resist: 'every seasonable line imaginable - no nonsense prices'. Bains Wines offer a good range of bottled beer, not least Bathams. There are Lidl and Aldi supermarkets; convenience stores, pharmacies, and a post office.

## Things to Do

BUMBLE HOLE VISITOR CENTRE - Tel: 01384 814100. Interesting and friendly centre devoted to Windmill End and its post-industrial environs.

## Connections

BUSES - frequent services to/from Dudley etc. Nearest railway station at Old Hill.

# 40 WYRLEY & ESSINGTON CANAL Wednesfield 4mls/0lks/2hrs

HOARDINGS herald the development of a new 'Canalside Quarter' at Horseley Fields where the Wyrley & Essington Canal embarks on its lockless, contour-clinging journey to Brownhills and beyond, justifying its nickname - affectionate or otherwise - "Curly Wyrley". The point of departure is far from salubrious. One squeezes through the narrows beneath the railway square-jawed, honour-bound to enjoy oneself, however high the emotional cost. The W&E opened - independently of the Birmingham Canal - in 1797; extending for 24 miles from Horseley Fields, Wolverhampton to Huddlesford Junction on the Coventry Canal (Map 30) near Lichfield. Its fidelity to the 473ft contour was absolute until Ogley (Map 42) beyond which there were no less than thirty locks in the seven mile stretch down to Huddlesford. Several branches blossomed, so that by the mid-19th century there were half a dozen or more junctions adding traffic to what had become a route of much significance. Huddling together in the face of railway competiton, the W&E merged with the BCN in 1840.

Alan Godfrey's reprint of the Ordnance Survey 25 inch map of Wolverhampton and Heath Town dated 1902 depicts a lost world of engineering works and railway basins. Indeed, just how multi-layered cartography can be is evidenced by the presence of the Osier Bed Iron Works, erected on a marshy site once given over to harvesting of willow trees for basket weaving and hurdle making. On the opposite bank the all but entirely derelict New Griffin Works cry out for tender loving care.

After the disappearance of trade from this canal, it fell into neglect. Technically it remained navigable, but it was too ugly to appeal to all but the most perverse of pleasure boaters. And to all intents and purposes, despite the march of redevelopment along its banks, together with a general mellowing in atmosphere, the 'Curly Wyrley' remains an unloved orphan of neglect and official indifference, displaying little pride in its appearance as it heads dolefully towards Wednesfield.

Wood End

Moat House

Devils Elbow

Olinthus

Wards

Castle

A4124

Trapmakers Church

park

Pinfold

New Bentley

New Cross

Rookery

Heath Town

A4124

Heath Town

Deans Road

Swan Garden

Horseley Fields Junction

Town Centre

Wednesfield

'Passengers No More'
1: Heath Town - closed 1910
2: Wednesfield - closed 1931

Perry Hall

New Invention

Pool Hayes

Knights

A462

Lane Head

Adam & Eve

continues foot of Map 41

Rookery

W'HAMPTON RD.

New Cross

Bentley Bridge

NORTH

○ Key
A site of Osier Bed Iron Works
B rems of Midland Railway boat dock
C site of Midland Railway basins
D former New Griffin Tool Works
E Coltham Basin

○ Key
A Bentley Canal
B Neachells Branch

126

At Heath Town an aqueduct carries it across the Grand Junction Railway, forty years its junior. Furthermore, blue brick abutments recall the existence of another railway which meant that the canal was once sandwiched vertically - and as far as we know uniquely - between two railways. Largely vanished under redevelopment, the Midland Railway line between Wolverhampton and Walsall was abandoned - as far as passengers were concerned - upon the inauguration of a trolleybus service between the two towns in 1931, though the local station had already ceased functioning, doubtless rendered obsolete by the trams which predated the trolleybuses.

In his learned treatise of 1686, *The Natural History of the County of Stafford*, the Oxford University academic Robert Plot alluded to a battle between the Saxons and the Danes in the vicinity of Wednesfield in 910AD. A thousand years later Phil Drabble referenced it in *Black Country*, one of Robert Hale's Regional Books series, published in 1952. "King Edward, with an army of West Saxons and Mercians, overtook the Danes at the village of Wednesfield, overthrew them in bloody battle, wherein he killed Edwills and Halfden, two of their kings, and Othea and Scurfer, two of their earls, and nine other noblemen of which great slaughter there are no remains ...". You'll just have to take our word that Wednesfield's become more peaceable since then ... comparatively.

The Curly Wyrley glides serenely enough through Wednesfield. The towpath well-surfaced and well-loved by the locals, even if they only use it as a short cut to the shops. Apart from a roving bridge spanning a truncated stub (which provides secure 48 hour visitor moorings) most traces of the Bentley Canal, which until its closure in 1960 linked the W&E with the Walsall Canal at Darlaston (Map 46) have been exorcised. A flight of half a dozen locks led down to a junction with the Neachells Branch, a short three furlong arm opened in 1845 and abandoned in 1953. The redoubtable Richard Chester-Browne explored what he could in the 1970s and tantalizingly described his discoveries in *The Other Sixty Miles*, but redevelopment has been remorseless in the subsequent half century.

Beyond Wednesfield the canal finds itself adrift in nebulous galaxies of housing, some of whose more juvenile occupants, it must sadly be said, occasionally display a Neanderthal aggression towards strangers. Coltham Basin, at Lane Head, remains invitingly in water, but no longer do mineral trains come clangorously down from the coal mines at Hilton Main and Holly Bank, though one of the latter's locomotives is preserved on the Chasewater Railway. There are secure (though not the most prepossessing) offside visitor moorings at Lane Head alongside a pub disingenuously named 'The United Kingdom'. A lot of water under the bridges of the Wyrley & Essington since that was the case.

## Wednesfield      Map 40

The big brick church of St Thomas - topped by a gold cockerel weathervane in homage, perhaps, to the Black Country's cock-fighting heritage - lures you off the cut into Wednesfield's busy main street. Equally imposing, in its contrasting way, is the Guru Nanak Gurdwara on the opposite side of the road. Strange how these tangential Black Country communities contrive to stay so purposeful and relevant. This town's particular contribution to the industrial revolution was in the painful art of trap-making - Sidebotham's trap factory has been reconstructed at the Black Country Living Museum.

### Eating & Drinking

COSMO - Bentley Bridge (adjacent 48 hour visitor moorings). Tel: 01902 722233. 'All you can eat world buffet'. Lunches from noon, dinners from 5.30pm. Food served throughout on Sundays. WV11 1BP
NICKLEODEON - Bentley Bridge Way. Tel: 01902 305741. Greene King 'Fayre & Square' pub/restaurant open from 11.30am daily. WV11 1BP
ROYAL TIGER - High Street. Tel: 01902 307816. Wetherspoons open from 8am daily. Former bakery with terrace to rear beside canal. WV11 1ST
*KFC, Pizza Hut, Bella Italia, McDonald's, Nandos, Chiquito etc in retail park.*

### Shopping

Large Sainsbury's by Rookery Bridge. Small street market Tue, Fri & Sat, Post office, banks, butcher and pharmacy in old town centre. Bentley Bridge Shopping Park: Next, JD Sports, Laura Ashley, T K Maxx etc.

### Things to Do

WOLVERHAMPTON SWIMMING & FITNESS CENTRE - Planetary Rd. Tel: 01902 384777. WV13 3SW *Bentley Bridge hosts a cinema and bowling alley.*

### Connections

BUSES - National Express 59 provides frequent links to/from Wolverhampton. Tel: 0871 200 2233.

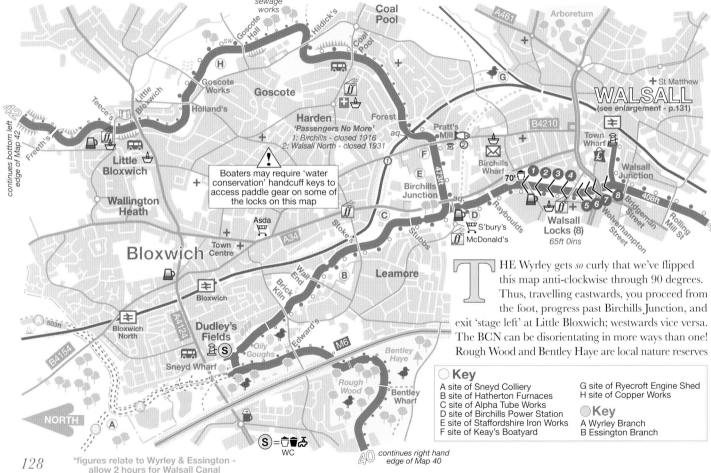

# 41 BCN WYRLEY & ESSINGTON CANAL  Walsall  6mls/0lks/2hrs*

Boaters may require 'water conservation' handcuff keys to access paddle gear on some of the locks on this map

THE Wyrley gets *so* curly that we've flipped this map anti-clockwise through 90 degrees. Thus, travelling eastwards, you proceed from the foot, progress past Birchills Junction, and exit 'stage left' at Little Bloxwich; westwards vice versa. The BCN can be disorientating in more ways than one! Rough Wood and Bentley Haye are local nature reserves

## Key
A site of Sneyd Colliery
B site of Hatherton Furnaces
C site of Alpha Tube Works
D site of Birchills Power Station
E site of Staffordshire Iron Works
F site of Keay's Boatyard
G site of Ryecroft Engine Shed
H site of Copper Works

## Key
A Wyrley Branch
B Essington Branch

*figures relate to Wyrley & Essington -
allow 2 hours for Walsall Canal

continues right hand edge of Map 40

continues bottom left edge of Map 42

reclaimed from 19th century coal workings; ditto Oily Goughs, as opposed to an esoteric strand of sub-culture.

Only mildly more eccentric than journeying along the Wyrley & Essington, is exploration of its long abandoned branches. From Sneyd the erstwhile Wyrley, Wyrley Bank and Essington canals once proceeded northwards to a number of obscure colliery basins. Indeed, the former was originally deemed the W&E's 'main line', pending completion of the easterly extension from Sneyd to Huddlesford in 1797. And, of course, therein lies the source of one half of the canal's title, Essington (at 533ft, the highest point above sea level reached by the network, and the 'Tollington' of Meera Syal's *Anita and Me*) its immortal partner. Happily the Wyrley and Wyrley Bank canals - partially 'in water', partially 'dry' - can be comfortably and enjoyably followed on foot northwards beyond the borders of this map. A well surfaced footpath runs throughout, much of it given the protective status of a linear nature reserve, and there are fairly frequent buses back from the terminus at Cheslyn Hay to Bloxwich.

Secure 'off-side' visitor moorings and other boating facilities are provided at Sneyd Wharf. Unnervingly, as if it has forgotten something, the canal appears determined to head back the way it's come, but it is only circumspectly sniffing out Walsall. A built-up zone ensues: half commercial, half residential; wholly lugubrious. Birchills Junction marks the egress of the W&E's Walsall Branch. The local power station, for many years the dominant feature of the area, was closed in 1982, its six cooling towers, a landmark for miles, being demolished five years later. A sizeable unloading basin was serviced by overhead travelling cranes whose grabs lifted vast tonnages out of fleets of Joey boats. Somewhat inevitably, the site is now a retail park.

The Walsall Branch terminated, prior to the construction of the Walsall Junction Canal and its flight of eight locks, at Birchills Wharf. Here, in 1900, a Boatmen's Mission or 'Rest' was built under the aegis of the Incorporated Seamen & Boatmen's Friendly Society. Its function was similar to that at Tipton (Map 12) but at Birchills an upper storey provided dormitory facilities for day boatmen as well. Unfortunately,

although the building had found appropriate use as a canal museum for a number of years, it closed due to shortfalls in local authority funding. Manned by volunteers, its overheads would surely be negligible, and how much better to have it open and welcoming, than the crumbling eyesore it is well on the way to becoming.

## Walsall (Locks & Town Arm)

Walsall Locks were first mooted to link the Wyrley & Essington and Walsall canals in 1825, but the W&E and BCN companies were suspicious of each other's motives and proposal was followed by counter-proposal for fifteen years before the canal and its flight of eight locks, rising 65 feet, materialised. The flight seems almost impervious to the landscape it occupies, as solitary in its predisposition as the men who invariably haunt it: with, or without, dogs; with, or without, cans of cheap lager; with, or without, motive.

Christ comes to the rescue in the form of a war memorial attached to the end wall of St Andrew's parish church. At street level there's a Madonna, adding weight to the suspicion that the church's congregation must belong to an especially devout Anglo-Catholic tradition; a quixotic notion now in terraced streets multicultural in atmosphere. Alongside Lock 7, fronting Wolverhampton Road, the old Albion (aka Smiths) flour mill has been

*Albion Flour Mill*

*Leaving Lock 7*

## Birchills - Little Bloxwich

Sunken wooden narrowboat hulls lie masked in reeds east of Birchills Junction, eloquent testimony to the BCN's busy past. There are no tangible remains, however, of the boat docks which once stood by Pratt's Mill Bridge - which, before being rebuilt in the 1930s, carried one of Walsall's tramway routes. Bowaters and Worseys - both famous Black Country boatbuilders - had premises here. In latter years the yard west of the bridge - now covered by housing - was operated by Peter Keay & Son, one of the last wooden canal boat builders. Keays went into business after the Great War, based at first on the Daw End Branch, and were also known as canal carriers by virtue of their fleet of tugs which towed 'Joey' boats down from the Cannock coalfield. Joey was a BCN colloquialism for day boats without living accommodation used for short haul work. Tugs would pull 'trains' of these unpowered craft, or they might be worked singly by horses. They were equipped with transferable helms for bi-directional working.

An aqueduct carries the canal over the Walsall to Cannock railway, electrified in 2019. The original course of the canal was by-passed when the railway cutting was excavated, thus allowing the aqueduct to be built without disrupting canal trade. At Harden, Coal Pool and Little Bloxwich, housing borders the canal. Walsall Corporation's blue liveried trolleybuses used to weave their way through these estates until the extensive system fell into the hands of the West Midlands Passenger Transport Executive in 1969 and was abandoned within a year. An evocative photograph of one of the fleet at the Beechdale Estate terminus, against a backdrop of Birchills Power Station, appears in Howard Piltz's *The Heyday of the Trolleybus*.

Poverty stalked these post-war housing schemes and pilfering was commonplace when the coal boats passed by. The easiest approach was to board a boat at one bridge-hole, fill a bag with the black stuff, and alight at the next. At Freeth's Bridge eastbound canal travellers discover a sudden and surprising rurality: pastures, ploughed fields and ruminative cattle. Paradoxically, the working boatmen of the past would be passing from farmland into an area of collieries and iron works.

converted into stylish apartments. Lock 6 is unique to the flight in having mitred bottom gates; the rest being of BCN design with single leaves.

Walsall's Town Arm has been regenerated and then, as often seems to be the case, quietly left to its own devices. Nevertheless, it forms an off-beat gateway to the town's New Art Gallery, whose hundred foot high, terracotta-tiled tower provides a suitable climax. The boom is there to keep flotsam and jetsam out of the basin, not boaters, and your bow should automatically push it aside. Anecdotal evidence, however, would have it that boat passages (BCNS Explorer Cruises and Challenges apart) are rare, which is a shame, both for the canal and the town itself. We must all try much, much harder! The Walsall Canal between Walsall and Great Bridge - an assault course of a canal by any standards - is described in the text accompanying Map 46.

# Walsall

Map 41

'A place of very considerable character' wrote our hero, the peerless Henry Thorold, in *Staffordshire: A Shell Guide* published in 1978, exhorting discerning visitors to 'climb first to the parish church'. Five decades later, there are those who feel the town has never really recovered from abandoning its annual autumnal 'illuminations' in 2010. Yet there remains so much to admire about Walsall, that one is inclined to overlook its tendency to scruffiness. Heaven knows it must be hard for the Wolverhamptons, Walsalls and West Bromwichs of this world to compete with Big Brother Birmingham when it comes to sourcing funding. So approach the town with an open mind and keep your eyes peeled for some of its most imposing buildings. The baroque Council House of 1905 - whose foundation stone was ceremoniously laid by Prince Christian of Schleswig-Holstein (one of Queen Victoria's son-in-laws) three years earlier - would not look out of place in a city setting, whilst its neighbours exude barely less municipal swagger. As an intriguing aside, the Danish born prince had taken part in the First Schleswig-Holstein War (1848-1852) of which Lord Palmerston famously remarked: 'Only three people have really understood the Schleswig-Holstein Question: one is dead, one has gone mad, and I've forgotten the answer'. From its (not so far away) green hill at the summit of High Street, St Matthew's parish church brokers grandstand views across the Black Country. In the open space where Park Street becomes Digbeth stands a statue to local heroine Sister Dora, reputedly the first statue erected for a non-royal female in the country. Jacob Epstein's exhortation to his muse and mistress, Kathleen Garman - "Be There Saturday Sweetheart" - displayed in blue neon script on the roof of the coffee house adjoining Town Wharf rarely fails to raise a smile.

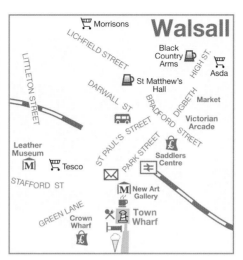

## Eating & Drinking

BLACK COUNTRY ARMS - High Street. Tel: 01922 640588. Black Country Brewery town pub. Kitchen open 12-7pm Tue-Sat. Twenty real ales! WS1 1QW
COSTA - Town Wharf. Tel: 01922 624510. Coffee shop with big glass window views over the basin. WS2 8LG
GEORGE STEPHENSON - canalside, Birchills. Tel: 01922 630458. The 'Father of Railways' links with Walsall seem slender at best, notwithstanding this 'Harvester's' location overlooking the trackbed of the old Midland Railway line to Wolverhampton, but there are mooring rings on the adjacent canal and Sainsbury's and Lidl stores adjacent. WS2 7EU
ST MATTHEW'S HALL - Lichfield Street. Tel: 01922 700820. Wetherspoon conversion of former library/court in imposing Greek Doric style. WS1 1SX

WATERFRONT - Wolverhampton Road. Tel: 01922 616382. Green King 'Hungry Horse' pub/restaurant open from 11am weekdays and 10am weekends, food served throughout. WS2 8DH
*Bella Italia, Brewers Fayre, Nando's, Piri Fino, Starbucks, Subway etc. within easy reach of the canal terminus.*

## Shopping

Walsall's market dates from 1219 and attracts shoppers from all over the region. There are several busy precincts burgeoning with all the usual chain stores. Crown Wharf retail park abuts the canal terminus. The Victorian Arcade is full of soaring glass and faded charm.

## Things to Do

THE NEW ART GALLERY - Gallery Square. Open Tue-Sun admission free. Tel: 01922 654400. Lucky Walsall to have such a fine cultural facility. Surprisingly cosmopolitan range of exhibits by the likes of Cezanne, Van Gogh and Picasso. But we were especially taken with Stanislas Lepine's French landscape *The Canal*; discount the beam of the vessel depicted and it might have been the Wyrley & Essington. WS2 8LG
WALSALL LEATHER MUSEUM - Littleton Street. Tel: 01922 652288. Homage to the town's stock in trade; saddle making, lorinery, leather goods etc. Admission free. Open Tue-Sat 10-4 (5 Apr-Oct). WS2 8EW

## Connections

BUSES - alas no trolleybuses now - both the blue liveried vehicles of Walsall's fleet and the olive & primrose of Wolverhampton's are long gone - but from the town's imposing modern bus station frequent services will take you to Wolverhampton, Wednesfield, Pelsall and Brownhills and other nodal points along the Wyrley & Essington Canal. Tel: 0871 200 2233.
TRAINS - WM local services to/from Rugeley (via Cannock), and Birmingham. Tel: 0345 748 4950.

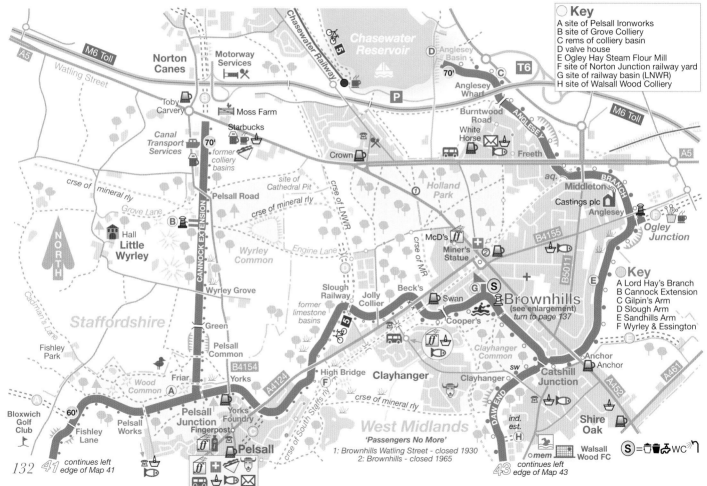

# 42 WYRLEY & ESSINGTON CANAL Brownhills 4mls/0lks/2hrs

**Key**
A site of Pelsall Ironworks
B site of Grove Colliery
C rems of colliery basin
D valve house
E Ogley Hay Steam Flour Mill
F site of Norton Junction railway yard
G site of railway basin (LNWR)
H site of Walsall Wood Colliery

**Key**
A Lord Hay's Branch
B Cannock Extension
C Gilpin's Arm
D Slough Arm
E Sandhills Arm
F Wyrley & Essington

M6 Toll
A5
Watling Street
M6 Toll
Norton Canes
Motorway Services
Chasewater Reservoir
Chasewater Railway
Anglesey Basin
70'
T6
Anglesey Wharf
Burntwood Road
ANGLESEY BRANCH
M6 Toll
A5
Toby Carvery
Moss Farm
Starbucks
Canal Transport Services
70'
former colliery basins
Crown
White Horse
Freeth
Middleton
Castings plc
Anglesey
aq.
Ogley Junction
crse of mineral rly
Grove Lane
Pelsall Road
site of Cathedral Pit
crse of mineral rly
crse of LNWR
Holland Park
McD's
Miner's Statue
B4155
B5011
Little Wyrley
Hall
Wyrley Common
Engine Lane
crse of MR
Slough Railway
Beck's
Brownhills
(see enlargement) turn to page 137
Wyrley Grove
Jolly Collier
Swan
Cooper's
Green
former limestone basins
Clayhanger Common
Anchor
Anchor
Staffordshire
Pelsall Common
High Bridge
Clayhanger
sw
Catshill Junction
A461
A452
Fishley Park
Fishley Lane
Friar
Yorks
B4154
Wood Common
A
A4124
crse of mineral rly
DAW END
ind. est.
Shire Oak
Bloxwich Golf Club
60'
Pelsall Works
Pelsall Junction
Fingerpost
Yorks Foundry
Pelsall
West Midlands
'Passengers No More'
1: Brownhills Watling Street - closed 1930
2: Brownhills - closed 1965
mem
Walsall Wood FC

NORTH

Cadman's Lane

crse of South Staffs rly

132 41 continues left edge of Map 41

43 continues left edge of Map 43

Ⓢ = 🚻 WC

LOCK-WHEELER will let you into a well-guarded secret. Of all the hundreds of maps he has drawn (and redrawn!) down the years for the Canal Companion series, this is pretty much his favourite; cartographically and emotionally. There is a pervasive alchemy in the relationship between the area's vanished industries and its present natural wildness which chimes with his own split personality; a mirror image in a stagnant, heron-haunted pond.

Picking up coverage of the Wyrley & Essington at Fishley Lane - at the left hand foot of the map - the first point of interest is the junction of the former Lord Hay's Branch. Barely a mile in length, it opened in 1800 to serve several collieries. They were disused by the end of the century, but the branch wasn't officially abandoned until 1954. It may enjoy a fresh lease of life, however, if the Lichfield & Hatherton Canals Restoration Trust's plan to provide a new link to the Hatherton Branch of the Staffordshire & Worcestershire Canal (Map 36) comes to fruition.

## Cannock Extension Canal

Wittily known as 'the cut to the Chase', the Cannock Extension Canal opened in 1863 to tap the Cannock coalfield. It was five and three-quarter miles long, lockless, and terminated at Hednesford, a colliery town at the very foot of Cannock Chase. En route there was a junction at Church Bridge, where a precipitous flight of thirteen locks linked with the Hatherton Branch of the Staffs & Worcs Canal.

Paradoxically, mining subsidence brought about abandonment of the Cannock Extension above the A5 at Norton Canes at the end of 1962, a year shy of its centenary. Malcolm Braine's entertaining account of a pleasure boat convoy's last cruise along the abandoned length appeared in the Summer 2011 edition of *Narrow Boat* magazine.

The Extension was probably the last narrow gauge canal of any significant length to be built, and it has a distinctive character, for even in its dotage, it retains an uncanny sense of purpose. Blue 'Utopia' engineering

Pelsall Common

*Old Railway Bridge & Irises*

more coverage in the national press had the tragedy not coincided with the crash of the airship R101 over northern France. We all know how fickle the Fourth Estate can be.

Little Wyrley Hall stands behind high walls and security gates and barriers. Parts of its fabric can be traced back to Tudor times. Nikolaus Pevsner was much taken with the diversity of its shaped gables. British Railways Western Region Hall class locomotive 7913 bore its name. The Extension ends with a whimper at the A5; though, by virtue of a public right of way (nettle-prone in summer), a short length (replete with a ruined overbridge) may be explored on foot beyond the M6 Toll road, enabling those of a certain bent to summon up the ghosts of the canal's past.

## *Pelsall - Ogley*

Pelsall Junction hosts boat rallies from time to time, and the BCNS lead an annual convoy of adventurers, but few boats cruise these shallow, weed-

*Brownhills*

bricks line its banks; BCN concrete fencing posts can be glimpsed in the undergrowth; and hefty, name-plated overbridges - more railway-like than canal - parenthesise its passage across the moody, back to nature landscape. White-clawed crayfish are reputed to reside beneath the surprisingly transparent surface.

Two old BCN cottages (No.s 211 & 212) adjoin the massive proportions of Friar Bridge. Opposite, former stables have been painstakingly renovated to form a delightful dwelling. Wasteland extends westwards across Wood Common, a heathery, pock-marked site of a huge ironworks. Grove Colliery ceased production in 1952, though the basins continued to be employed as a loading point for boats until 1966 and remain used for moorings. In 1930, Grove pit was the scene of an underground explosion which killed fourteen miners. Ten of them are buried in a poignant row in the overflow of St James's churchyard, Brownhills. The miners' deaths might have attracted prone waters, let alone negotiate the junction and head for Norton Canes. A shame, because this really is an evocative location to moor overnight, soaking up the haunted setting of post-industrial inactivity; murmuring pines, skeins of geese, loping foxes, and bull-rushy ponds where once there were slag-heaps and mineral railways. Follow the footpath which leads to Fishley Park and you'll come upon a ruck of stones where John Wesley is said to have preached.

Pelsall Ironworks closed as early as 1892 and all the neighbouring coal pits had ceased working by 1903, but the canal remained commercially busy into the 1960s. York's Bridge (with or without the apostrophe) has a keystone dated 1866. Edward Paget-Tomlinson's charming drawing of it, along with an informative historical essay by Ray Shill, appears in *A-Z of the Birmingham Canal Navigations* published by the BCNS in association with the Canal Book Shop, Audlem in 2016. Controversial plans exist for a side-by-side replacement which will dwarf/suffocate the original.

Modern housing creates a domestic interlude between Yorks Foundry and High bridges. There was an extensive railway marshalling yard at Norton Junction. The Slough Arm was disused by the end of the 19th century. A lock lead to a short summit fed by local springs and colliery pumping. Follow the course of the old mineral railway north from Slough Railway Bridge, and at Engine Lane you'll come upon the reasonably well preserved remains of an old hump-back bridge.

Jolly Collier Bridge recalls the presence of a former inn whose premises remain, refurbished and privately occupied, behind a high self-effacing hedge. Turning sharply under Beck's Bridge, the canal passes beneath the old South Staffordshire Railway which can be walked west of here. The decorated cast iron parapets of the bridge are replicated at Golds Hill and Great Bridge (Maps 13A & 46).The blue brick abutments of the Midland Railway's Walsall Wood branch stand stubbornly alongside Cooper's Bridge which was originally a swing-bridge, lending its name to a nearby farm.

Tentatively the canal approaches Brownhills, like someone unsure of a warm welcome. There are times on these BCN backwaters when you fear the world has experienced a cataclysm, and only you and mutant

Catshill Junction

Canada geese have survived. A rewatered arm extends into the former railway interchange basin at Brownhills, whilst a canoe centre provides boating facilities and visitor moorings. Pier Street footbridge effects access to Clayhanger Common, ninety acres of former mine workings redeveloped as an admirable public open space. Long ago a canalside pub called The Fortunes of War stood here.

Catshill Junction is overlooked by a solitary tower block where previously, if our memory serves us well, there were three. Both routes narrowed here to facilitate toll taking. The W&E proceeds from Catshill to Ogley passing the long vanished course of the Sandhills Arm, known to working boatmen as the 'Apple Arm' because it traversed an area of orchards. There are said to be some interesting wharf buildings on private land at its terminus. Sources variously suggest that it was dug to bring sand from a neighbouring quarry, or to convey lime as a fertiliser. Pupils at Millfield Primary School on the off-side are in the enviable position of

*Ogley Hay Flour Mill*

having a floating classroom in the shape of former Grand Union Canal Carrying Company Star class motor *Tucana*. A little further on, a former flour mill has been converted into apartments with 'Juliet' balconies.

Farmland falls bucolically away to the east as the canal enters a shallow cutting of bracken and broom to reach Ogley Junction. East of Ogley, the Wyrley & Essington fell through a flight of locks which will have to be restored if the canal is to reconnect with the Coventry Canal at Huddlesford (Map 30). Encouragement has been given by the provision of an as yet unwatered aqueduct over the M6 Toll Road. Regrettably, much of the course of the W&E has been obliterated. Not far from here, the 'Staffordshire Hoard' of Saxon treasure was discovered by a metal-detecting enthusiast in 2009. Further items were found three years later.

## Anglesey Branch

Chasewater Reservoir (aka Norton Pool) was opened in 1800 to supply the Wyrley & Essington main line with much needed water. Fifty years later, with the development of coal mining in the area, the feeder to Ogley was upgraded to navigable standards. Nowadays the branch represents the furthest north you can travel on the BCN. There are views north-east beyond the M6 Toll road of the three spires of Lichfield Cathedral. An aqueduct carries the canal over the trackbed of the South Staffordshire Railway, before you pass beneath the A5 - alias Watling Street - and the M6 Toll to reach Anglesey Basin, as remote as anything the inland waterways system has to offer. The last consignments were loaded here in 1969; the Clean Air Act had reduced the demand for coal. There is evidence of former coal loading chutes near the M6 Toll bridge.

## Daw End Branch

Say D'oh! End, like Homer Simpson, and you'll soar in the esteem of local canal aficionados. Walsall Wood Colliery opened in 1864 and had just marked its centenary when the NCB declared its coal reserves exhausted. Following closure its shafts and galleries were filled with toxic waste. Old photographs - readily accessible on the internet - depict a lunar landscape of slag heaps and craters threaded by mineral lines and a canal basin thronged with cabin-less dayboats. Luke Perry's memorial, in the form of a winding gear headstock, can be found at the edge of a neighbouring playing field, and very photogenic it is too!

The navvies who laboured to build the Daw End Branch of the Wyrley & Essington Canal would be hard put to recognise it now. When it opened in 1800, as a link to the limestone quarries at Hay Head (Map 43), it was a classic contour canal, traversing a district largely innocent of industry and wholly unfamiliar with the prospect of urbanisation. But it soon became apparent that its hinterland was rich in clay deposits, and brick and tile making became the staple activities of the area. Coal mining prospered too, bequeathing a legacy of subsidence which wrought havoc with the canal bed, necessitating continual heightening of its banks. Old-stagers would furrow their brows to see their cut twisting and turning high above the rest of the brittle landscape and all those interloping houses.

# Pelsall
Map 42

The centre, a mile south of the canal, is grouped around a pleasant sequence of green open spaces. In St Michael's churchyard stands a memorial to the victims of the Pelsall Hall Colliery disaster of 1872. In the immortal words of the *Walsall Observer* in December 1887, a boiler explosion at one of the local mines, "hurried three fellow creatures into eternity".

## Eating & Drinking
FINGER POST - Yorks Bridge. Tel: 01922 276450. Canalside pub formerly known as the Royal Oak. Bar and restaurant food lunch and evening. WS3 5AU
OLD HOUSE AT HOME - Norton Road. Tel: 01922 682011. Marston's 'all-day' food orientated pub near the centre of Pelsall. WS3 4NT
*Several fish & chips and fast food outlets in the vicinity.*

## Shopping
There's a convenience store 5 minutes stroll south of Pelsall Works Bridge, but a much wider range of shops (see map) group about the green a little less than 10 minutes from the junction or Yorks Bridge.

## Connections
BUSES - NatEx service 8 operates half-hourly to/from Walsall and Lichfield. Tel: 0871 200 2233.

# Norton Canes
Map 42

STARBUCKS - Watling Street. Tel: 01543 378667. Seattle-based coffee shop chain. WS11 9NA
*Plus ASDA convenience store & Greggs take-away.*
TOBY CARVERY - Watling Street. Tel: 01543 373292. Open from 8am, food served throughout. WS11 9ND

# Brownhills
Map 42

Brownhills provides a sense of purpose on a Wyrley & Essington otherwise prone to nebulousness. Whether Brownhills fits your idea of a 'destination' is down to personal taste, though probably you

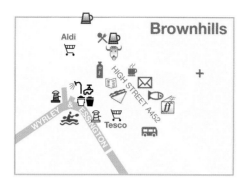

wouldn't be expecting too much being on the BCN in the first place. A forty feet high miner's statue sets the tone, towering over the town like a Soviet Bloc sculpture of Stalinist proportions, reminding us all (very necessarily now) why the town was built here in the first place. Bracing walks on Clayhanger Common.

## Eating & Drinking
THE ANCHOR - Chester Road (by Anchor Bridge near Catshill Junction). Tel: 01543 360219. Modern Marston's pub, food and Sky Sports. WS8 6DP.
THE BOAT - Muckley Corner. Tel: 01543 361692. Well off the map, but well worth a detour, this now Michelin listed establishment was formerly a modest boatmen's boozer alongside the course of the W&E. Charming stained glass window features a realistic narrow boat. Fine-dining Thur dinner (from 6pm) and Fri-Sun lunch and dinner (from 6pm). WS14 0BU
JIGGERS WHISTLE - High Street. Tel: 0785 435 6976. Micropub open from 3pm Mon-Thur (ex Tue) and noon Fri-Sun. Potent selection of real ales. WS8 6ED
MARIO'S FISH BAR & RESTAURANT - High Street. Tel: 01543 371487. Eat in or take-away. WS8 6HL
MCDONALD'S - Chester Road. Tel: 0775 461 7498.

Fast food outlet in former police station! WS8 7JP
SWAN - Pelsall Road (accessible off towpath between Beck's and Jolly Collier bridges). Tel: 01543 820628. Cosy local serving Holdens and guests. WS8 7DL

## Shopping
There are Tesco and Aldi supermarkets adjacent to the canal's Silver Street visitor moorings. Incongruously engulfed by suburban streets, Edmund Hurdle of Clayhanger has been ministering to the voracious appetites of local carnivores since 1935.

## Things to Do
CHASEWATER RAILWAY - Tel: 01543 452623. Trains operate on Sundays most of the year and additionally on selected days in summer along two miles of old mineral lines. Museum/cafe/souvenir shop. WS8 7NL

## Connections
BUSES - in a country with a transport policy more rational than the UK's, the Lichfield to Walsall railway would still be flourishing. In its absence bus 10 links Brownhills with Walsall, 937 with Birmingham.

# Aldridge
Map 43

Surprisingly large and prosperous 'village' more akin to to the Home Counties than the Black Country.

## Things to Do
ALDRIDGE TRANSPORT MUSEUM - Shenstone Drive. Tel: 01922 454761. Open Tue, Sat & Sun 10.30am to 4pm. Splendid collection of road vehicles. Running days with trips aboard preserved buses chugging up to Barr Beacon etc. WS9 8TP

# Rushall
Map 43

An Indian restaurant (Royal Oak - Tel: 01922 614947) and two pubs (Boat House 01922 615032 and Manor Arms 01922 642333) provide canalside refreshment opportunities at Daw End Bridge. Just west of the canal is a Chinese takeaway - Tel: 01922 624255.

**B**LACK COCK BRIDGE brings out the worst in motorists, who honk their horns aggressively across its narrow span. Walsall Wood was the location of the Travellers Rest Inn, probably the last pub in England to offer stabling for canal horses. Tom Foxon recalled when the landlord was a retired boxer and the stone-flagged bar was patronised by boatmen, busmen and miners. Sadly, it was demolished in the 1960s, a victim of subsidence. A branch of Screwfix occupies the site today. A spanner in the works of time!

Those Utopia bricks we spotted on the Cannock Extension were made in a canalside works at Northywood Bridge. The

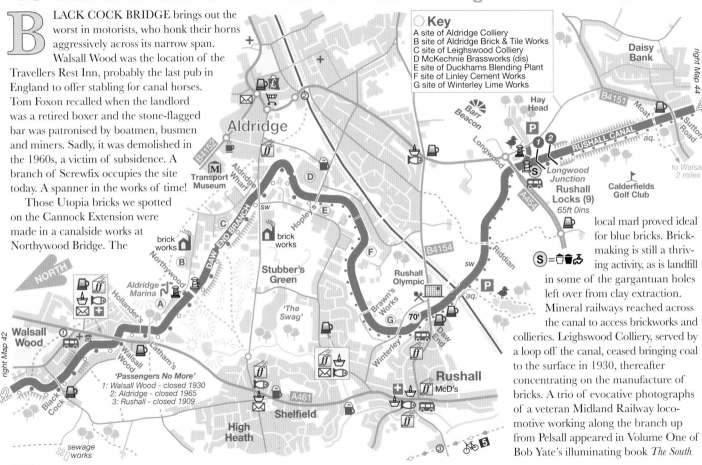

**Key**
A site of Aldridge Colliery
B site of Aldridge Brick & Tile Works
C site of Leighswood Colliery
D McKechnie Brassworks (dis)
E site of Duckhams Blending Plant
F site of Linley Cement Works
G site of Winterley Lime Works

Daisy Bank

Hay Head

Barr Beacon

Longwood

RUSHALL CANAL

Sutton Road

aq.

to Walsall 2 miles

Longwood Junction

Calderfields Golf Club

Rushall Locks (9)
65ft 0ins

Aldridge

Transport Museum

Aldridge Wharf

DAW END BRANCH

sw

Hopley's

Stubber's Green

brick works

brick works

Northywood

Aldridge Marina

Hollander's

Latham's

NORTH

Walsall Wood

Walsall Wood

Black Cock

'Passengers No More'
1: Walsall Wood - closed 1930
2: Aldridge - closed 1965
3: Rushall - closed 1909

'The Swag'

Rushall Olympic

Brawn's Works

70'

Winterley

Daw End

Riddian

sw

aq.

Rushall

McD's

Shelfield

High Heath

A461

A4154

sewage works

continues bottom right Map 42

continues top right Map 44

local marl proved ideal for blue bricks. Brickmaking is still a thriving activity, as is landfill in some of the gargantuan holes left over from clay extraction. Mineral railways reached across the canal to access brickworks and collieries. Leighswood Colliery, served by a loop off the canal, ceased bringing coal to the surface in 1930, thereafter concentrating on the manufacture of bricks. A trio of evocative photographs of a veteran Midland Railway locomotive working along the branch up from Pelsall appeared in Volume One of Bob Yate's illuminating book *The South*

*Staffordshire Railway* published by The Oakwood Press in 2010.

The uninvasive hum of industry going about its business off-stage characterises the Daw End Branch. Some, however, are forlornly defunct. Witness McKechnie's former brass-works, exactly the sort of derelict factory which attracts growing numbers of 'urban explorers'. Lock-wheeler was sorely tempted to join their ranks until he visualised the reception he would have received from Mrs Pearson had he been arrested for breaking and entering … at his age! In its 1960s heyday the workforce topped a thousand and the management were altruistic enough to provide them with a ballroom. Solely the extensive sportsground remains in use by Red Star Athletic, an affiliation of junior football sides.

Walsall Wood

Having shifted base from beside the Thames at Hammersmith (a site now occupied by the Michelin starred River Cafe) Duckhams, the lubricant manufacturers revered by the motor racing fraternity, opened a new plant canalside at Hopley's Bridge in 1968. Mooring rings, stubbornly embedded in the towpath, play silent witness to a regrettably short-lived initiative between Duckhams and the Birmingham & Midland Canal Carrying Company in 1970 to bring in oil from Stanlow, on the Manchester Ship Canal, by narrowboats fitted with special tanks. Thwarted by deteriorating levels of canal maintenance - in particular a lack of depth in numerous places along the 87 mile route via the Shropshire Union, Wolverhampton Twenty-One and Wyrley & Essington, only nine round trips were made, averaging a morale-sapping, commercially unsustainable two and a half weeks apiece.

From time to time we've day-dreamed of boating through a football season, attending fixtures at grounds beside, or at most a hefty goal kick from the canal or river bank. Indeed, there are enough venues in this guide alone to keep one pretty occupied through the winter months. From Stourport Swifts via Wolverhampton Wanderers to Rushall Olympic, whose Doles Lane ground lies alongside the canal at Daw End. You can't miss the floodlights! 'The Pics' can trace their roots back to the 19th Century when miners from Aldridge Colliery formed an ad hoc side. Delightfully, in match reports, they are apt to refer to their No.1, not as a mere goalkeeper, but as a 'custodian'. Truly the olympic ideal lives on in this unjustly overlooked corner of the Black Country.

At Longwood the Daw End Branch turned eastwards to reach the limestone workings at Hay Head, and there was no canal link southwards until the merger of the BCN and W&E in 1840. The Rushall Canal was an offspring of this union though, maintaining the connubial metaphor, there is reason to believe that the resultant waterway was by way of being an accident of careless family planning. Apparently the BCN began to have doubts about the viability of the proposed link, only to be reminded that Government money borrowed under the Act of Union with the W&E would have to be returned should the Rushall Canal not be built.

Longwood Boat Club (establised 1970) have moorings on the Daw End's original terminus. Twenty four hour visitor moorings are designated above the top lock, and water, refuse and Elsan facilities are laid on. Not a bad place to pause, ponder on the meaning of life, and plan your next move.

S HUNNED, even by BCN standards, you're more likely to be vouchsafed a vision of the Virgin Mary - or, indeed, any virgin - than a boat on the Rushall or Tame Valley canals. Which is not to imply that they collectively lack interest: if canal exploration has taught you anything at all, you will know by now that the most beguiling can manifest itself in the least promising of circumstances.

Characterised by mitred tailgates, Rushall Locks were nicknamed 'The Ganzy' by working boatmen, reputedly because of the thick Guernsey style sweaters favoured by steerers on this windswept cut. 'Handcuffed' nowadays they seem prone to seepage. Grass growing out of the silt in the bottom pound suggests it is often bereft of water. In the pound between locks 6 and 7 stood Bell Wharf, one of the few predominantly agricultural basins to be found on the BCN.

To the east looms Barr Beacon, a worthwhile ascent - once you've shrugged off the housing estates - along country lanes, if you've that increasingly elusive commodity, time, at your disposal. At 774 feet above sea level, the summit commands, on a clear day at least, views of eleven counties, not all of them English - answers on a postcard, please! Nearer the canal lie various sports grounds. West Bromwich Albion, aka 'The Baggies', have an impressive training facility here.

Prior to the advent of post-war urbanisation and the arrival of the motorways, Rushall Junction lay very much out in the wilds. The BCNS signpost which suggests that Salford Junction is eight and a half miles away appears a tad awry - we make it more like five.

Black Country seagulls cry nasally over the Tame Valley Canal, a late addition to the BCN network,

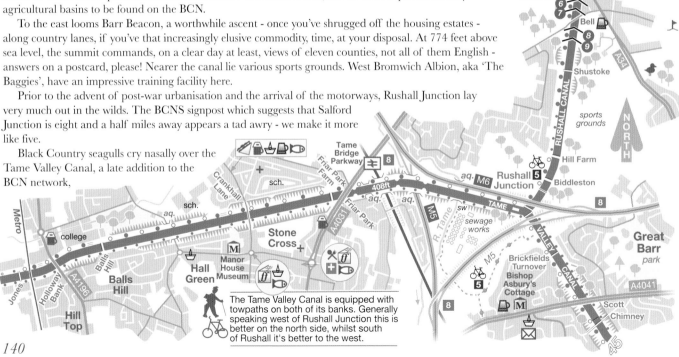

The Tame Valley Canal is equipped with towpaths on both of its banks. Generally speaking west of Rushall Junction this is better on the north side, whilst south of Rushall it's better to the west.

43 continues right hand edge of Map 43

We were intrigued by the proliferation of side bridges. Our trusty 1904 6" Ordnance map showed them to have spanned arms serving sandpits and small collieries. The TVC's most dramatic gesture is its crossing, on an imposing three-arch aqueduct, of the Grand Junction Railway; a rare case of a railway pre-dating an adjoining canal. The floodlights of Bescot's marshalling yard illuminate the northern horizon on dull days, a pale, weed-strewn, rusty-siding, graffitied rolling stock shadow of its 1960s heyday; shunting wagons these days is as outdated a notion as carrying goods by canal.

At Rushall Junction the Tame Valley Canal bears southwards towards Perry Barr and the outskirts of Birmingham. In contrast, the Rushall Canal heads practically due north, having arranged a clandestine assignation with the Daw End Branch of the Wyrley & Essington.

*Tame Valley Pylons*

opened in 1844: a brave attempt to forestall the Railway Age; as obstinately akin, perhaps, to publishing guidebooks in the GPS era.

Half on embankments, half in cuttings, the Tame Valley Canal slices across the landscape like a surgeon's incision. Post-war housing estates notwithstanding, a profound sense of alienation is engendered by the long, pylon-accompanied straights; one might almost be on another planet.

Holloway Bank Bridge carries Telford's Holyhead Turnpike across the canal at Hill Top. Apparently the road here was so steep that passengers had to climb the hill on foot whilst horses strained to haul their carriages up unloaded. The region's Metro system crosses the canal, on tracks formerly part of the Great Western Railway's main line between London Paddington, Wolverhampton and Wales.

*Rushall Junction*

C HAMELEONIC in its capacity to remind you of other canals, the Tame Valley essays a largely north-west/south-east course across a landscape densely urbanised to the point of suffocation. And yet the canal traveller appears innoculated against these pressures: one minute they could be on Burnley Embankment (albeit without the heady allure of the bus station), the next in densely wooded cuttings reminiscent of 'The Shroppie' at its most mysteriously arboreal. Foxgloves thrive in a fecund environment both rocky and damp.

Being primarily an avoiding route - enabling boats to by-pass central Birmingham - the TVC at first attracted scant industry to its banks, a notable exception being a basin by Gorse Farm Bridge linked to Hamstead Colliery by a precipitous mineral tramway. Trade, however,

held up throughout the 1950s, predominantly in the shape of coal from the Cannock coalfield destined for canalside works in and around Birmingham. Tugs handled much of this traffic, hauling up to four boats at a time, the vessels being bow-hauled through the locks at Rushall and Perry Barr.

Two aqueducts - one masonry, one steel - carry the canal above the rooftops of Hamstead. Access to the road below and the facilities of Hamstead is only feasible via steps from the metalled south side towpath at the easternmost aqueduct. The local colliery closed in the early Sixties. In 1908 there was an underground fire at the pit which claimed the lives of twenty-five miners. One of the trapped groups, anticipating their doom, chalked their names on a nearby door together with the poignant inscription:

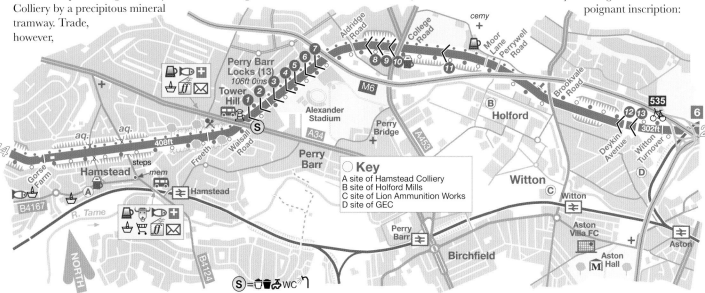

Key
A site of Hamstead Colliery
B site of Holford Mills
C site of Lion Ammunition Works
D site of GEC

*Perry Barr Top*

throughout: all the top paddles, and some of the bottom require the use of water conservation T keys. There's a middle cluster of four, and a final pair within half a mile of Salford Junction (Map 25). Interesting relics of a recirculating pumping system are encountered: a Gauging Weir House by the top lock; Reflux Valves by locks 7 and 11; and a Grid House at the tail of the bottom lock. Boating facilities are provided at the top of the flight, though one suspects, rarely used.

Beyond the towpath there is much to induce exploration. The Alexander Stadium was a focal point of the 2022 Commonwealth Games. The City of Birmingham (or Witton) Cemetery was opened in 1863 and extends to over a hundred acres encased by a brick wall two miles in length. It contains six hundred Commonwealth War Graves. Perry Bridge is a four-arch packhorse affair dating from 1709. Holford Mills began life in medieval times grinding corn, but by the 19th century had progressed - if that's the correct expression - to the manufacture of gun barrels. Armament manufacture

"The Lord preserve us for we are all trusting in Christ." Rescue teams with special breathing apparatus were sent from the Yorkshire coalfield, and one of these men, John Welsby, lost his own life, heroically searching for the trapped men. A touching little memorial (pictured opposite) in the form of a colliery wagon filled with simulated coal can be found at the junction of the B4124 and B4167.

Talking of road numbers, the A34 encounters its fair share of canals on its long, weary way from Winchester to Manchester - ten at a rough count. These old trunk roads have fallen into obscurity in the motorway era, but hark back to a time when it was usually necessary to put up overnight in some unlikely town in order to get anywhere in England.

Perry Barr Locks - nicknamed the 'New Thirteen' (as opposed to the 'Old Thirteen' at Farmers Bridge on Map 16) boast double bottom gates

was also the principal occupation of the Lion Ammunition Works. During the First World War eighteen thousand people worked there, the female employees being known as 'Kynoch's Angels' after the Scots founder of the firm; notwithstanding that he ignominiously absconded to South Africa to escape his creditors.

One of the largest industries to develop alongside the canal was the General Electric Company whose sumptuous offices were the work of the same architectural practice who designed Victoria Coach Station.

*143*

S OONER or later, sadness overtakes all but the most unsusceptible traveller on the Walsall Canal. A sadness, furthermore, which comes in all shapes and sizes: sadness that it is so underused; sadness that every time you revisit it less and less manufacturing appears to be going on along its banks; sadness that it resembles nothing so much as a linear recycling facility; and a more general and insatiable sadness that we're incapable of doing anything about it. But didn't someone once wisely point out that they'd happily exchange all the happiness of the west for the way the Russians have of being sad? And, yes, there is indeed a perverse kind of pleasure to be found in exploring a canal at the nadir of its fortunes. Certainly one's imagination is given full rein: either to picture the canal in all the panoply of its working past; or how it might be in a more caring and Utopian future.

Unwittingly (one assumes), Pleck sets the tone for the Walsall's woebegone wanderings, its one syllable, oath-like

**'Passengers No More'**
1: Pleck - closed 1965
2: Darlaston - closed 1965
3: Wednesbury Town - closed 1964
4: Ocker Hill - closed 1916
5: Princes End - closed 1916

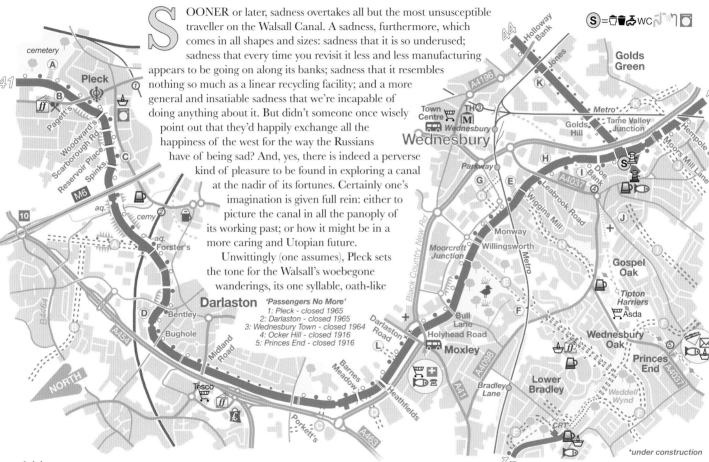

*under construction

name fitting the mood perfectly. Walsall gasworks was a relatively late user of canal transport: coal in and waste products out. Thomas Clayton's very last run was from here with crude tar to Oldbury on 31st March 1966 aboard the motor boat *Stour* now resident at the BCLM. A former warehouse catches the eye on the opposite bank, and a substantial mosque breaths fresh life into an otherwise predominantly debauched scene. We'd

*Gasworks side-bridge*

*Pleck*

been promising ourselves a refreshing glass of mild at Pleck Working Men's Club, advertised at a mere £1.50 the previous time we'd passed, but it had pulled its last pint.

The canal slips through a sandy cutting strewn with detritus and passes the levelled site of James Bridge copper works. Nip up the steps at Reservoir Place Bridge, turn right, and you'll come upon the once proud premises of the South Staffordshire Tramways Electric Generating Station, erected in 1892. Coal was brought in by canal boat to feed the furnaces. In the neighbouring business park J&E Sedgwick & Co, bastions of Walsall leathermaking, have been manufacturing goods for the equestrian market since 1900.

Emerging from beneath the M6 motorway - on which the traffic

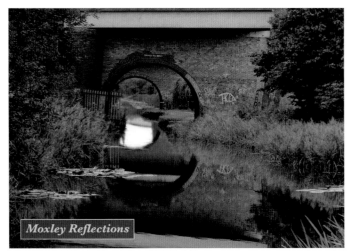

**Moxley Reflections**

appears benighted in a nose to tail crawl - the canal rides upon a considerable embankment carrying it over a by-road and the infant River Tame. On one side of the embankment stands a casino, on the other a cemetery: the long and short odds of life in eloquent juxtaposition. Bullrushes thrive at the entrance to the Anson Branch which connected with the Bentley Canal, abandoned in 1961 (see also Map 40). Breeds of duck conspicuously absent from naturalists' handbooks patrol the canal.

Crossing the Grand Junction Railway, the canal essays a loop around the old metal-bashing town of Darlaston. By Bughole Bridge the Black Country New Road makes itself known to southbound canal travellers for the first time - you are not expected to become bosom pals. Telford's Holyhead Road (see also Maps 8 and 44) crosses the canal at Moxley. Ernest Thomas - a well known operator in the twilight years of canal transport - employed the worked-out Moxley Sand Beds to dispose of refuse brought in by narrowboat. Disused lorries await scrapping with the same sense of despondency as the working boats which preceded them.

Redevelopment has eroded much of the latent atmosphere of the canal as it reaches Moorcroft Junction, a textbook example of a regeneration 'initiative' abandoned to its own devices. Until its highly regrettable closure in 1961, the Bradley Branch led off from here to the Wednesbury Oak Loop, ascending to the Wolverhampton Level through a flight of nine locks, the first two of which are straddled by a bridge carrying the Metro, formerly the GWR main line. This, if the graffiti can be relied upon, is the haunt of the 'Moxley Crew': Gav, Reece, Jay & Luke. Presently one finds oneself - literally and spiritually - with the whippet walkers and tethered ponies in Weddell Wynd.

Of the once vast Patent Shaft Steel Works there is no trace. In its heyday it spread over five hundred acres and employed three thousand men. Neither does the Gospel Oak Branch lead anymore to Willingsworth furnaces. Opposite its reedy remains - shot like a green arrow into the entrails of a housing estate - a side bridge spans the entrance to the Great Western Railway's Wednesbury rail/canal interchange basin.

The trio of cooling towers at Ocker Hill's coal-fired power station, once a significant landmark in this part of the Black Country, were demolished in 1985, having survived closure of the generating plant by eight years. The contemporary face of transport, in the shape of lorry-served warehouses, taunts the emasculated canal as it reaches Tame Valley Junction, where boating facilities are laid on in boarded-up premises erected by British Waterways to house area office staff. By all accounts, they couldn't cope with the sense of isolation, and were suitably counselled and swiftly relocated.

THIS LENGTH OF CANAL IS NOT RECOMMENDED FOR BOATING

Off-Cuts

153

## Uncaptioned Photographs

## Acknowledgements

High fives to Karen Tanguy, Meg Gregory and the Short Run Press. Fist bumps to Los Lumsdenos, Chris & Terry Rigden, David Hymers, Jenny Tyte, Sister Davina Sharp, Tony Ford, Roger Ireland, Brian & Brenda Ward, Andrew & Debbie Shephard, John & Gill Wilkinson, and all participants of the 2019 BCNS Explorer Cruises, Lizzy Perkins (and James aged 5!) of Worcester Cathedral Ferry, Hugh Humphreys of Lapal Canal Trust, and Dave Constable and the team at CRT Bradley Workshops. Mrs Jackie Pearson stoically bore Lock-wheeler's prolonged absences for the greater good!

## This Guide

Pearson's Canal Companions are a long established, independently produced series of guide books devoted to the inland waterways and designed to appeal equally to boaters, walkers, cyclists and other, not readily pigeon-holed - though no less deserving - members of society. Considerable pride is taken to make these guides as up to date, accurate, entertaining and inspirational as possible. A good guide book should fulfil three functions: make you want to go; interpret the lie of the land when you're there; and provide a lasting souvenir of your journeys.

## The Maps

There are forty-eight numbered maps whose layout is shown by the Route Planner inside the front cover. Maps 1-24 show the route of the Stourport Ring; and Maps 25-37 and 9-16 the route of the Black Country Ring. Maps 38/39 cover the Stourbridge and Dudley Canals, whilst Maps 40-46 cover the northern area of the Birmingham Canal Navigations.

The maps - measured imperially like the waterways they depict, and not being slavishly north-facing - are easily read in either direction. Users will thus find most itineraries progressing smoothly and logically from left to right or vice versa. Figures quoted at the top of each map refer to distance per map, locks per map and average cruising time. An alternative indication of timings from centre to centre can be found on the Route Planner.

Obviously, cruising times vary with the nature of your boat and the number of crew at your disposal, so quoted times should be taken only as an estimate. Neither do times quoted take into account any delays which might occur at lock flights in high season. Walking and cycling times - not indicated on the maps - will depend very much on the state of individual sections of towpath and the stamina of those concerned.

# INFORMATION

## The Text

Each map is accompanied by a route commentary placing the waterway in its historic, social and topographical context. As close to each map as is feasible, gazetteer-like entries are given for places passed through, listing, where appropriate, facilities of likely benefit to users of this guide.

## Walking

The simplest way to go canal exploring is on foot along the towpaths originally provided so that horses could 'tow' boats. Walking costs largely nothing and you are free to concentrate on the passing scene; something that boaters, with the responsibilities of navigation thrust upon them, are not always at liberty to do. The maps set out to give some idea of the quality of the towpath on any given section of canal. More of an art than a science to be sure, but at least it reflects our personal experiences, and whilst it does vary from area to area, none of it should prove problematical for anyone inured to the vicissitudes of country walking. We recommend the use of public transport to facilitate 'one-way' itineraries but stress the advisability of checking up to date details on the telephone numbers quoted, or on the internet for trains and buses respectively.

## Cycling

Bicycling along towpaths is an increasingly popular pastime, though one not always equally popular with other waterway users such as boaters, anglers and pedestrians. It is important to remember that you are sharing the towpath with other people out for their own form of enjoyment, and to treat them with the respect and politeness they deserve. A bell is a useful form of diplomacy; failing that, a stentorian cough. Happily, since the inception of the Canal & River Trust in 2012, it is no longer necessary for cyclists to acquire a permit to use the towpath.

## Boating

Boating on inland waterways is an established, though relatively small, facet of the UK tourist industry. It is also, increasingly, a chosen lifestyle. There are approximately 38,000 privately owned boats registered on the canals, but in addition to these, numerous firms offer boats for hire. These range from small operators with half a dozen boats to sizeable fleets run by companies with several bases.

Most hire craft have all the creature comforts you are likely to expect. In the excitement of planning a boating holiday you may give scant thought to the contents of your hire boat, but at the end of a hard day's boating such matters take on more significance, and a well equipped, comfortable boat, large enough to accommodate your crew with something to spare, can make the difference between a good holiday and one which will be shudderingly remembered for the wrong reasons.

Traditionally, hire boats are booked out by the week or fortnight, though many firms now offer more flexible short breaks or extended weeks. All reputable hire firms give newcomers tuition in boat handling and lock working, and first-timers soon find themselves adapting to the pace of things 'on the cut'.

## Navigational Advice

Newcomers, hiring a boat on the inland waterways for the first time, have every right to expect sympathetic and thorough tuition from the company providing their boat. Boat-owners are, by definition, likely to be already adept at navigating. The following, however, may prove useful points of reference. **Locks** are part of the charm of canal cruising, but they are potentially dangerous environments for children, pets and careless adults. Use of them should be methodical and unhurried, whilst special care should be exercised in rain, frost and snow when slippery hazards abound.

Apart from the basin locks at Diglis, Worcester and the automated locks on the River Severn between Worcester and Stourport, all the locks on the canals covered by this guide are of the familiar narrow-beam variety. All gates should be closed on leaving each chamber (unless courteously leaving them open for

an approaching boat) and all paddles wound down. A high proportion of locks in urban areas are fitted with security gear to combat hooliganism, and boaters should ensure that they are equipped with 'handcuff' (aka 'T' or water conservation) keys to release the paddle gear. These are obtainable by post from CRT or from boatyards and chandleries.

The River Severn locks at Bevere, Holt and Lincomb are mechanised and manned. It's not a bad idea to telephone ahead when joining the river at Worcester or Stourport to Bevere or Lincomb locks respectively

to let them know you are on the way if you're not intending to stop en route. Once you've negotiated one lock the grapevine tends to alert the keepers to your progress. Be guided by the colour light signals, but wait for the signal to turn green and the gates to open before approaching too closely. The chambers of these locks are large and you may be sharing with other craft. Steadying straps and chains are attached to the chamber walls and these can be hand held to control your boat if there is any turbulence. Always follow the lock-keeper's advice. He will be in his control cabin as you pass through the lock.

The basin locks at Worcester and Stourport are only open during timetabled hours - as indeed are the river locks mentioned above. Hire craft are likely to have up to date timings in their boat manuals, but private boaters can obtain details from the Canal & River Trust.

Finally, it behoves us all to be on our best behaviour at locks. Remember to exercise a little 'give and take'. The use of fists to decide precedence at locks is one canal tradition not worthy of preservation. **Floods** can occur on the River Severn at any time of year at short notice. Officials should be on hand to help and advise at such times. If you are already on the river you must tie up at the nearest official moorings and remain there until further notice. At times of flood you may be denied access to the river. Boat hire companies are familiar with the Severn's moods and will be sympathetic to genuine delays. **Mooring** on the canals featured in this guide is per usual practice - ie on the towpath side, away from sharp bends, bridge-holes and narrows. A 'yellow' bollard symbol represents visitor mooring sites; either as designated officially or, in some cases as recommended by our personal experience. Of course, one of the great joys of canal boating has always been the ability to moor wherever (sensibly) you like. In recent years, however, it has become obvious, particularly in urban areas, that there are an increasing number of undesirable locations where mooring is not to be recommended for fear of vandalism, theft or abuse. It would be nice if local authorities would see their way to providing pleasant, secure, overnight facilities for passing boaters who, after all, bring the commerce of tourism in their wake. Few boaters would object to making a small payment, as is the custom on a number of river navigations.

**Moveable Bridges** are an occasional feature of the canals. Some 'swing', some 'lift', some are manually or windlass-operated, some mechanised. Some require either a CRT 'facilities' Yale key and/or 'handcuff' key to facilitate their moving. Always return them to the position you found them in after use unless it is obvious that another boat is approaching to use them.

**Tunnels** occur at a number of points on the canals included in this guide and are great fun to negotiate. Pets and young children should be kept 'indoors'. Steerers are advised to wear waterproofs, and not to forget to turn their headlight off on exiting the tunnel!

**Turning** points on the canals are known as 'winding holes'; pronounced as the thing which blows because in the old days the wind was expected to do much of the work rather than the boatman. Winding holes capable of taking a full length boat of around seventy foot length are marked where appropriate on the maps. Winding holes capable of turning shorter craft are marked with the approximate length. It is of course also possible to turn boats at junctions and at most boatyards, though in the case of the latter it is considered polite to ask permission before doing so.

**Rubbish** round the prop is a largely unavoidable hazard on the BCN and can result in your boat losing power or steerage. Often this can be solved simply by putting the engine into reverse for a moment or two to free the offending item(s). But sometimes you may

need to stop the engine (take the key out) and access the weed-hatch to remove the impediment by hand.

**Boating facilities** are provided at regular intervals along the inland waterways, and range from a simple water tap or refuse disposal skip, to the provision of sewage disposal, showers and laundry. Such vital features are also obtainable at boatyards and marinas along with repairs and servicing. An alphabetical list of boatyards appears opposite.

**Dimension** restrictions vary from waterway to waterway. Up to date details can be obtained from the Canal & River Trust.

**Closures** (or 'stoppages' in the arcane parlance of the canals) traditionally occur on the inland waterways between November and April, during which time most of the heavy maintenance work is undertaken. Occasionally, however, an emergency stoppage, or perhaps water restriction, may be imposed at short notice, closing part of the route you intend to use. Up to date details are posted at key locations throughout the inland waterways network. They are also available from CRT online or from most hire bases.

## Amendments

Updates to current editions can be found on our website: *www.jmpearson.co.uk*. Feel free to email us if you spot anything worth notifying others about.

## Canal & River Trust

CRT are the charititable body responsible for the canals and rivers in this guide. Their head office address is: First Floor North, Station House, 500 Elder Gate, Milton Keynes, MK9 1BB Tel: 0303 040 4040 *www.canalrivertrust.org.uk*

## Societies

The Inland Waterways Association was founded in 1946 to campaign for retention of the canal system. Many routes now open to pleasure boaters may not have been so but for this organisation. Membership details, together with a list of the IWA's regional branches, may be obtained from: Inland Waterways Association, Island House, Moor Road, Chesham HP5 1WA. Most of the canals featured herein are also supported by individual groups - visit internet for details.
BCN Society
Lapal Canal Trust
Lichfield & Hatherton Canals Restoration Trust
Staffordshire & Worcestershire Canal Society
Stourbridge Navigation Trust
Trent & Mersey Canal Society
Worcester-Birmingham & Droitwich Canals Society

## BCNS Explorer Cruises

Boating on the remoter, less visited parts of the BCN is encouraged by the Birmingham Canal Navigations Society by means of escorted convoys, typically lasting a week. A reassuring sense of 'safety' is engendered, together with the opportunity to explore these fascinating, but challenging waters with like-minded souls. Talks and presentations are an added attraction. Visit the BCNS website for further details.

## Hire Bases

**ABC BOAT HIRE** - Coventry Canal Map 30; Staffs & Worcs Canal Map 36; Worcester & Birmingham Canal Maps 1, 20 & 24;. PO Box 232, Worcester WR1 2SD. Tel: 0808 296 6720.

**ANGLO WELSH WATERWAY HOLIDAYS** - Worcs & Birmingham Canal Map 21 and Staffs & Worcs Canal Map 33. 2 The Hide Market, West Street, Bristol BS2 0BH. Tel: 0117 304 1122

**BLACK PRINCE HOLIDAYS** - Worcester & Birmingham Canal Map 21. Stoke Prior, Bromsgrove, Worcestershire B60 4LA. Tel: 01527 575115

**NAPTON NARROWBOATS** - Staffs & Worcs Canal Maps 8 & 37. Oxley Moor Road, Wolverhampton WV5 9HW. Tel: 01902 789942

**STARLINE NARROWBOATS** - Staffs & Worcs Canal Map 3. Engine Lane, Stourport-on-Severn, Worcs DY13 9EP. Tel: 01531 632003.

**TRINITY BOATS** - Worcester & B'ham Canal Map 23. Dunhampstead Wharf. WR9 7JX Tel: 01905 779048.

## Boatyards

**ALVECHURCH MARINA (ABC)** - Alvechurch, Worcester & Birmingham Canal, Map 20. Tel: 0121 445 1133. B48 7SQ

**ANGLO WELSH** - Gt. Haywood, Staffs & Worcs Canal, Map 33. Tel: 01889 881711. ST18 0RJ

**ANGLO WELSH** - Tardebigge, Worcester & Birmingham Canal, Map 21. Tel: 01527 873898. B60 1LR

**ASHWOOD MARINA** - Ashwood, Staffs & Worcs Canal, Map 6. Tel: 01384 295535. DY6 0AQ.

**BLACK PRINCE** - Stoke Prior, Worcester & Birmingham Canal, Map 21. Tel: 01527 575115. B60 4LA

**BOURNE BOAT BUILDERS** - Penkridge, Staffs & Worcs Canal, Map 35. Tel: 01785 714692. ST19 5RH

**CAGGY'S** - Tipton, BCN Map 12 Tel: 0121 663 6144. DY4 8NA

# BOATING DIRECTORY

**CANAL TRANSPORT SERVICES** - Cannock Extension Canal Map 42. Tel: 01543 374370. WS3 5AP

**COOMBESWOOD CANAL TRUST** - Hawne Basin, Dudley No.2 Canal, Map 39. Tel: 0121 550 1355. B62 8AW

**CRAFTED BOATS (PINDER)** - Stoke Wharf, W & B Canal, Map 21. Tel: 01527 876438. B60 4JZ

**DIGLIS BASIN MARINA** - Worcester & Birmingham Canal, Maps 1 & 24. Tel: 01905 356314. WR5 3BW

**DROITWICH SPA MARINA** - Droitwich Junction Canal, Map 22. Tel: 0797 062 6807. WR9 7DU

**FAZELEY MILL MARINA (ABC)** - Birmingham & Fazeley Canal Map 28. Tel: 01827 261138. B78 3SE

**FRADLEY MARINE SERVICES** - Fradley, Map 30. Tel: 0797 168 6516. DE13 7DN

**GREAT HAYWOOD MARINA** - Trent & Mersey Canal, Map 33. Tel: 01889 883713. ST18 0RQ

**GRIST MILL BOATYARD** - Diglis Basin, W&B Canal, Maps 1/24. Tel: 0795 608 4107. WR5 3GL

**HATHERTON MARINA** - Staffs & Worcs Canal, Map 33. Tel: 0791 946 6368. WV10 7DU

**JD BOAT SERVICES** - Staffs & Worcs Canal, Map 36. Tel: 01902 791811. ST19 5PR

**J F BOATBUILDING** - Kings Bromley, Trent & Mersey, Map 31. Tel: 0794 904 3455. WS13 8HS

**KINGS BROMLEY MARINA** - Trent & Mersey Canal Map 31. Tel: 01543 417209. WS13 8HT

**KINGS ORCHARD MARINA (ABC)** - Coventry Canal Map 30. Tel: 01543 433608. WS13 8SP

**LIMEKILN CHANDLERS** - Stourport, Staffs & Worcs Canal Map 3. Tel: 01299 821111. DY13 9EL

**NAPTON NARROWBOATS** - Autherley, Staffs & Worcs Maps 8 & 37. Tel: 01902 789942. WV9 5HW.

**OXLEY MARINE** - Autherley, Staffs & Worcs Canal Maps 8 & 37. Tel: 01902 789522. WV10 6TZ

**PINDER** - Diglis Basins Drydock - see Crafted Boats.

**OTHERTON BOAT HAVEN** - Penkridge, Staffs & Worcs Canal Map 30. Tel: 01785 712515. ST19 5NX

**SHERBORNE WHARF** - Birmingham, BCN, Map 16. Tel: 0121 455 6163. B16 8DE

**STAFFORD BOAT CLUB** - Stafford, Staffs & Worcs Canal, Map 34. Tel: 01785 660725. ST17 4SG

**STOURPORT MARINA** - River Severn, Stourport, Map 3. Tel: 01299 827082. DY13 9QF

**STREETHAY WHARF** - Lichfield, Coventry Canal Map 30. Tel: 01543 414808. WS13 8RJ

**WORCESTER MARINA** - Worcester & Birmingham Canal, Maps 1 & 24. Tel: 01905 734160. WR1 2RS

## Day Boat Hire

**ABC BOAT HIRE** - Alvechurch, Worcester & Birmingham, Map 20. Tel: 0121 445 1133. B48 7SQ

**ANGLO WELSH** - Tardebigge, Worcester & Birmingham, Map 21. B60 1LR Gt Haywood, Staffs & Worcs, Map 33. Tel: 0117 304 1122. ST18 0RJ

**DEBBIE'S DAYBOATS** - Birmingham & Fazeley Canal Map 28. Coleshill Road, Fazeley, Tamworth, Staffs. B78 3RY Tel: 0752 216 9241.

**GEORGIE'S** - Penkridge, Staffs & Worcs Canal, Map 35. Tel: 0794 649 0203. ST19 5RH

**STREETHAY WHARF** - Coventry Canal, Map 30. Tel: 01543 414808. WS13 8RJ

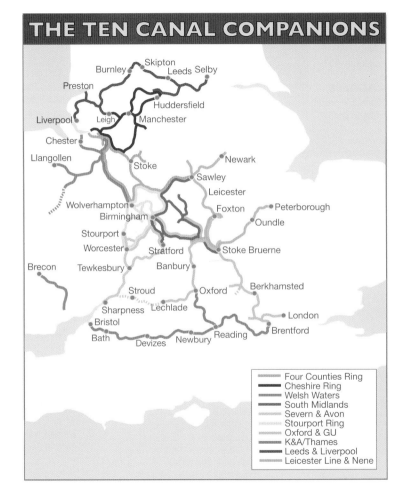

# THE TEN CANAL COMPANIONS

Skipton
Burnley
Leeds Selby
Preston
Huddersfield
Liverpool    Leigh    Manchester
Chester
Llangollen    Stoke    Newark
Sawley
Leicester
Wolverhampton    Foxton    Peterborough
Birmingham    Oundle
Stourport
Worcester    Stratford    Stoke Bruerne
Tewkesbury    Banbury
Brecon
Stroud    Oxford    Berkhamsted
Sharpness    Lechlade
Bristol    London
Bath    Brentford
Devizes    Newbury    Reading

Four Counties Ring
Cheshire Ring
Welsh Waters
South Midlands
Severn & Avon
Stourport Ring
Oxford & GU
K&A/Thames
Leeds & Liverpool
Leicester Line & Nene